D1708012

Grazia Gobbi Sica

THE FLORENTINE VILLA
Architecture History Society

Translated from the Italian by Ursula Creigh

CONTENTS

Published 2007 by Routledge
2 Park Square, Milton Park, Abingdon, Oxon OX14 4RN

Simultaneously published in the USA and Canada
by Routledge
270 Madison Ave, New York, NY 10016

Routledge is an imprint of the Taylor & Francis Group, an informa business

English language edition: 2007

Original Italian edition published 1998 by Alinea Editrice
La villa fiorentina: Elementi storici e critici per una lettura

Translated from the Italian by Ursula Creigh

Publisher's note
This book has been prepared from camera-ready copy supplied by the author.

Additional typesetting by Florence Production Ltd, Stoodleigh, Devon
Printed and bound in China by Everbest Printing Co. Ltd

British Library Cataloguing in Publication Data
A catalogue record for this book is available from the British Library

Library of Congress Cataloging in Publication Data
Gobbi, Grazia.
[Villa Florentina. English]
The Florentine villa: architecture, history, society/Grazia Gobbi Sica.
p. cm. – (Classical tradition in architecture)
Includes bibliographical references and index.
1. Country homes – Italy – Florence (Province).   2. Architecture
and society – Italy – Florence (Province).   I. Title.
NA7565.G613 2007
728.80945 51 – dc22   2007010940

ISBN10: 0–415–44397–0 (hbk)
ISBN10: 0–415–93925–5 (ebk)
ISBN13: 978–0–415–44397–5 (hbk)
ISBN13: 978–0–415–93925–3 (ebk)

PREFACE

Recalling the origins of this book and my reasons for writing it means retracing the steps that first led me to tackle the subject of the villa, in a regional analysis and historical architectural study of an area as remarkable as the surroundings of Florence. Here, as nowhere else, the form given to the landscape by agricultural activities was joined by some of the finest expressions of urban art and culture.

The study is the outcome of research carried out in the orbit of the university, its objective being to provide a historical framework for any planning measures in this area. The basis of the present volume was a short work in four chapters, published in 1980, in which I investigated the various aspects of the phenomenon of the villa as a source of production, fruit of literary and philosophical culture, architectural form and, lastly, in its relationship with nature as expressed by the gardens. In 1998 an enlarged edition was published; the original four chapters were expanded by a second section analyzing the area between Florence and Sesto in a study of its morphology, history and forms of representation. A map expressly produced for this purpose illustrates the figurative and morphological features and qualities of the area. A third section consists of the description of the villas in the same area. A chapter on the villa during the 19th century and an appendix with descriptions of six villas are now included in the English-language edition. These latter villas are open to the public and, together with several others studied in this volume, particularly the Medici villas of Castello and Petraia and the Villa Corsini, State-owned and easy to visit, they provide a useful background for an understanding of the evolution of the villa in the Florentine area.

The background and development of the Florentine villa provide a record of the continual and unbroken pattern of reciprocal use and exchange with the walled city of Florence from the 13th century right up to the present day. It is this "other city", the one outside the walls, which has engaged the attention of historians, chroniclers and travellers, spellbound by the unique harmony of the landscape that lies before them.

In the antithetical relationship between the city and the countryside the villa assumed a symbolic role, a place for gathering agricultural produce (although agricultural investment came from the capital accumulated from commercial and industrial activities in the city), but also a place which brought social advancement. The villa thus presents an architectural and ideological paradigm. Myth and fantasy were used to mark the privileges of an improved social status, initially achieved through trade and commerce, which opened the doors to a more gracious way of living, the ideology of which was supported by literature.

A study of the Florentine villa within the parameters chosen here, those of careful research, means making a contribution to the protection of the landscape and its historic buildings, and, as a result, it supplies an informative guide for monitoring any form of change.

Of the many who have helped me in different ways I want to thank the architects Luciana Capaccioli, Donatella Donatini, Teresa Gobbò, Luigi Lazzareschi; Giulia Maraviglia, Silvana Benedetti and the staff of the Libraries of Dipartimento di Progettazione dell'Architettura, of the Kunstihistorishes Institut in Florenz, Biblioteca Nazionale Centrale, Archivio di Stato and particularly, Elena Cotta and Marina Laguzzi; Lucia Monaci Moran of Gabinetto Disegni e Stampe Uffizi, Gabriella Battista Crestini for the translation and interpretation of documents in the State Archive, Enzo Crestini for the photos around the countryside and in the State Archive, Carletta Scano of the Dipartmento of Progettazione, Kate Eadie for the layout of the book and my daughter Beatrice for the meticulous and helpful refinement of the text.

For the English edition I want to thank particularly Ursula Creigh, Gian Luigi Maffei for his help in the general organization, Giancarlo Cataldi and Benedetto Di Cristina for their continuous support, Roberto Corona, and particularly Massimo Battista for his enormous patience in the creation of the new layout of the book.

A special thank you to Giovanna Balzanetti Steiner who enriched the English edition with her precious, original drawings of the six villas in the appendix, and to Lina Bolzoni for her invaluable help.

PART ONE

CHAPTER ONE

Origins and Development of the Villa

[1] On agricultural questions in the Middle Ages the writings of M. Bloch are fundamental. See M. Bloch, *Les caractères originaux de l'histoire rurale française*, Paris 1956; and the collection of essays *Lavoro e tecnica del Medioevo*, with a preface by G. Luzzatto, Bari 1970. For a picture of the situation on a European scale see G. Duby, *L'economia rurale nell'Europa medioevale*, Bari 1972. On the position of these transformations in Italy see G. Luzzatto, *Storia Economica d'Italia. Il Medioevo*, Florence 1970. There is an exhaustive collection of Italian studies conducted prior to 1960 by P. J. Jones in "Rivista Storica Italiana" LXXVI (1964), pp. 287–348. An important essay by the same author, *From manor to mezzadria: a Tuscan case-study in the medieval origins of modern agrarian society*, was published in *Florentine Studies, Politics and Society*, London 1968. Of fundamental importance is E. Conti, *La formazione della struttura agraria moderna nel contado fiorentino*, Rome 1965. On the connection between early buildings and the Medici estates in the 1400s, see V. Franchetti Pardo, G. Casali, *I Medici nel contado fiorentino. Ville e possedimenti agricoli tra Quattrocento e Cinquecento*, Florence 1979.

The origins of the extra-urban villas of Tuscany lie in the pattern of events – already the subject of well-known studies – arising from the dissolution of feudal estates and their replacement with properties owned by the bourgeoisie, with all the socio-economic differences inherent in the two different methods of organizing production, even if this was a gradual process and took place in stages.[1] As we know, during the 12th and 13th centuries the dramatic changes in urban life and the establishment of institutions to govern a communal society led to profound changes in the agricultural economy, making an impact on current terms of production and giving rise to new and more dynamic forms of capital accumulation. Alongside the feudally-inspired manorial order there developed a system of freedom of cultivation, whether through the allotment of land with rent being paid in kind, the usurpation of property, or the granting of concessions in exchange for services rendered. Much land came into the possession of the countrymen who worked it, with the accord of the secular or ecclesiastic owners of the feudal properties, while farmers paid in kind with farming produce and, later, money.

Left: Detail from Giusto Utens' *La Magia*. Below: March, the year's first farm work. Right: October, the month of tilling and sowing. Details from *The Très Riches Heures of Jean, Duc de Berry*, Musée Condé, Chantilly.

The affirmation of these new social forces culminated in around the mid-13th century with the complete dissolution of feudal ties, accompanied by a general movement to develop agriculture and to expand and intensify farming within a programme of a vast reorganization of land. The development of share-cropping (*mezzadria*) after the reform of the fiscal system in around the mid-13th century led to a transformation of the countryside which became based on the composition of a farming community. A farmer's presence on the land he worked encouraged settlements to spread and scattered houses began to appear in the countryside; the farming family became a unit of measurement on the agricultural scene. Thus, by the second half of the 14th century the countryside was no longer the hunting ground of feudal lords living defensively in their castles, supported by a closed economy (very close to running at a loss) and dependent on farmers who had little autonomy and were often subject to a regime of contributing free labour, of taxation and of legal obligations. What now emerged was a practice of share-cropping based on the traditional family identity of the producer and on property rights consolidated by a landlord which, at this level of organizing production, in legal terms implied the drawing of a surplus value that could be converted into cash. Conti writes: "*During the early 15th century in much of the area around Florence the basic agricultural structure was now a small share-cropping farm [*podere*]. Wherever a peasant's land was reduced to a minimal amount this represented the most rational way of organizing agricultural production and creating a meeting-place for the two worlds of the city and the countryside. Naturally, the same word,* podere, *was used to describe farms that in size, income and structure varied greatly from place to place, and from each other in the same area. However, the essential components of every true* podere *were the same: a farmhouse and an amount of arable, tree-planted, grazing or wooded land that would absorb the labours of a farming family and produce a net income that was at least double what was needed for its support. Indeed, after the usual deduction of seed, the harvest was divided 'into parts', half to the landlord, the master, and half to the worker, the share-cropper.*

A farm's land did not always form a compact or semi-compact block. Very often the central nucleus was surrounded by plots scattered here and there among nearby properties and adjoining farms. At times a farm was allotted fields, woods and grazing lands lying quite some distance off. The central nucleus was the most intensely cultivated part and here stood

Below and right: details from the *Nova Pulcherrima civitatis Florentiae Topographia* by don Stefano Bonsignori 1584 and details from the so called *View of the Chain* painted in the 19th century from the original xylography of 1470. Florence, Museo Firenze com'era.

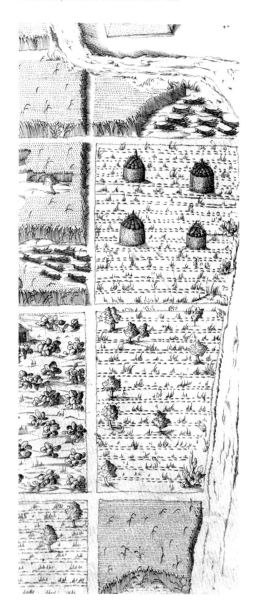

[2] E. Conti, op. cit., Vol. I, p. 2.

[3] G. Duby, op. cit., pp. 482–483.

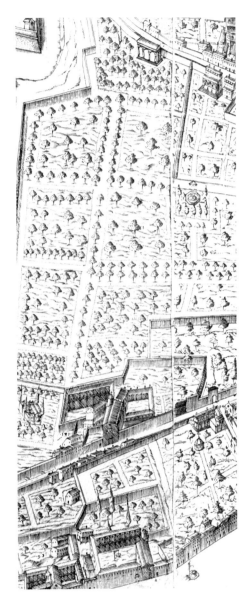

the farm buildings: the 'worker's house', a stall and barn for animals and forage, a bread-oven and a threshing floor; sometimes also a 'master's house', sporadically occupied by the landlord when he visited his 'villa' to check on the farmer and enjoy the pleasures of the countryside."[2] In his outline of the general process, but one that might well apply to the Florentine position, Duby states: *"The stimulus provided by entrepreneurs from the city and the urbanization of the countryside that they introduced was expressed, particularly during the 14th century, in an increasing adoption, especially in the hills, of a method of cultivating the soil which made its first appearance on the outskirts of large towns. This was mixed farming, combining the growing of vines, fruit trees and crops on the same irrigated plots of land, a blend of fruit and cereal farming. In creating the new landscape, first illustrated by 14th-century Tuscan painters, we see clear evidence of the remarkable prosperity that urban vitality brought to the countryside. The 'signori' here were almost all citizens, nobles of the plains who had resettled in the local city, or citizens who had bought land or rented Church property on favourable terms."*[3]

The accounts of both Conti and Duby thus present the basic issues in this new exploitation of agriculture including, as we see, the house of the "master", who operated not only by reinvesting the surplus value from the land back into agriculture but also, and to a greater extent, the capital produced by commercial and trading activities which, as we should not forget, formed the basis of the Florentine economy during the 12th and 13th centuries. It was particularly in the Florence area that this bourgeois colonization of the surrounding countryside coincided with the development of a trading economy; quite dissimilar from the course of events in the Venetian Republic, where the interest of merchants in land investment only became of any significance following the end of commercial hegemony. Considering the differences in the profit ratios of the two sectors, at least during the period of the greatest expansion in commercial activity, there can therefore be no doubt that the urge to invest in agricultural land shown by merchants and bankers must be ascribed, not to a move of a speculative nature, but rather to the need for social dialogue, full of political implications, which led the new classes to become landowners and develop a scale of values that went beyond mere financial goals and aided the establishment of their hegemony.

"Land, a house in the country", states Cherubini, *"just like property in the city, lent that prestige, that air of gentlemanly*

self-sufficiency, which even the man from the meanest lodging often regarded as the ultimate goal of his social advancement, almost the clearest sign of a change of condition."[4]

Thus, the constant availability of material goods should be considered in this light, that is, within the framework of the social differentiation that was taking place. We can imagine a bourgeois citizen's sense of security, autonomy and improved status (in a society continually threatened by fear of famine) on seeing his table spread with the fruits of his own fields.[5]

Below: Around the Lappeggi villa, detail from the painting by Giusto Utens, 1599.
Bottom: Giuseppe Zocchi, Florence 1744, Florence Museo Firenze com'era.
Right: Farmhouses of the Careggi farm (A.S.F. Piante RR Possessioni, Vol VIII)

[4] G. Cherubini, *Signori, Contadini, Borghesi*, Florence 1974, p. 382. On this question see also G. De Rossi, *Sviluppo economico e agricultura*, in *Un'altra Firenze*, Florence 1971.

[5] *"If you have money in hand and your children are gathering what they need. . . properties around Florence on good land . . . where there are plenty of workers . . . which you can resell any day"*, exhorts Giovanni di Pagolo Morelli in around the mid-14th century. G. di Pagolo Morelli, *Ricordi*, ed. V. Branca, Florence 1956, p. 231; and there are repeated references to the benefits of owning rural property in L. B. Alberti, *Libri della Famiglia*, English trans. by R. Neu Watkins, *The Family in Renaissance Florence*, Prospect Heights, Ill. 1994, pp. 187 and 192: *"I would make every effort to have estates from which my house would be kept furnished with grain, wine, wood and straw, all much more cheaply than by purchase in the market. I would there raise flocks, pigeons, chickens and fish . . ."*, and later, *"I would ensure that the property was capable of producing everything needed to nourish the family and, if not everything at least the basic necessities, bread and wine."* Still on the subject of produce to satisfy the needs of a proprietor and his family, he includes a passage which is a humanist and literary eulogy of agriculture: *"In the spring the farm supplies you with a multitude of delights, greenery, flowers, aromas, songs. It tries to please you; it smiles and promises a magnificent harvest, it fills you will high hopes as well as sufficient joy in the present. Then in summer it courteously attends on you. First one sort of fruit and then another arrives at your house, your house is never left unprovided for. Then comes autumn when the farm gives liberal reward for your labours, shows great gratitude for your merit – serving you gladly, copiously and faithfully! Your farm replaces what is old and stale in your house with what is new, fresh and clean. It brings you berries, grapes and other fruits to hang up and dry. To this add nuts to fill your house and beautiful fragrant apples and pears. The farm never stops providing you with periodic gifts of its later fruits. Even in winter it does not fail to be generous, it provides you with wood and oil, juniper and bay, so that when you enter your house in snowy windy weather you can build a cheerful sweet-smelling fire. And when you decide to lend it your company, the farm offers splendid sunshine, provides hares and bucks and deer for you to hunt, lets you enjoy the sport and shake off the harshness of the weather. I need not mention the chickens, kids, fresh cheeses and other delicacies produced by the farm and preserved to supply you the year round. The farm labours that you may lack for nothing in your house, that your spirit may be free of all melancholy, that you may be nourished with what is pleasant and good. If*

the farm also requires some work from you, this is at least unlike other occupations which depress and worry you. It does not sap your energies and make you weary but fills you with joy."

[6] Quoted by I. Origo, *La villa*, in *Storia dell'economia italiana*, ed. C. M. Cipolla, Turin 1959.

[7] G. Rucellai, *Zibaldone*, ed. A. Perosa, The Warburg Institute, London 1960, p. 9.

Veduta della Casa per il Lauoratore Posta in pianta alla lettera A ~

Veduta della Casa per il Lauoratore, posta in Pian lettera.V. ~~

ta della Casa per il Lauoratore a in Pianta alla lettera Y.

della Casa per il Lauorato posta in

It was not until around the mid-14th century that, with the aim of splitting financial risk, increased interest was shown in spreading investments. An entrepreneurial merchant tended to diversify the use of his capital, in commercial, banking and manufacturing activities, as well as through the purchase of property (houses and lands). In 1406, in order to persuade him to buy a piece of land adjoining his country property near Prato, Ser Lapo Mazzei wrote to Francesco Datini, "*… altogether, with the houses walls and barns would cost less than 300 florins. And for these 300 you would have a harbour on dry land and settle down.*"[6]

Importance was laid on knowing how to invest wisely as a protection against life's changing fortunes, with a balanced proportion of movable and immovable goods and property. In his Zibaldone Giovanni Rucellai cautions as follows: "*Therefore, I like neither all money nor all possessions, but some in this and some in that, and placed in different areas.*"[7] There is little doubt that when the great economic crisis hit Florence, a gradual replacement of sources of wealth was already largely under way, with agriculture prevailing almost exclusively over the other forms of production that were still typical of Tuscany up to the early 20th century, and this fact is of primary importance in assessing the particular characteristics of building and land, especially in the Florentine area.

These brief introductory remarks may help to clarify the impact of this occupation of the countryside, derived from the major transformations wrought in the 11th–14th centuries, on a changing and unchanging world which, moreover, was already deeply marked by man's presence and activities. This new colonization of the Florentine countryside may have taken place along the general lines of a use of the land whose most distant roots lie in Etruscan times, while, particularly during the early Middle Ages, developments took place on a much broader scale with the setting up of roads, paths and agricultural land, and the establishment of Church and lay settlements. But the process of reorganizing the division of land into farms, introducing changes in agricultural management, and increasing the land under cultivation was just as complicated and ramified. In this process one of the truly new features was the role that the villa-farm was gradually assuming, one strictly linked to the establishment of middle-class townspeople and their particular concerns and interests. The change in these interests, related to a landowner's presence in the country, caused a new balance among production, management and business control of the villa-farm with a display of social status and of a more stylish way of life.

In order to accurately identify and evaluate convincing historical evidence concerning the origins of a landlord's presence on his land and, more broadly, the role that his presence played in production and in subsequent developments in the Florence area, we must firstly address the question in strictly economic terms. As a yardstick we can use the criterion of an estate's management: adjustment of a unit of production's scale and structure, changes in crops and cultivation and the market return on agricultural surplus value by comparison with other possible uses of capital. Furthermore, in the case of Florentine villas, on the basis of present research there seems no doubt about the initially prevailing, if not exclusive, adoption of share-cropping farming agreements. A landlord of this period who had entrusted his property to a share-cropper frequently visited his lands and oversaw every activity that took place, keeping an eye on the stables and cellars and taking charge of the sale of produce; he thus appeared to participate fully in farming life. This moment, when the divisions between social classes rested on their role in the economy (and indeed conflicted in terms of production), preceded a radical difference in social customs and habits and is probably the period where we should place the type of villa described by de' Crescenzi in his agronomic treatise *De ruralium commodorum Libri XII*, published in 1305, in which the landlord's residence and the farm buildings appear bound together into one structural working body.[8]

In settling the terms for conducting share-cropping arrangements the conflict of financial interests between landlord and farmer became accentuated. The land-owning class, while consolidating its independent position in the city, was progressively breaking away from its traditional family roots, adopting a style of life and culture modelled on the customs of courtly circles. The "master's house", on the site of his agricultural property, now had a clear practical purpose: it enabled a proprietor to check the share-cropper's work on his land. Any common interest between proprietor and farmer, proclaimed by partisan sources and extolled as the cornerstone of the new system of operation, is belied by numerous surviving reports. We cannot fail to be aware of this conflict if we read between the lines of the abundant instructional literature that was available (either of a general or textbook nature), aimed at putting landowners on their guard against the dishonesty and greed of the peasants.[9]

Alberti, to cite the most highly respected source, becomes advocate for the bourgeois side when he dwells on the wick-

[8] Pier de' Crescenzi of Bologna, who was born in around 1233 and died in 1320, was a judge and the author of the treatise: *Ruralium Commodorum Libri XII*, written in Latin and published in around 1305. The treatise circulated the agrarian doctrine which responded to the needs of agriculture at a time in history when the bourgeoisie was asserting itself over the feudal order. The treatise became extremely well known and was translated, not only into Italian, but also German, English and Polish. The first French edition, commissioned by Charles V of France, appeared in 1373. On Pier de' Crescenzi and his treatise, see *Pier de' Crescenzi. Studi e Documenti*, Bologna 1933.

[9] Among others, it is interesting to read Paolo da Certaldo's account written in around 1350, in *Libro di buoni costumi*: "*When you want to use your villa take care not to arrive on a feast day . . . not in the square where all the workers are drinking and inflamed with wine and carrying their weapons and none of them in their senses, each thinking he is king and wanting to hold forth because they have been in the fields talking to no-one but their animals. Being heated with wine they do not even spare their betters, and if you had words with them you would not be spared either; if they laid their hands or their weapons on you it would be impossible to do anything about it, except leave them be on their feast day. If you have anything to say to workers go to them in the fields when working and you will find them humble and peaceful, thanks to the plough, mattock and spade,*" ed. G. Morpurgo, Florence 1921, p. 70. In his *Ricordi*, Giovanni di Pagolo Morelli advises a landlord "*. . . reproach him for poor work but praise him for the harvest of grain, wine and oil, hay and fruit and compare all other things to past years...ask him about his progress and his health; beware if he talks too much or is over-assertive, tells a lot of lies or boasts of his loyalty . . . Never trust such a person, keep an eye on them . . . you want to see the harvest in the field, on the threshing floor, and its amount. Always make sure you have your share down to the burrs. Never offer anything to the peasant or he will think it's owed to him, whereas he would finish you off for half what you have. Never ask to see him if it is not essential; never ask him to do anything without paying him, if you don't want it to cost you three times as much . . . don't be over friendly and don't talk to him too much . . . don't trust him at any game. In this way you will not be deceived and they will love you more than others and respect you and you will get the very best from them.*" G. di Pagolo Morelli, op. cit., pp. 234–235.

[10] " . . . it is hard to believe how much wickedness there is among the ploughmen raised among the clods. Their one purpose is to cheat you, and they would deceive you in anything. All errors are in their favour; they try constantly and by every means to get what is part of your property. First the peasant wants you to buy him an ox, goats, a sow, a mare too and then sheep. Next he asks you for loans to satisfy his creditors, to clothe his wife, to dower his daughter. Finally he asks you to reinforce the barn, to rebuild various structures and improve various parts of the building, and still he never stops complaining. Even though he is richer than his master, he is always bewailing how poor he is. He forever needs something and he never speaks to you but to bring you some expense or burden. If the crop is abundant, he keeps the better two thirds to himself. If through bad weather or some other reason the land was barren in a certain year, the peasant gives you only the damage and the loss. So does he always take for himself the most or the best of what is useful, while he passes on the unwanted and the burdensome to others." L. B. Alberti, I Libri della Famiglia, op. cit., p. 189.

A path connecting the villa with the farmhouse around Castello

edness and cunning of the "ploughmen raised among the clods". From the lips of this champion of healthy natural living, the "life in the country" myth already betrayed the deep rifts in a situation that was in fact one of exploitation and mistreatment by the landowners.[10]

But, when Alberti was writing the initial drive behind the share-cropping agreement (increase in productivity, expanded cultivation) had run its course in economic terms. This was in part because the new urban bourgeoisie failed to bring the same spirit of enterprise to property expansion and accumulation of profits in managing rural possessions that had inspired its commercial dealings. From this period onwards the use of land around Florence was sanctioned by turning a villa into a supportive element for a style of living in which the earlier productive purpose of the "master's house" became swallowed up in its new social use, a marked accent being laid (according to a family's social standing) on the need for *otium* and *delectatio*, etc., which bourgeois-humanist society identified as a way of life and a mark of social status. The leading families employed their capital on their villas and inspired the finest creative efforts of architects and artists who had previously chiefly worked only in the enclosed spaces of towns and cities. Commissioners asked them not only for architectural plans, works of sculpture and painting, landscaping of gardens and parks, but also for a veritable ideological model, complete and consistent in its use of space and time, a paradigm of their Utopian view of their status.

Looked at in this light, the villas of the nobles and the *signori* became of central importance to the development of the newly-dawning Renaissance culture, and later, to the expression of its full maturity, due to the fact that the villa drew, as we shall see, on all matters embodied by that culture, directing, stimulating and enhancing them.

All this was taking place, at least in the area of Florence, on quite another plain from agreements concerning production which, already outlined by around the mid-16th century, were to remain little changed until the first decades of the establishment of a united Italy, while still granting the reformist zeal of the Grand Dukes of Lorraine something more than a simple declaration of intent.

An analysis of typical examples in the Florentine area over this stretch of time, with particular attention to the great Medici properties, will help us to document the basic steps marking the transformation of bourgeois-humanistic culture between the early 15th century and the last days of the feudal-noble hegemony of the Grand Duchy.

CHAPTER TWO

The Ideology of Villa Life in Florentine Culture and Society

[1] G. Villani, *Cronica*, in *Croniche storiche di Giovanni, Matteo e Filippo Villani*, Milan 1848, III, p. 326.

Left: Villa Medici at Poggio a Caiano dominates the grounds.
Below: Two details of a Medicean tapestry of the 16th century in Palazzo Vecchio: Giuliano da Sangallo presents the model of the villa to Lorenzo, while the villa is under construction.

The cultural, artistic and literary contributions accompanying the economic changes we have just mentioned cannot simply be considered as descriptive or celebratory reflections of these events. They signify, instead, a new social awareness, advancement, consolidation and, frequently, far-sightedness. Thus, on the one hand, these additional forms of expression were of major importance in supporting the advancement of the middle-classes and their view of the world, and, on the other, they supplied the very soil which gave rise to the studies of the specialist treatises, an attempt to produce the kind of building that was relevant to their particular ways of life. We shall move on to examine some aspects of these cultural outposts and to trace the thematic variations related to the evolution of the productive and residential role of the extra-urban villa.

The movement of middle-class townsmen to the countryside was the most striking event of the time in the Florentine area and it coincided with the city's greatest period of expansion, following Arnolfo's enlargement of the city. The enthusiastic nature of this trend quite understandably amazed outsiders and foreigners, while being commended by contemporary local historians. Giovanni Villani, according to Burckhardt the leading authority on the fashion for building villas around Florence, wrote in his *Cronaca*, before the mid-14th century: *"There was no citizen, high or low, who had not built, or was not in the process of building, a large and expensive property in the surrounding countryside, with a handsome dwelling and fine buildings, much better than in the city. And all were guilty of this and were thought to be mad because of the extravagant expenditure. It was such a magnificent sight that those coming from outside and not familiar with Florence believed that the fine buildings and beautiful palaces in a three-mile band outside the town made it a Roman style city."*[1]

Villani's reference to "Roman style" should not lead us astray and suggest a pre-dating of the revival of *topoi* from the classical world, which was instead a result of the humanist studies of the next century. Rome is cited here in a general sense, in line with the ennobling and celebratory tradition of the city's

17

historical writing (Florence as Rome's daughter and heir, referred to by Dante) and, perhaps more specifically, as an indication of a model of the countryside drawn from current Utopian-symbolic iconography, both lay and religious. There is no doubt, that the move to take possession of the countryside described by Villani was in turn supported and reinforced by motives and ideas that were more typical of feudal times, re-evoked by the literary works of the communal era in the decisive shift from the Latin tongue to Italian. We need only mention the more important writers: the desire to escape to the country is the theme of Petrarch's *Vita solitaria*, "*domum parvam sed delectabilem et honestam struxi*", writes Petrarch, "*cumque oliveta et aliquot vineas abunde quidem non magna modestaque familia suffecturas*"[2] ("I built a small but pleasant and respectable house, with some olive-groves and vineyards, large enough for a small and unpretentious family"). In Boccaccio's work the villa symbolizes a refuge from evil and corruption and from the tragic nature of existence, as represented by the plague. If the significance here was one of foreboding and prophecy, it could nevertheless be later re-evoked for other historical conditions. Whatever the case, medieval literature frequently used the theme of nature and the landscape.[3]

[2] There is an excellent essay on the relationship between Petrarch's, and his followers' aspirations for a solitary life and the ideal of the villa by B. Rupprecht, *Villa zur Geschicte eines Ideals*, in *Wandlungen des paradiesischen und utopischen: Studien zum Bild eines Ideals (Probleme der Kunstwissenschaft,* II), Berlin 1966, pp. 210–220 from which the quotation from Petrarch is drawn.

[3] On the concept of *Locus Amoenus* in medieval literature, see E. R. Curtius, *European Literature and the Latin Middle Ages*, New York 1963; the chapter *The ideal landscape*, pp. 183ff. See also *La campagna in città. Letteratura e ideologia nel Rinascimento. Scritti in onore di Michel Plaisance*, ed. G. Isotti Rosowsky, Florence 2002.

A detail of the landscape around Florence, from Benozzo Gozzoli *Adoration of the Magi*, in the Medici Palace, Florence, 1459

4 The cult of country life, drawn from classical writers, gave rise to a whole genre of literature. *Hesiodi Opera et Dies* was printed in 1471 by Nicolò de Valle and Greco Conversio, and the Latin *Res rusticae scriptores* in 1482 in Venice, by Nicolò Jensen.

5 Among the many descriptions of humanist writers, Michele Vieri's letter to Pietro Ridolfi is of particular interest: "*Here I am to satisfy your curiosity about how I pass my time in my villa at Lecore, in what way I consume the summer days and what are my literary diversions. I rise early, go for a walk in my dressing-gown in a little garden, where I am refreshed by the cool morning breeze, I retire to my study, glance through some poet, study the precepts of Quintillian, read with wonder the Orations of Cicero. I enjoy the letters of Pliny, my greatest delight, compose epigrams or, more willingly, elegiac verse. After lunch I sleep a little. My father, who is here with me, dedicated as he is to literary pursuits, corrects, adds, adorns and reorders my compositions here and there, as needed. After sleeping I enjoy myself at checkers or the royal board. Near the villa is a vineyard with much fruit and in the middle runs a stream of freshest water full of small fish, the hedges are thick and day and night the nightingales lament past wrongs. Here I read a little and sing some improvised or familiar verses to my lute. When the sun goes down I take some exercise with the ball. This is how I spend the summer, while the spread of diseases in the city continues. I do not cultivate my fields but engage myself with letters. I do not have the library of the Sassetti or the Medici but I have a small shelf of the right books which are dearer to me than the richest possessions.*" Compare this letter with Pliny the Younger's IX Epistula where he describes a typical summer day at his villa Tusci: "*. . . then I sleep a little more, walk, and read a Greek or Latin oration aloud and with emphasis, not so much for my voice as for my stomach, though it strengthens both. I walk again, am oiled, exercise and bathe. Then, if I am dining with my wife or a few friends, a book is read and after dinner a play is performed or the lyre is played. Again I walk a little with members of the household, a number of whom are well educated . . . Friends come from nearby towns, sometimes* providing a welcome interruption when I am tired. . ." quoted by B. Patzak, Palast und Villa in Toscana, Leipzig 1913, II, p. 183.

6 Agriculture became a respected and privileged occupation. "*La vita in villa*" offered the opportunity to create a distance from the city merchants, something which was increasingly important to the wealthy and educated Florentine bourgeoisie. As Vespasiano da Bisticci reports, Agnolo Pandolfini provides a perfect example: "*. . . in the summertime he went to his well-ordered villa, a man in the fullness of his*

The rediscovery and reading of classical writers in the early days of humanism therefore provided important confirmation of aspirations that were already widespread in Florentine society at the end of the 14th and beginning of the 15th centuries. But the *Rei rusticae scriptores* who now took the stage – including the Romans, Cato, Varro, Columella, the *rusticus* Palladio, and the Greek, Hesiod – provided further food for thought, adding value to the literary notion of a house in the country as a refuge, corresponding to the classical *topos* of the joys of country life, and the practical and educational concept of farming as the purpose and *magistra* of life. The ideology of the paired words *utilitas-delectatio*, a humanist concept, dates back to classical times and appears in works of the most authoritative Latin writers, including Cicero, Seneca and Pliny.[4]

This philosophical and literary position was reflected in works and commentaries by humanist writers at the very time when the particular fashion for suburban villas became part of the larger scene of events and changes in Florentine life and, especially, the waning of the climate of civic renewal which had spanned the late 14th and early 15th centuries. The relationship between politics and culture, made possible at the peak of the communal era, was already crumbling at the very moment when individual contributions of artists and intellectuals were coming to be appreciated. In its increasing estrangement from political and social reality, the humanist debate found in contemplative life an opportunity, and perhaps one of the conditions, for a new moral equilibrium.[5] The doubts which troubled humanists during the second half of the 15th century sought to find appeasement in an *ubi consistam*, in an idealistic approach, a return to the happy natural life. The fusion of the literary tradition of Petrarch's *Vita solitaria* and specialized practical and ethical writings, such as de'Crescenzi's treatise, and newly discovered philosophical works from antiquity, gave birth to a literary output that made villa life (*la vita in villa*) the basis and mirror of a particular ideal of a way of life. In the years following 1460 the finest and more sophisticated literary masters of this school became part of the Arcadian-bucolic inspired stream, bent on showing the advantages of country life as a means both of escaping the commercial world and of realizing a "virtuous life".[6]

The father of this line of thought was Leon Battista Alberti, the first to set out the ethical principles forming the basis of rural life. In his essay on the villa he writes: "*Buy a villa to nourish and sustain your family, not to give pleasure to other people . . . Buy it from one who loved his property, not from one who attempted to sell it many times . . . The best villa is the one that needs you to improve it with your work, without great expenditure... Having bought your villa, the first aim will be to establish good relations with your neighbours...*"[7] In *Libri della Famiglia* too, where in the dialogue between Lionardo, exponent of the culture of the new generation, and Giannozzo, spokesman for the last, both agree that the concept of the villa and living in the country embody the moral bases of existence: "*Who would not take pleasure in his villa? The villa is of great, honourable and reliable value. Any other occupation is fraught with a thousand risks, carries with it a mass of suspicions and trouble, and brings numerous losses and regrets. There is trouble in purchasing, fear in transporting, anxiety in selling, apprehension in giving credit, weariness in collecting what is due to you, deceit in exchange. In all other occupations you are beset by a multitude of worries and suffer constant anxiety. The villa alone seems reliable, generous, trustworthy and honest. Managed with diligence and love, it never wearies of repaying you ... You cannot praise the villa half as much as it deserves. It is excellent for our health, helps maintain us and benefits the family. Good men and prudent householders are always interested in the villa and the farm which are both profitable and a source of pleasure and honour. There is no need, as with other occupations, to fear deceit and fraud from debtors or suppliers. Everything is above board, visible and public. You will not be cheated nor need to call upon notaries and witnesses, bring lawsuits or engage in other irritating and depressing matters, most of which are not worth the vexation of the spirit involved in settling them. Consider too that you can retire to the farm and live there in peace, caring for your family, dealing with your own affairs, and chatting pleasantly in the shade about oxen and wool, or wines and seeds. You can live undisturbed by murmurs and tales and by the strife that breaks out periodically in the city. You can be free of the suspicions, fears, slanders, injuries, feuds, and other miseries which are too ugly to mention. Among all the subjects discussed on the estate there is none which can fail to delight you... Everyone teaches and corrects you where you erred in planting or in the manner of sowing. The cultivation and management of fields does not give rise to envy, hate, and malevolence... and what is more, while enjoying your estate you can escape the violence, and unrest of the city, marketplace and palace. At the villa you can hide yourself and avoid seeing all the stealing and crime, and the great numbers of evil men who are always in sight in the city, always murmuring in your ear, screaming and bellowing hour after hour like frightful wild beasts. What a blessing to live in a villa, what unheard of happiness.*"[8]

years, with family and horses, escaping the mediocrity that the townsman was obliged to support. There were few citizens who did not want to stay with him and his children at Signa where there was then a beautiful house, equipped with everything a gentleman could wish, dogs, birds and every sort of net for catching birds or fish. Everyone coming to the house was received with honour. He was extremely liberal... when his sons appeared from Florence on feast days without bringing guests he was very unhappy and reprimanded them... When the working day was over and there were no visitors he would send to the road to see if someone was passing by who could be invited to dine with him. When they arrived they were given water to wash their hands and seated at table. When they had eaten, he thanked them and sent them on their way, saying he did not want to inconvenience them further. The sports were those of gentlemen, hunting with hawks and dogs. On these excursions there were never less than twenty on horseback, not counting those on foot with the dogs. They hunted deer and hare and went fishing, so that no time was wasted but spent on healthy pursuits. This is how Agnolo's sons passed their time..." Vespasiano da Bisticci, *Vite degli uomini illustri del secolo XV*, ed. P. D'Ancona and E. Aeschlimann, Milan 1951, p. 470ff.

[7] L. B. Alberti, *Villa*, in *Opere Volgari*, ed. C. Grayson, Bari 1960, pp. 359–363. Alberti's work on the villa was discovered, and edited, by Grayson in Cod. Pal. 267 of the National Library of Parma and is an example of the humanistic revival of the didactic tradition of the *Rei rusticae scriptores*.

[8] L. B. Alberti, *The Family in Renaissance Florence, I libri della famiglia*, op. cit., p.190.

Giuseppe Zocchi, *La Real Villa di Careggi*, Florence, 1744

[9] Ficino's view of nature is, like Poliziano's, "*Full of mythical forces and gods: the beauty of the flowers and the silence are themselves muses; wondrous events resound in the sky. The sight of animals, the energy in the air, the murmur of fountains and rustle of leafy branches seemed for these sensitive and myth-filled spirits to hold a welcoming freshness, a grace waiting to be interpreted in allegorical form. Statues, shrines and symbols soon began to appear in the landscape, reminders of the ways man extends and embellishes the natural world*". A. Chastel, *Arte e Umanesimo a Firenze ai Tempi di Lorenzo il Magnifico*, Turin 1964, p. 158.

[10] "*When my noble master Pico della Mirandola and I were wandering among the hills of Fiesole we saw all Florence spread out beneath us – fields, houses, and, in the middle, over the Arno, mist, and on the other side, steep mountains. We imagined a house placed on the slopes of the hill in such a manner as to escape the fog of Boreas, but without being in a hollow, to allow it to receive breezes when the weather is warm. We wished in addition that it be situated at equal distance from the fields and the woods, be surrounded by springs and turned towards the south and the east, as Aristotle counsels in his treatise on the administration of the family in respect of the building. While we were giving ourselves up to this imaginary invention, suddenly we had it before our eyes. Pico cried, 'Dear Ficino, is what we see before us not what we were imagining and wishing for so strongly, as in a dream? Perhaps we created the form we were imagining in our minds by the sole power of our imaginations? No less than a sage has erected it according to the correct rules and physical principles of architecture.*" 27 October 1489, M. Ficino, letter to Filippo Valori, *Opera Omnia*, Turin 1959, I, 2, pp. 893–894; translation in P. E. Foster, *A Study of Lorenzo de' Medici's Villa at Poggio a Caiano*, Yale Univ. Press 1986.
A 1478 letter to Marsilio Ficino from Poliziano ends: "*When you are inconmoded with the heat of the season in your retreat at Careggi you will perhaps think the shelter of Fiesole not undeserving of your attention. Set between the sloping sides of the mountain, we have water in abundance and since we are constantly refreshed by moderate winds we are little inconvenienced by the burning sun. As you approach the house it appears embosomed in the wood but when you reach it you find it commands a full prospect of the city. Populous as the vicinity is, yet can I enjoy the solitude so gratifying to my disposition. But I shall tempt you with other enticements. Wandering beyond the limits of his own estate, Pico sometimes steals unexpectedly on my retirement and draws me from my shade to partake of supper with him. You well know the kind of supper that, sparing indeed but neat and favoured by the charm of the conversation. But come and be my guest. Your supper shall be as good and your*

From Alberti's right-minded and slightly limited realism we move to Marsilio Ficino's more scholarly and literary escapism.[9] In Ficino's treatise *De vita*, when he advises the literati to take walks in the Tuscan hills as an antidote to melancholy and a restorative tonic for both body and mind, or when he discusses the ideal residence in a letter to Filippo Valori, expanding on the advantages of position and exposure, the places he describes still seem to evoke a religious aura, a sacred quality which evokes a blend of religious and pagan themes. In his letter to Valori, the Pandolfini family's villa and Leonardo Bruni's, glimpsed during a walk in the hills of Fiesole, literally take on the appearance of apparitions, since in this way they appear transformed, the outlines growing blurred here and there, the perfecting of an ideal style. Details concerning the typical, real and ideal character of a villa are overshadowed by its "salutary" and "hallowed" position, sheltered and cool in the summer, "among fields and woods".[10]

Ficino's descriptions are also drawn from his personal experience as proprietor of a villa at Careggi. This was given to him by Cosimo de' Medici and christened the "*Academiola*", a name which, with its polite and respectfully modest use of the diminutive, reminds us of the villa's use as a meeting-place for writers and artists in the outskirts of Florence, thanks above all to the Medici, a supplement and complement to the cultural life of the city. As we know, the Medici villa at Careggi became the seat of the Platonic Academy, at the wish of Cosimo the Elder. The founding members gathered here, making it one of the leading Italian centres for intellectuals in the mid-15th century, the cradle and disseminator of the humanist movement. The most important exponents of the cultural and artistic world gathered together here included: Ficino, Niccolò Niccoli, Poliziano, Pico della Mirandola, Brunelleschi, Alberti, Michelozzo, Donatello, Landino, Scala and Marsuppini. It was here, in the summer of 1464, that Cosimo died, expressing as his last wish that Ficino bring him a copy of his most recent translation of one of Plato's works.

The villa at Poggio a Caiano, the favourite residence of Cosimo's successor Lorenzo the Magnificent, came to be considered the most perfect exemplar. This was in part due to its *ex novo* construction and originality, its importance as a prototype of a particular typology and its fusion of different idioms and symbolic canons. As the temple of the Florentine intelligentsia and of humanist thinking (the "Florentine Trianon", to quote A. Chastel's happy definition) Poggio a Caiano became of central importance to the life and history of the Medici family, as Vasari was to recall a century later when referring, in *Ragionamenti*, to "*highly learned men with whom, when at the villa at Careggi or the one at Poggio a Caiano for their greater peace, (Lorenzo) carried out noble studies*".

Of all the grand villas, Poggio a Caiano best reflected the celebratory mythology of Florence's new cultural season, so that its contents and stylistic features became models for other Italian courts.

The Careggi villa was described in laudatory terms in a work of elegiac verse by Avogadro (Alberto da Vercelli) entitled *De religione et magnificentia Cosmi Medicis*.[11] In the literature that flourished at Lorenzo the Magnificent's court references to delightful visits to the villa at Poggio a Caiano and to its splendours occur frequently. Courtiers praised the building, Michele Verino described the Poggio's gardens, parks and aviaries in a letter[12] to his friend Canigiani, and Poliziano actually dedicated one of his most elegant elegies to the villa, *Ambra mei Laurentis amor*. Lorenzo the Magnificent himself dedicated an unusual mythological poem to the villa, *Ambra*, in which the surroundings forming the villa's natural

Above: Eleonora di Toledo's nuptial train to Poggio a Caiano, painting by Giovanni Stradano, Palazzo Vecchio Florence.
Right: The entrance to the villa Medici at Poggio a Caiano as a temple-like portico.

wine perhaps better, for in the quality of wine I shall contend for superiority even with Pico himself". A. Poliziano, *Angeli Politiani Opera*, Basel 1553, p. 559, trans. by W. Roscoe, *Life of Lorenzo de' Medici*, 2nd ed., London 1891, p. 275. Roscoe tells us that Poliziano was Lorenzo's long-term guest at Fiesole.

[11] E. H. Gombrich's essay, *Alberto Avogadro's descriptions of the Badia of Fiesole and of the villa of Careggi* in *Italia Medievale e Umanistica V*, 1962 p. 217. "*I came to the villa at Careggi not to cultivate my field but my soul. Come to us, Marsilio, as soon as possible. Bring with you our Plato's De summo bono which by now I imagine you have translated from the Greek tongue into Latin as you promised. I desire nothing more ardently than to know the route that leads most conveniently to happiness. Farewell, and come not without your Orphean lyre*". This excerpt comes from a letter in Latin from Cosimo to Marsilio Ficino, edited without date or source by A. Fabronio, *Magni Cosmi Medicei Vita*, I, Pisa 1789, p. 137 (an English translation appeared in J. Ross, *Lives of the Early Medici*, London 1910, p. 73). J. S. Ackerman, *The Villa Form and Ideology of Country Houses*, London 1990, p. 289, n.17. Life in the villa at Fiesole, commissioned from Michelozzo by Cosimo the Elder for his son Giovanni shortly before 1455, must have been conducted in the same manner.

[12] "*Ad Simonem Canisium, Superioribus literis promiseram tibi Caiani Ruris laudes describere, ut libentius ad Agellum nostrum Caiano vicinum accederes. Vicus est celeberrimus, in colle lenitur acclivi. Is distat ab Urbe decem millibus passuum via est plana et patens, pervia multis simul curribus, sine luto heme, sine lapide, glarea operta. Umbro fluvius ambit, profundus, amoenus; ibi maxima copia Piscium, hinc inde, et supra semper vernantibus Avibus. Ambra Villa dicitur, sive ab Anne, sive a pulchritudine, quam Medices, ut in caeteris mirabilis, Aquaeductu per multa millia, per montes et anfractus derivata irrigat aqua saluberrima, et in colle sicco per necessaria, viatoribus, ut spero potum preabitura suavem Moles nondum structa, sed jacta sunt Fundamenta. Haec Pistorium, Florentiamque Urbes media insecat. Ceaterum ad Aquilonem iuxta Umbronem Amnem Planities iacet maxima: Florentissima Prata quae cingit Ager immensus, ne forte auctus imbribus Amnis limo oblimet pabula: Rigantur aestate perennibus rivis, ut ter Foeni copia resecetur…. Stercorantur alternis annis Fimo Vaccarum, ne assiduo foetu sterilescant. In medio, loco paulo editiori, Stabula multa et longissima facta, lapide area stradata, ne fimo et luto vaccae sordescant, moenibus et fossa latissima cincta inter Castelli, quatuor turribus. Vaccarum numerus magnus, faecundissimae quaeque, Cascique pinguissimi in hyeme copia magna fit, qui Urbi Florentiae, et*

*Agro supersit; neque ut olim ex Gallia Cisalpina
necessit sit nunc adportare. Lactentium vitulorum
caro suavissima. Est ibi Stabulum Porcorum, qui
Sero pingui magnopere crassescunt. Incredibilis
est Avium numerus, Aquatilium presertim, et in
pratis degentium: inter domesticas Silvestris
Anser et Anata pescuntur. Aucypium sine labore
uberrimum. Praeterea in silvis vicinis, et id Medicis industria, Phasides Aves, et Phoenicopteri,
quas ille usque ex Sicilia devexit. Qui Coturnicum?
Quid Hortulanorm? Quid Ficedularum numerum
espresserim? Pomeria pulcherrima, et Hortus
iuxta ripas fluminum: Mororum Sylva copiosa, ut
iam inde speretur utilitas Serici. Se quid Te plura?
Veni iam: dicis illud quod Sabaerrum Regina
visa gloria Salomonis asserui longe famam mi-
norem, quam esset rei veritas. Vale.*" Letter from
Michele Verino to Simone Canigiani, in C. von
Stegmann, H. von Geymüller, *Die Architektur
der Renaissance in Toscana*, Munich 1885–93,
pp. 180–181.

[13] B. Rupprecht, *L'iconologia della villa veneta*, in
"Bollettino del Centro Internazionale di Studi
di Architettura A. Palladio" "BCISA", Venice
1968, p. 234.

setting are taken up and celebrated in mythological terms (the current threatens to carry away the remains of the nymph Ambra, Ombrone's beloved, now transformed by Ombrone into an island close by the villa). An important point, and a complementary one here, is the extolling of country life in allegory and myth represented by the symbolism of the seasons of the year portrayed on the majolica frieze ornamenting the villa's entablature with agricultural motifs (the growing of vines and wheat). Furthermore, to give an example of a sequence of elements following a harmonious order, this frieze was used by Ficino as an illustration in a letter to Lorenzo which, according to Rupprecht, represents a document marking the villa's foundation.[13]

At the beginning of the Cinquecento this enthusiasm for villa life was widespread among the noble, merchant, banking and intellectual élite of Italian society. Time was given to creative activities which, to varying degrees, included residential and farming matters, courtly life and all the necessary for diversion and relaxation, or was reserved for withdrawing into poetic quietude.[14] The Medici court's Florentine villas, either

visited and known personally or reproduced by architects and artists, played a leading role in disseminating this style of life. Giuliano da Maiano and Sangallo went to Naples, and Florentine artists gravitated to Rome, especially when a member of the Medici family rose to the papal throne. L. Puppi has attempted to demonstrate the creation and arrangement of a type of "humanist villa" that bridged the 15th and 16th centuries, before Palladio's great season, modelled on the examples we have described above.[15] In the mid-16th century another versatile talent, Anton Francesco Doni, in a work entitled *Le Ville*, succeeds in giving us a remarkably broad picture of the social and practical characteristics of an out-of-town villa.

Above: Giuseppe Zocchi, *La Real Villa di Cafaggiolo*, Florence, 1744.
Below: Giuseppe Zocchi, *Villa della Magia*, Florence, 1744.
Right: Giuseppe Zocchi, *La Real Villa dell'Ambrogiana*, Florence, 1744.

[14] *La vita in villa* was lauded and explored in a series of literary works which were chiefly produced in the area of the Po valley and the Veneto around the mid-1500s. Among these we should mention: *Lettera in laude della villa*, 1543, by Alberto Lollio of Ferrara; *Vinti giornate dell'agricoltura e de' piaceri della villa*, 1550, by Agostino Gallo of Brescia; *La nuova vaga et dilettevole villa*, by Giuseppe Falcone of Piacenza, first edition 1559. In these and other works life in a villa is presented as the complete antithesis of city life. Gallo writes: "*Here at the villa you do not hear people slandered as you do under the loggias in the city, or in workshops or other places . . . People here are not ambitious, envious, proud or underhand; they are not disloyal, hot-tempered, vindictive or murderous; they are not cuckolded by their wives; still less will you find them acting as false witnesses, dishonest notaries, lying officials, false lawyers, unjust judges or devious legal clerks . . . Nor will you see here debtors languishing in jail, criminals dragged off by force, swindlers sent to the galleys, slanderers having their eyes put out, blasphemers having their tongues slit, malefactors branded on the face, false witnesses having their hands cut off, murderers being beheaded, thieves being hanged by the neck, traitors being quartered . . . Who would want to live anywhere but in the country? Here we have complete peace, real freedom, tranquil security and sweet repose. We can enjoy pure air, shady trees with their abundant fruit, clear water and lovely valleys; we can make use of the fertile farmland and the fruitful vines, as well as enjoying the mountains and hills for the view, the woods for their charm, the fields for their spaciousness and the gardens for their beauty. Another source of enjoyment is being able to watch the hard work of the farmers and the discipline of their teams as they skillfully plough and sow the fields, and then see the crops flourishing and being harvested; and hear the songs of the peasants, the pipes of the shepherds, the rustic bagpipes of the cowherds and the sweet singing of the birds.*" Quoted by J. S. Ackerman, op. cit., p. 129. The scholar Ortensio Lando takes a similar if more extreme stance, advising men to abandon not only cities and palaces, but even villages and villas, to withdraw into utter solitude. On this position of 16th-century literary men and the crisis in urban values see P. F. Grendler, *Critics of the Italian World 1530–1560. A. F. Doni, N. Franco and O. Lando*, Wisconsin Press 1969. The exhortations to go into retreat are accompanied by exaltation of the rural life as a path to Virtue, a position earlier sustained by Alberti and taken up again by Palladio in his *Four Books of Architecture*.

[15] L. Puppi, *Le residenze di P. Bembo* in Padoana, in "L'Arte", 7/8 (1969), pp. 30–65, which emphasises the close links that Pietro's father, Bernardo Bembo, had with Florence, Medici circles and

leading figures such as Ficino. Links which, according to the author, were enough to "*have a profound influence on cultural directions and even on ways of life*", strong enough to give rise to a "*desire to build, on the family land near Padua, a dwelling modelled on the extra-urban examples of his Florentine humanist friends*". There are accounts of other humanist country houses in the Veneto, aside from Bembo's, such as the "*the modest and isolated villa, almost just a small house surrounded by shady trees*", dreamt of by Trifon Gabriele. Bartolomeo Pagello, a humanist of Vicenza, gave the following instructions to Bernardino Leoniceno, who wanted to build a villa at Monticello di Lonigo: "*My needs are modest . . . It will suffice me if only one doorway leads from the house to the garden, rising only two steps from the courtyard. On either side there should be rooms, not luxurious but supplied with the usual amenities. The reasonably elegant library, my only treasure, should lead off the bedroom. Many apple, pear, pomegranate and Damascene plum trees, and plentiful vines; many plane trees around the house and clipped box, a beautiful bay tree, and a clearer- than-crystal spring, dedicated to the Muses.*" The quotations are taken from Puppi, op. cit. Giangiorgio Trissino's villa at Cricoli, which he designed to be the seat of the Academy of Bernardino Partenio for the education of young noblemen, was a famous villa in its day and is included by Serlio in his *Treatise*. We have the following description by Trissino himself in 1537: "*. . . the place is less than half a mile outside Vicenza, wonderfully convenient, and its situation and those of the vegetable and flower gardens is very pleasing. The whole place is called Cricoli, surrounded by walls and crenellations, built like a fortress, and courtyards with fountains and loggias, and many comfortable and noble rooms, far from distraction and disturbance.*" W. Wolters, *S. Serlio e il suo contributo alla villa veneziana prima del Palladio*, in "BCISA", Venice (1969), XI, p. 83.

[16] This is the description of Bellocchi who edited *Le Ville*, including the unpublished manuscript in the Library in Reggio Emilia and others from the Correr Museum in Venice, the Trivulziana in Milan and the 1566 Bologna edition, a pen and ink copy of which exists in the Biblioteca Ambrosiana in Milan. U. Bellocchi, *Le Ville di A. F. Doni*, Modena, Aedes Muratoriana 1969.

[17] B. Rupprecht, in *L'Iconologia della Villa Veneta*, op. cit., p. 233.

[18] The quotations are taken from the text, note 16, p. 32 of the quoted edition.

We should linger a little on this distinctive figure, man of letters, artist and courtier, "*mystical and calculating, a mixture of contrasting principles and contradictory aspirations*".[16] He was a restless traveller who spent much time outside his native city and an indefatigable writer and editor whose troubled existence embodied the crisis in a world based on the *studia humanitatis* entrusted with providing a civilized education. Doni's studies in Florence and important contacts with areas of the Po Valley and the Veneto form a link between two parallel worlds. However, according to Rupprecht, the cultural roots of the treatise *Le Ville* are more obviously identifiable as Tuscan than Venetian in the author's concept of culture.[17]

Doni's idea of classifying villas according to the social standing of their commissioners was not new. A categorization of this kind, traced by scholars and essayists to Vitruvius, appears in both Alberti and Francesco di Giorgio (as well, in a certain manner, in Pier de' Crescenzi's 14th-century treatise). However, what is significant about Doni's work, as we shall see, is the precision of the classifications and his use of a scale of social values. Doni begins by first describing a town villa: "*of a King, a Duke, and powerful and valorous lord*", specifying that "*There is no difference between the outside and the inside*". Indeed, the features of the structure which he describes as, "*a space of two hundred or more yards each way*", with, "*at the top . . . a beautiful palazzo which was entered from a stairway . . . with three parts, in fine and varied style, like that in the San Lorenzo Library in Florence*",[18] could well be the description

of a sumptuous city palazzo. The princely examples which Doni is referring to (the Castello of the Duke di Fiorenza, Coppare of Ferrara, Marmirolo of Mantua and the Palazzo Imperiale, Urbino) give some idea of the size of these early villas. The *Codice Reggiano*, which we shall quote from, contains a lengthy passage concerning this type of lordly villa, which we cite below, offering precious first-hand information on the life that five or six times a year a lord conducted in the country during his week-long visits.

"On arriving in his Village on a Sunday morning he paid an honorarium for a Mass to be performed, with music, instruments and wonderful decorations, in which the whole Villa took part. After this, at the Villa there was horse racing and jumping … with lances and other devices, as the master of the stables had instructed his riders. Then the table was set in the pillared loggia overlooking the square, and with trumpets, pipes and music his lordship came to table, cheering the whole village with his friendly manner and his happy court. When the table was prepared, everyone from the estate appeared with venison, kid, hare, game birds, fruit and other things, everything presented with goodwill. Whereupon with a happy expression he accepted and thanked them graciously, praising the gifts and inviting them to eat, because a Prince, Lord or gentleman may not lack good manners. After lunch the peasants had a wrestling match, until only one was left. It was certainly a fine thing to see the pride and skill of those strong men. The young girls ran a race, and then the young men. Then it was time for the Play, sometimes performed before and sometimes after dinner, and with music and dancing the day of entertainments and festivities drew to a happy end. On Monday morning bright and early, as had been arranged for the deputies, they went hunting for wildlife, boar and deer. Lunch was served in some pretty hillside spot with a good view, a suitable place having been found for such a prince, and for the gentlemen; or atop a pleasing hill shaded by the thick branches of a wood, where some good spring rises with sweet fresh water, and all day was spent hunting with nets, snares and dogs. In the evening they returned with a large bag, everyone happy after the chase and pleased with the game, thinking of their daring exploits with spears, the ferocity of the dogs and the struggle of the wild creatures to defend themselves. With peaceful hearts they ate their dinner at the palazzo with good appetite, and after all their exertions went happily to bed. On the following day he [the prince] attended to farming matters, doing some pruning himself and ordering various fruit trees and vines to be planted. He had roads improved, gardens ornamented and spent the whole day engaged on the farm, except after lunch when he

[19] U. Bellocchi, *Le Ville . . .* , op. cit., pp. 42–46.

Left: from the top: Villa Collazzi; Villa Corsini; Villa Medici at Poggio a Caiano; Villa Petraia; Villa Medici at Lappeggi, from Giuseppe Zocchi, 1744.
Below: Villa Medici at Castello by Giuseppe Zocchi; the same villa by F. B. Werner, 1730; Villa Medici at Cafaggiolo, Villa Ambrogiana by Bernardo Rosaspina, 1830.

passed some time in amusements. On Wednesday morning, the falconers prepared their birds and at a given time they had truly royal sport, taking enormous pleasure in the battles in the air, the flight of the wild birds and of the trained falcons, and one could find no greater happiness. On one day, it was a Thursday, he had the Villa prepared and with dogs and greyhounds went hunting for small game, hare and foxes, giving the gentlemen the greatest possible pleasure. After lunch, sheltered from the heat, the gentlemen turned to games … with poles and balls etc. On this special festive day his lordship was wont to bestow many favours, taking note of requests and giving alms generously. He then rode about the property, to see if the rivers were causing damage and, with artful engineering, when necessary he gave orders for bridges, the digging of ditches and clearing of drains, before returning home where he lunched alone. Meanwhile, the men prepared themselves and the fishing nets for the best possible catch (according to the place), attended by his lordship and the rest of the court with that pleasure which in the opinion of many is keener than all other delights of the Villa. Fishing only tires the eye, and for those who find this too peaceful, they may hunt when they wish, whether hunting or bird-netting, whichever is preferred, and I enjoy both, and I believe that one is worth the other . . . ."[19]

The second villa to be defined is the country house for the recreation and relaxation of the gentleman, and also, "*this is the farm for scholars*". The classical notion of a country house being the place for scholars and men of letters, makes its first appearance in gentlemanly circles in Doni's essay. Here we find, albeit in terms of exaggerated grandeur compared with the previously cited accounts, both the actual and ideal characteristics of the villa so admired by the humanists: "*A closed courtyard with surrounding walls all painted with Flemish landscapes*" (Doni is here describing a villa that he knew in Reggio), "*and through a broad and well-proportioned entrance with posts, architraves, cornices, columns and foundations; on either side narrow urns, and others that allow you to sit comfortably on the rim provided by the width of the worked stone, and these are planted with sweet oranges, the rest are filled with juniper, flowers and fragrant herbs, and all that most delights the master of the house. There should be two loggias on this level, one for summer and one for winter. Between these lies the entrance to the house, comfortable in all parts and supplied with all necessary rooms, and this building should be at the head of the courtyard… given an elegant appearance by vases, paintings and architecture, with a generous number of windows giving onto the courtyard with carved balustrades and balconies*

... Gardens, fruit trees, pergolas and groves of trees should be arranged in suitable places around the building". [20]

Doni continues his essay by comparing this type of villa to the one "*the great Lorenzo de' Medici gave to Marsilio Ficino*". He includes Cafaggiolo in this category, since in his view it embodied the very essence of this type, designed to bring together gentlemen and men of letters: "*when a nobleman is troubled by his efforts for the Republic, while another governs in his place he seeks some quiet retreat two or three times a year to more easily support the bothersome matters and intolerable travail that so frequently afflict him in government. So that he is not overwhelmed by wearisome books, he climbs a hill, walks the plain, pausing with some pleasing small volume in his hand, and amid the greenery of some lovely glade he restores himself, his eyes weary from reading many books of another kind; and some take pleasure in grafting and pruning, planting fine fruit trees and doing a little gardening, but only insofar as this labour provokes no sweating...*" [21]

These observations give a clear picture of the basic concepts of the humanist villa, a harmonious balance between entertainment, escape from the preoccupations of city life, and working on the land, understood, naturally, as a pleasurable activity.

The third villa is classified as "merchant property" and Doni does not give a particular architectural type but describes

[20] Ibid., pp. 46–48.

[21] Ibid., p. 52.

Giusto Utens, *Cafaggiolo*, 1599

[22] Ibid., p. 56.

[23] Ibid., p. 64.

instead a *de facto* social situation, noting the tendency of a newly wealthy merchant to buy a villa of a different size and status, as a place for undemanding relaxation. This was a setting in which merchants: *"caper over the flowery meadows to recover from their days spent labouring over troublesome accounts, which has half atrophied their bodies!"*[22]

With the fourth villa, defined as an "economy house", Doni is describing a more modest construction, the outcome of a worker's savings, providing the owner with wine, grain and wood, and with a purely utilitarian appearance. This would seem similar in type to the traditional farmer's house, built to satisfy the simple practical needs of a family and, as the writer stresses, with no particular style of a typological kind, apart perhaps from the very casualness of the additions: *"These houses are built without a plan, there is a room for the grandfather in the summer, a stall for a horse, the great-grandfather; a pigeon-loft for the old grandmother who is fond of birds; an oven, barn and an extra roofed shelter turn a poor house into a handsome lodging. However, it should have its own elm tree on the road for withdrawing into the shade, the workers' gossip and the neighbours stories."*[23]

The "villa", or "utility hut", occupying the fifth and last position on this scale is the home of the peasant and Doni does not describe it as being of any particular type or pat-

Giusto Utens, *Il Trebbio*, 1599

tern, but he uses the category to weave in a general eulogy of country life – *"Oh the happy, free and lovely life of the Villa, the tranquil peaceful life"* – which outlines the course of a farm-worker's day, from rising at dawn, working in the fields and eating his rustic meal before finally retiring for the night. This confirms Doni's view of villa life as an escape from urban life, while nevertheless insisting on the innate superiority of city life and the negative side of the concept of rusticitas professed by Alberti and the Florentine humanists. *". . . we of the Villa, born of gentlemen; we are here while they go to dig . . . and there the fields will bear crops, while here we live in suitable style . . . Thus, the Villa should be used as a Villa and the City as a City. You cannot lie with dogs without getting fleas . . . "*. [24]

In the Venetian area the economic and cultural climate of the Cinquecento was very different, the new ethical dimension that farming assumed was the "sacred agriculture" praised by Cornaro, which came to fruition with the Palladian villa.

To return to the larger villas in the Florence area, events in the second half of the 16th and following centuries corroborate the idea that their position was alternative and, more frequently, supplementary to an urban residence. They were frequently a refuge for those privileged men of letters who enjoyed the benefit of princely patrons; ivory towers for creative minds troubled by moral reasoning, settings for academic debate,[25] perfect places for indulging in idyllic or

[24] Ibid., p. 79. The quotation is taken from the 1566 edition; it is not included in the manuscript in Reggio.

[25] Raffaello Borghini gave his treatise on painting and sculpture the title *Il Riposo*, the name of the villa between Ponte a Ema and Grassina that was made available to him by his friend Bernardo Vecchietti. According to literary tradition, the villa supplied the setting for a discussion that takes place between the learned friends, Vecchietti himself, Ridolfo Sirigatti, Baccio Valori and Girolamo Michelozzi. On the villa see M. L. Benevento, G. Fanelli, *Il ninfeo della villa il Riposo*, in "Ingg-Arch.", n.11–12 (1961).

Giusto Utens, *Artimino*, 1599

[26] See U. Pirotti, *Benedetto Varchi e la cultura del suo tempo*, Florence 1971.

[27] Quoted by C. O. Tosi, *Castello nel comune di Sesto Fiorentino*, Florence 1905, p. 39.

sometimes mawkish sentiments, or passionate yearnings for Arcadian graces or, at times, the transaction of official or business matters, where, in this instance, the poet and man of letters provided a counterbalance to courtly ritual and political negotiation.

Following the intercession of Cosimo I, Benedetto Varchi returned to his native Florence in 1543, after living in Venice, Ferrara, Padua and Bologna, and in 1558 the Grand Duke actually made him a gift of Villa la Topaia, part of the ducal estates of the Castello farm. Here, Varchi could surround himself with his faithful friends, Bonsi, Oradini and Girolamo Razzi, far from the more wearisome debates of Academicians and scholars. Here, he could devote his time to writing the *Istorie Fiorentine*, commissioned by Cosimo;[26] here too he was also to write *Dialogo delle Lingue*, known as *Ercolano*, which is set against the background of Villa la Topaia. Lasca, a humorous poet and leader of lively gatherings and pranks (himself the owner of another famous villa in the neighbourhood of Castello, Il Pozzino) buried his earlier literary diatribe with Varchi to sing the praises of the Topaia's delights in verse: *Varchi! / la vostra villa è posta in loco / ch'ella volge le spalle al tramontano, / sicchè soffi a sua posta, o forte, o piano / nuocere non vi può molto nè poco, / (. . .) Penso doman venire (e non è baia) / Con esso voi a starmi alla Topaia.*[27]

To thank the Duke for his favours Varchi wanted to rename his villa "Cosmiano", while Lelio Torelli suggested the name

Giusto Utens, *Castello*, 1599
Next pages: *Lappeggi* and *Ambrogiana*

"Varchiano", until lack of agreement finally led the villa to keep its original name. After the property had returned to the Medici following Varchi's death, Scipione Ammirato also stayed there, before Grand Duke Ferdinando generously gave him, according to Moreni, *"the use and amenities of the Petraia villa so that, in this gracious setting, he could conduct his studies in greater tranquillity and give the final touches to completing* Istorie Fiorentine *and his other works."* [28]

As places for official gatherings, the Medici family's Florentine villas became particularly important at the end of the 16th century, when the Grand Ducal residences had been established throughout Tuscany (on the basis of Buontalenti's designs[29]) and the earlier properties situated immediately around the Grand Duchy's capital served as alternatives to the Pitti Palace for state occasions. There are numerous accounts of the role the villa played in life of the court, including theatrical performances and wedding celebrations,[30] hunting (among the most famous grounds in Europe); sumptuous scenic displays,[31] or simply a pleasant stay in the country with all the trimmings demanded by the customs of court. Some houses were also to be the scenes of bloody events and mysterious deaths, all faithfully recorded by the chroniclers of the day, while others were to serve as gilded cages for the exile of rebel wives.[32]

Furthermore, use of the various villas followed a seasonal pattern which depended on their location and the opportuni-

[28] D. Moreni, *Notizie istoriche dei contorni di Firenze*, Florence 1791, letter IX, Vol. I, p. 90.

[29] In the mid-16th century Bernardo Buontalenti carried out complete or partial transformation of almost all the Medici villas, working at Pratolino, Magia, Ambrogiana, the Coltano villa, Petraia, Artiminio, Cerreto Guidi and Lappeggi, before Ferri's intervention. See A. Fara, *Le ville di Bernardo Buontalenti nel tardo Rinascimento toscano*, in "Storia dell'Arte", 29 (1977), pp. 25–38.

[30] The route taken by the Medici's foreign brides to reach Florence always included a stay at a grand ducal villa. Eleonora of Toledo, wife of Cosimo I, was received with her retinue at Poggio a Caiano. Grand Duchess Johanna of Austria, the bride of Francesco I, travelled from Firenzuola *"passing by the villa at Cafaggiolo where she was received by Alessandro Salviati and other leading gentlemen. Later, she and her retinue stayed also at the Poggio villa, prepared for her repose, where they were received by Cardinal Sforza and Don Luigi of Toledo."* Maria Maddalena of Austria, before her triumphal entrance into Florence for her marriage to Cosimo II, was a guest at the Castello villa. The villa at Pratolino was to be visited by Princess Violante Beatrice of Bavaria before her triumphal entrance for her marriage to Grand Prince Ferdinando in 1688, while Margherita Luisa d'Orleans, after sailing from France to Livorno, stopped at the Ambrogiana villa where she met her future husband Cosimo III. See *Memorie de' viaggi e*

*feste per le reali nozze de' Serenissimi sposi Vio-
lante Beatrice di Baviera e Ferdinando Principe di
Toscana*, Florence, Stamperia di S.A.S. 1688, by
A. Segni, who had also celebrated the wedding
of Cosimo III in 1662.

[31] The famous "musical plays" by Ferdinando,
Cosimo III's son, the last Medici patron of
the arts, were performed at the Pratolino villa.
In 1689 Ferdinando had a theatre built at the
Pratolino villa, directing operations himself
and calling on the leading composers and stage-
designers, such as the Bibbiena family. L. Puliti,
*Cenni storici della vita del Serenissimo Ferdinando
de' Medici Granprincipe di Toscana e delle origini
del pianoforte*, Florence 1874.

[32] Don Pietro, Francesco I's brother, murdered
his wife Eleonora at Cafaggiolo for her infidelty.
In the Cerreto Guidi villa Isabella, daughter of
Cosimo I, met a mysterious end, perhaps at the
hand of her husband the Duke of Bracciano,
as contemporary historians report. Margherita
Luisa, Cosimo III's wife, intolerant of life at
court and of her husband, was confined to the
villa at Poggio a Caiano for almost two years
before their final separation.

[33] The Lappeggi villa had its finest hour when
Cosimo III entrusted it to his brother Cardinal
Francesco Maria who made it his chosen place
for entertaining guest, having it converted by
Antonio Ferri and embellishing it with splendid
gardens. There is an instructive account of the

ties they offered for amusement and relaxation. According
to the accounts of contemporary chroniclers, Grand Prince
Ferdinando, son of Cosimo III, used the Poggio a Caiano
villa chiefly in the springtime *"where he was entertained by the
comic performers he kept for the purpose"*. In the summer he
preferred to stay at the Poggio Imperiale villa, while he almost
invariably passed the autumn at Pratolino, devoting his time
to hunting and music. During the 17th and 18th centuries not
only the Grand Duke but various family members also held
court while occupying a villa whose use had been ceded to
a younger son. During the reign of Grand Duke Ferdinand
II, the Castello villa was made over to his brother Cardinal
Giovan Carlo, and in 1664 the Lappeggi villa was given to
another brother, Prince don Mattias.[33]

From the correspondence of Francesco Redi, poet and doctor to the court during Cosimo III's reign, we gain many
illuminating insights into courtly life in a villa at a time when
princely pomp and wasteful expenditure, shared by the para-
sites in Cosimo's entourage, were modelled on the lavish style
of the Spanish court, financed by a levying of taxes which was
increasingly crippling to the Grand Duchy's subjects. As court
doctor, Redi accompanied the Duke's family in its moves and
he applied himself to poetry not *"as a profession, but rather as a
pastime and to avoid sloth, while he was staying with at the villa
with the court."* He obviously writes of the joys of rural life, as
in *Bacco in Toscana* where he refers to the famous vineyards

of Petraia and Castello.[34] Redi was also to be present at the signing of the treaty between Cosimo III and his wife Margherita Luisa d'Orléans, on the eve of her final departure from the Grand Duchy to return to France.[35]

With the passing of the House of Medici, the enormous estates the family had accumulated[36] were redistributed, part of the far-reaching scheme of reformist measures embarked on by Pietro Leopoldo of Lorraine. A certain number of properties were alienated, despite the dogged opposition of those – tenants or administrators – who made lavish profits out of their situations. In the general scheme to reorganize the Grand Duchy's lands and properties only five estates were to remain under personal administration: *"The estates of Poggio a Caiano and the ten annexed farms, Castello with its vineyards and four annexed farms, and Cascine dell'Isola with its eleven annexed farms, and Poggio Imperiale with its twelve annexed farms, may continue to be administered for the purpose of retreat and pleasure."*[37]

The villas which were to remain the property of the ducal family were also designed to be used for "the court's recreation". The Grand Duchy of Lorraine's interest in these recreational visits is shown by the works of restoration and improvement that they carried out, making changes to conform, especially in the gardens, to the fashionable taste of the day (among others, note the changes introduced to the gardens at Petraia and Castello). However, a certain desire to cut down on expenses by the Lorraine family resulted in the loss of at least two splendid Medici residences, the villas of Pratolino and Lappeggi, destroyed to avoid the costs of restoration.

Under French rule, and after Princess Elisa's move from Lucca to Florence, the Medici properties around the city had a new hour of splendour due to the princess's preference for these outlying villas, and also to her keen interest in the arts. Elisa spent most summers at Poggio a Caiano where, besides attending to the interior decoration of the rooms and alterations to the double staircase leading to the terrace encircling the first floor, she opened a majestic avenue, twenty metres wide, planned to extend as far as Prato. In Elisa's day forty gardeners, aside from the farm-workers and gamekeepers, were employed on the enormous farm and hunting reserve. The lively society which attended the court could enjoy boat trips on the river Ombrone whose wandering course created little islands, linked by bridges built from bank to bank. Elisa held court at Villa del Poggio and during the summer she organised outdoor festivities and concerts which were performed by famous musicians (including Paganini), as well as more modest entertainments. One of Elisa's court ladies, Madame Ida Saint-Elme, wrote in her

lavish festivities that the Cardinal laid on in 1709 in honour of the visit to Florence of King Frederick IV of Denmark: *"Early in the morning His Highness Prince Giovan Gastone, on behalf of his uncle the Cardinal, went to escort him to the villa at Lappeggi. When the time came to go to table even His Highness admired the lavish board, and its elegant display. All the royal pages waited at table. The table was reset four times. Later, when the cloth was removed, another cloth was revealed which in no time was set with a great array of sweet dishes. Once again the table was cleared and covered with highly prized liqueurs and a pyramid of glasses. A great silver coffee-pot shaped like a fountain with four spouts was placed before the King. On the four sides of his square table four gold trays, on two of them three cups of chocolate and two of water. The four spaces between were filled with Savoy biscuits and other dunking pastries. The two round ones had a similar setting, on a larger scale, with two silver vases. When the coffee-pot was removed it was replaced by a centrepiece filled with little flasks of San Lorenzo wine and other precious wines, and all the ornamented glassware was from Bohemia. We should mention that during the meal instruments were played and these same musicians accompanied the King for the rest of that day so that they were always ready to entertain him... Having seen the fine chamber, painted with Indian lacquer, the Kaffehaus, they went to look at the beautiful large garden of lemon trees below the villa, and from there to pass along the pleasant avenues to the other casino, called La Fattoria. On returning to the first garden they at once greeted by a table laden with a cold picnic including dairy products, soaked bread, capons from Galera, chilled fruits and cakes of every kind. What made most impact was the chilled fruit, being quite new to His Majesty and all his court . . . candied fruit of every kind and water-ices shaped like fruits . . . a separate table with another ornamental centrepiece full of little flasks of rare Tuscan wines . . . After the repast, a ball was proposed to round off the day and the King himself led the dancing. But it was drawing late and the air was damp, so to safeguard the ladies His Majesty entered the villa to find a place to dance indoors. And since the countryside gave a feeling of freedom and merriment French dances were set aside and instead there were country and folk dances, familiarly known as* alla spalmata, alla mestola *and* alla scarpettaccia, *and words cannot describe how the King enjoyed himself."*
G. Conti, *Firenze dai Medici ai Lorena*, Florence 1909, pp. 659–662.

[34] G. Imbert, *Francesco Redi, l'uomo. Dal carteggio edito e inedito*, Milan 1925. See also *Le usanze fiorentine del secolo XVII*, ed. P. Fanfani, Florence 1863.

[35] The Grand Duchess was given leave to say goodbye to her children before her departure.

The abbot Marucelli wrote the following to her on 3 June 1675: *"on Tuesday at around 20 hours, the three young princes will come to pay their respects to Your Serene Highness as the Most Serene Grand Duke has ordered, if Your Highness gives no orders to the contrary."* G. Conti, op. cit., p. 21.

[36] *"In February 1749 the grand ducal lands in Tuscany consisted of 49 estates, divided into 5 groups: 13 in the area of Florence-Arezzo; 10 in the immediate outskirts of Florence; 10 in the Pisa-Lucca area; 7 in the area of Pisa-Livorno; 9 in the Maremma. Ten or so of these farms had no organic unity of land, cultivation or management."* I. Imberciadori, *Campagna toscana nel '700*, Florence 1953, p. 96.

[37] In *Relazioni sul Governo della Toscana*, Pietro Leopoldo gives an exact account of the organization: *"The Office of Properties covered the management of possessions, farms, houses, and leases owned by the house of Medici. There was much graft in this department at the time of Medici rule, and they were so poorly administered that during the last years of the house of Medici the farms supplied almost no income. At the time of His Imperial Highness's government it was sought to remedy the position by letting the farms belonging to the Office of Properties with all the proceeds of the land, and particularly the farms, houses, shops and rural possessions. A good deal of graft accompanied these leases; they were now for all the farms together as one body, now for some separate farms; and as the leases expired they were renewed on different terms and conditions, never of benefit to the Medici but only to the tenants, and embroilment was such that on some occasions it offered tenants the opportunity to completely ruin a peasant's goods and family, and also to bring ruin on each other. The early ones made a good deal of money, because business was still little known, those coming later ruined themselves by dint of quarrelling, falling behind with their payments and building up debts to the Office of Properties which were never paid because of the clauses and conditions which had perhaps deliberately been included in the contracts to give rise to litigation. This is the state in which S.A.R. found the Office of Properties on his arrival in Tuscany."* A. Salvestrini, *Pietro Leopoldo, Relazioni sul Governo della Toscana*, Florence 1968, p. 343.

[38] I. Saint Elme, *Mémoires d'une contemporaine*, Paris 1895, p. 222. See also P. Marmottan, *Les Arts en Toscane sous Napoléon Ier. La Princesse Elisa*, Paris 1901.

Right: Poggio a Caiano aerial view.
Next page: The Villa Imperiale in a page for a fan, etching XVII century Uffizi, Gabinetto Disegni e Stampe, Florence.

memoirs: *"Dans les soirées intimes de la Grand-Duchesse, on riait, on jouait au billard, quelquefois à cache-cache. Les amusements les plus simples devenaient, par le contraste du lieu et des personnages, les plaisirs les plus agréables et les plus piquants. Les glaces, les sorbets, le punch circulaient sans cérémonie avec les bons mots. La Princesse me faisait lire les verses . . .".*[38]

The formal and official role of the Medici villas around Florence drew to a close over the few years that Florence was capital of the new realm, when the villas of Poggio a Caiano and Petraia became satellites of the court at Palazzo Pitti. However, this period proved of minor overall importance since it was short-lived and left little mark apart from a few points of detail arising from the less than perfect taste of the House of Savoy.

CHAPTER THREE

Typological Research and Renaissance Treatises

[1] Wölfflin identified two basic types of villa in the Italian tradition: "*a spacious country villa, of noble proportions, well-equipped for long visits, and a smaller extra-urban villa, not far from the city gates.*" H. Wölfflin, *Renaissance and Baroque*, Cornell Univ. Press 1967, the chapter on the villa. One of those to take up this subdivision by function was Frommel who identifies the "*palazzo-villa*", "*farm-villa*", "*castle-villa*" and "*rural villa*", and Heydenreich who subdivides the villas into three categories: the "*castle-villa*", based on a fortress, later turned into a villa for pleasure and entertainment; the "*suburban villa*" and its variations, including the princely villas in the outskirts of the city; the "*villa in the proper sense*", a landowner's country house expanded into a villa. C. L. Frommel, *La villa Madama e la tipologia della villa romana nel Rinascimento*, in "BCISA", Venice 1969, XI (1969), p. 47; and L. Heydenreich, *La villa: genesi e sviluppi fino al Palladio*, ibid., p. 12.

[2] Some restrictive interpretations (see, among others, L. Douglas, *Il problema della villa e le plantations americane*, in "BCISA", XII (1970), p. 231) make a distinction between one type of extra-urban construction, defined as the true villa, and other types of country houses. This criterion is based on a philological study of the word "villa" in classical times, recorded and codified by Vitruvius, for whom the villa was a profit-making agricultural property worked by slaves. In *De Architectura*, the word "villa" would always seem to be used of farm buildings and houses which formed part of a large property. Vitruvius's only allusion to the proprietor's residence appears in the well-known phrase: "*si quid delicatius in villis faciundum fuerit, ex symmetriis quae in urbanis supra scriptae sunt constituta ita struantur uti sine impeditione rusticae utilitatis aedificentur*" (Chap. VI, 6, V). This provided the basis for the distinctions already drawn by Pliny between "urban villa" or administrative central body encompassing the proprietor's residence, and *villae rusticae*, consisting of separate farms inhabited by farm workers, or peasants. The urban villa and rustic villas made up a large estate. The terminology of these distinctions goes back at least as far as Cato's treatise *De Agricoltura*; in the

Although typological-historical research has produced a wealth of detailed contributions on the theme of the Italian villa, particularly from the time of its codification by Renaissance writers (including developments in the various regional areas where the most remarkable examples are to be found), the question of the origins and first typological conversions of villas does not appear to have received the same exhaustive and systematic treatment from specialized historians. The reasons for this deficiency are probably not to be attributed to a continuing prejudice of a purist nature, but are chiefly related to the impossibility of reconstructing, in documented fashion, a sufficient quantity of typologically significant and classifiable original material covering the period of the urbanization of the city and region during the time of the Commune. The task is rendered more difficult by the lack of an unequivocal definition of sufficient available structural elements to identify this particular category in its earliest phase which, as has been shown in the previous chapter, was accompanied by the numerous unspecified functions of this particular period, when the commissioners were just emerging as a social class. We shall avoid adopting restrictive interpretations of the meaning of the word "villa", which lean towards the rigidly typological-functional classification proposed by some scholars (such as that introduced by Wölfflin[1] and followed by others) and risk missing, moreover, the highly varied expressions of this suburban phenomenon as an instance of upper and middle-class culture.[2]

As we have said, the country around Florence was already becoming settled by the 12th century, leading to a connection between the *extra muros* "master's house" – built to serve the dual purpose of monitoring a farm and holidaying in the country – and the pre-existing fortified-castle residence and rural house. In many cases this relationship proves useful for localizing new structures in already well-established areas of the region's network of settlements, but the effect is chiefly recognizable in the specific influence that pre-existing structures exercized on the birth of new types of buildings, developing and crystallizing into the first residences for signori not connected with purely productive interests. This involved designing procedures and a range of medieval models which were to appear in the grander buildings of the early 15th century, delaying, in a certain sense, the subsequent cycle of architectural expression. The problem therefore, from a typological point of view, lies more in the area of evolution and range than in that of origin. Nor, as has been mentioned, is there any absence of possibilities for verifying this transition in other parts of Italy, where the recurring elements of rural characteristics are sometimes more marked than in the Florentine area.[3]

It is quite natural, in any case, that this continuous process should have come about through the grafting or juxtaposition of certain pre-existing elements drawn from other contexts, firstly the urban palazzo and then the monastic cloister complex, even though these elements were undoubtedly all produced according to empirical choices (and only later more sophisticated ones), in accordance with the gradual nature of the process we have mentioned. Amongst the most common interventions to be found accompanying a building's changing use and status in preparation for its typological shift were, either singly or together: the enlargement of some areas (entrance); the particular character of some features (vaulted ceilings); the insertion of areas designed to serve as places of relaxation and rest (loggias, interior courtyards); the dawning of a rational order; an awareness of spatial volumes; introduction of decorative architectural features (such as crenellations); more carefully considered positioning of entrances, and even demarcation of an outdoor area and of a hortus. A study of a large number of examples – certainly not easy due to the limited availability of the material to which reference is made – should lead to confirmation of the studies we were able to carry out on a more limited number of structures from the first stages of their evolution, possible to reconstruct on the basis of historical records.

Certainly, it is far more legitimate to study the origins, derivations and references to pre-existing buildings and specific models in the case of the first major villas built by the leading families in the early 15th century (for the Medici family: Trebbio, Cafaggiolo, Careggi, Fiesole). For one thing, these work were "signed" and were already full participants in that early affirmation of humanist thought whose orientation we have outlined in the previous chapter. Although discovery of the Ancient world was a decisive factor in the ensuing artistic direction of the early Renaissance, at this stage knowledge of it appears not to have been absorbed, nor its models or prototypes adopted, in this area of architecture

Oxford Classical Dictionary, London 1960, the entries: agriculture (p. 24), latifundia (p. 480) and villa (p. 947).

[3] "Moreover, the same differentiated regional diffusion adopts a different nomenclature for some types of building which, arising more directly from the world of rural architecture and thus more influenced by usage, could be included in the general typology of the villa since they have a part for the landowner's occupation with specific emerging ornamental and structural features. Many regional areas reveal differences of this kind: cascine in the Po Valley, corti around Mantua, the Roman vigne, and casene and bagli around Palermo. In these examples the name frequently refers to some earlier tradition, predating the heyday of the villa which lacked this centuries-old historical background. In these instances it is not easy to make firm demarcations or investigate the stylistic and historical implications which led to these examples." P. F. Bagatti Valsecchi, Tipologia ed evoluzione storica della villa italiana, in Ville d'Italia, Milan 1972, pp. 180–181.

[4] Of interest concerning the structure of the Roman villa is "the connection, phsyically verifiable by a study of the remains, between the residential section and the structures for the pars fructuaria, a connection which exists from the period of the earliest known villas of Republican times to the dwelling-places of the late Roman potentiores. This connection was given concrete form by the enclosure surrounding all the components of a villa, whether physically or structurally orchestrated, or in simple paratactic order. In both Republican, more recent late-Roman times, and obviously in Africa, this enclosure had a defensive purpose, so there is good reason to hold that the villa is an antecedent of the feudal castle. But even without a defensive purpose, an established enclosure still serves to mark a boundary, besides safeguarding privacy. While there is no single definition of a villa, open to all the most varied and sometimes whimsical architectural interpretations, we can say that an enclosure, with the ensuing gravitation towards the interior, remains a constant." G. A. Mansuelli, Problemi della villa romana, in "BCISA", XI (1969), p. 23.

[5] As far as "sources" for the villa are concerned, on the broader basis of the relationship between the Renaissance and classical antiquity, it is difficult to trace a direct line from the Roman villa to the first Renaissance examples. As J. S. Ackerman has pointed out early Renaissance architects were quite unfamiliar with the appearance of a Roman villa. The only firm information was in literary form, but the attention that Cato, Varro, Columella and the other rei rusticae scriptores of classical times paid to the villa, concerns only its existence as a unit of production and ignore

the architectural aspects. The only writer to offer detailed descriptions of large and sumptuous villas is Pliny the Younger. But Pliny's villas were not in harmony with the taste or possibilities of the Renaissance gentleman and, at least in the early Renaissance, their features were not even imitated. J. S. Ackerman, *Sources of the Renaissance villa*, in *Studies in Western Art*, Vol. II: *The Renaissance and Mannerism*. Acts of the XXth International Congress of the History of Art, Princeton 1963, pp. 6–19. See also L. H. Heydenreich, *La Villa: genesi e sviluppi fino al Palladio*, op. cit.

[6] On the surprising knowledge and diffusion of Vitruvius's work in the Middle Ages and the early Renaissance, see L. Ciapponi, *De Architettura di Vitruvio, nel primo umanesimo*, in "*Italia Medievale e Umanistica*" III, 1960, pp. 59–99. Also *2000 anni di Vitruvio. Studi e Documenti di Archtettura*, edition of the School of Architecture, Florence 1978, n.8.

in the Florentine world, although it was to produce some of the most outstanding examples of secular late Renaissance architecture. Undoubtedly, we should not underestimate the role of ideological consolidation that the knowledge of antiquity came to play in trends that were already beginning to emerge, allowing, among other things, interesting analogies to be made between the past and present, in the dual role of the villa as both a place of retreat and a centre of agricultural exploitation. The former purpose is well-documented by literary sources: Cicero's villas, Catullus's villa at Sirmione, Horace's Villa in the Licenza valley, the renowned villas described by Pliny in his letters; and, the latter, by the *de re rustica* writers, from Cato to Columella, careful as they are to stress the productive aspect of the villa by distinguishing between the residential part and the *pars fructuaria*.[4] Ruins of the great Roman villas, to be found all over Italy, are completely ignored, nor is their presence acknowledged in copies and reconstructions of ancient monuments or in architectural drawings until at least the beginning of the Cinquecento.[5]

Alberti was the only writer to make some attempt to codify precepts on the theme of the villa, while making abundant use of classical sources, particularly Vitruvius,[6] for the purpose of evaluating ecological questions of settlement, determining the optimal distance from a city and the location in relation to other uses of the surrounding area; however, even he appears largely tied to the late-medieval model.

In an attempt to fill this gap, various scholars have sought to form hypotheses and conduct research into similarities

Right: Reconstruction of a Pliny's Laurentinum villa by Leon Krier.

of form and type in the search for the direct antecedents – outside the classical tradition – of the early Florentine examples. In summarizing the conclusions of these studies, beyond the hypotheses that can be outlined as their descent being from the fortified medieval castle, according to Patzak,[7] and the late-medieval urban palazzo, it is of value to indicate a study by Swoboda, written around eighty years ago but taken up again,[8] which relates the villa with projecting side-wings – the *portikusvilla mit ekrisaliten*, of which the first completed example is considered by Swoboda to be the Belvedere of Innocent VIII in Rome – to the direct influence of the late-Gothic Palazzo Loredan in Venice, and through this the Fondaco dei Turchi, a building that in itself would constitute a link in the chain between the palatial architecture of the late Empire and Renaissance developments. However Swoboda's hypothesis, clarified by J. S. Ackerman in a more recent interpretation which emphasises the symmetry of volumes, openness towards the outside world and surrounding countryside, two-floor façade, central block with loggia on the ground floor and projecting enclosing side-wings, *"the tripartite façade with central loggias and corner towers"*,[9] finds few exemplars in Tuscany. Ackerman identifies the building facing the courtyard of the Badia Fiesolana as a structure that is related to the one discussed, while a further example may be found in a building depicted in a fresco in the cemetery in Pisa, although its architectural type appears uncertain. According to Bierman,[10] instead, the 13th-century Palagio ai Torri near Compiobbi, with a loggia flanked by two towers, would approach this pattern. It should be said that Patzak upheld the Venetian influence on the Medici's Fiesole villa, because its creator, Michelozzo, was familiar with the Venetian area, having stayed there between 1433 and 1444. According to many of these writers a Venetian contribution, favoured by a natural geographic position rendering the use of fortifications and defensive measures in the buildings superfluous, would have been of importance to the development of a domestic architecture notable for the lightness of its structure and its general tendency to open onto the outside world with large windows or arcades, as is the case with the Palazzo Loredan mentioned above.

Whatever the true basis of these similarities of form and typology – certainly insufficient, however suggestive, to clarify all the features that are characteristic of the dignified Tuscan villa, or the links, connections and history of their fruition – we must state that a standard definition of types of buildings, or at least those showing an explicitly geometric

[7] B. Patzak, *Palast und Villa in Toscana*, Leipzig 1913.

[8] K. M. Swoboda, *Römische und romanische Paläste*, Vienna 1924. Of the same author, see *Palazzi antichi e medievali*, in "Bollettino del Centro Studi per la Storia dell'Architettura", II (1957), pp. 3–32; and *The problem of the iconography of late antique and early medieval palaces*, in "Journal of the Society of Architectural Historians", XX (1961), pp. 78–79.

[9] J. S. Ackerman, *Sources of the Renaissance Villa*, op. cit., p. 13.

[10] H. Bierman, *Lo sviluppo della villa toscana sotto l'influenza umanistica della corte di Lorenzo il Magnifico*, in "BCISA", XI (1969), p. 38. In the same essay Bierman rejects Ackerman's hypothesis that the building appearing in the painting in the Pisan cemetery is a villa, sustaining that it is a cloister with one open side.

Below: Palagio ai Torri near Compiobbi, plan of the ground floor.
Right: Reconstruction of the second panel by Filippo Brunelleschi with the perspective view of Piazza della Signoria; sketch by Baldassarre Peruzzi of a thermal bath in Villa Adriana at Tivoli; Sebastiano Serlio, some examples for central plan churches.

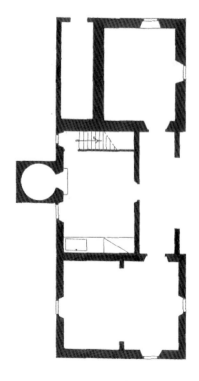

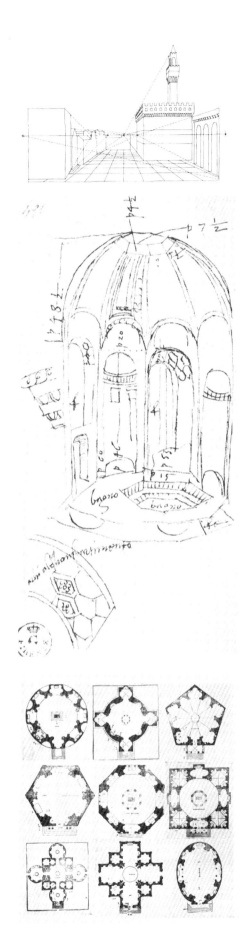

rationalization of layout and design, only emerged in the second half of the 15th century, a lapse of almost fifty years with respect to the model of the urban palazzo; but naturally adopting previously employed architectural elements.

Now, we have to consider what was the novelty of the project processes defined by the new theories of the Renaissance. Medieval man had always sought to avoid relating architectural issues with theoretical speculation. Projects were evaluated on the basis of empirical considerations, as a sequence of choices between alternatives of equal weight and possibility. If at times this choice fell to geometrical schemes and proportional calculations, these had a religious or cabalistic meaning, or were simply for structural convenience.

On the other hand, according to humanistic theories, every single problem can be seen as a particular case of a more general problem, dependent on precise laws from which it acquires internal measure and congruence. The two acts that define the new vision of operations carried out on architecture and on the city are the planned and canonical references to the classical orders, and the control instituted and permitted by the use of the science of perspective.

Perspective, in general use beginning in 1425, provided the possibility of rationally controlling space, and of dominating it on the paper and in the real world. In the perspective system, for example, from reduction in size one can deduct the distance between objects. One point on the paper can represent the encounter of two lines in the infinite, that is to say, represent the infinite in a finite way. One of the consequences of this technique is that reality is no longer a simple inventory of things, but a system of relations. Everything is known by proportional relationship: knowledge, according to Alberti, happens "by comparison".

The conventional forms of the Roman architectural orders, assumed independently of building-type as ideal models to be conformed to allow us to define, a priori, in their proportions, the forms of construction. Design becomes the assembly of a geometric scheme of these elements, fixed with relationship to the building structure, so as to constitute a closed system that at least theoretically can be extended to the urban scale, connecting every man-made environment in a system of rational relationship. On the other hand, it need hardly be stressed how the acquisition of these elements, and in particular of perspective, is much more than a merely technical and artistic act, but is in part the result of and in part the catalyst for a "world vision" having at its centre man born from the dissolution of the medieval universe.

The result of these choices is the foundation of a precise sector of activity – to which the word "art" is applied – removed from the environment of the medieval *artes*, separate from technical operations, and independent of the levels of experience it was earlier pervaded with (science, theology, morality).

Architecture was given a new working method, consisting of the preparation of a "project" in advance, with drawings and models which are the work of the architect, and the actual execution, which is a later and material event, reserved for the construction workers.

The idea of the project presupposes the concept of creative invention, while the drawing makes communication possible. Codification of typical elements gives rise to a language, and architecture acquires a cultural dignity that brings it in relationship with other creative arts, science and literature. These new events cast into crisis the tradition of collective behaviour on which the guild organisation of the first Florentine commune was based. Artists now signed their own works, and they established solid allegiances with the new moneyed aristocracy in Florence and abroad.

Both components of the new method – the geometric theory of perspective and the reference to the normalized elements of antiquity – represented a fundamental break with and reaction against the imperial practices of the Middle Ages. Regularity, symmetry, proportion now had to govern all architectural design.

The Renaissance movement had a special link for "perfectly" regular forms which are the basis for innumerable patterns of decorative planning, from the plan for the ideal city, to the details of ornamental parts. Alberti mentions in his Book VII ch. IV the delight of Nature herself in creating such forms as the bird's circular nest or the hexagons in the hives of "bees, hornets, and all kinds of wasps". Such examples are not chosen at random but with the purpose of demonstrating that the laws of beauty are eternal. Return to precise outlines, and concern for regularity led inevitably to a search for symmetry.

Every building, church, palace or suburban villa, was based on an axis or two perpendicular axes. According to the principle of regularity in classical architecture the bays of colonnades are all equal, and this allowed easily to emphasize the axis. Proportion, or the relationship between dimensions, was one of the overriding concerns of the Renaissance. Alberti went back to classical theories of harmony and proportions: architecture would possess the same natural harmony as music, and the idea that the two arts were interconnected became current in treatises on harmony.

Below: Fra' Giocondo, sketch for a circular temple and for the circus in piazza Navona; Ludovico Cigoli, from Michelangelo, plan of St. Peter in Rome.
Right: Leonardo's sketches of central plan churches, Giorgio Vasari Jr plan of the church of Santa Maria delle Carceri in Prato; Unknown Tuscan artist plan of Santa Maria degli Angeli in Florence (G.D.S.U.).

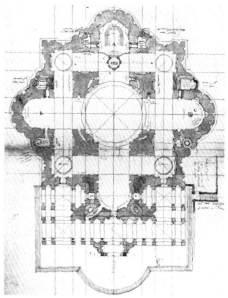

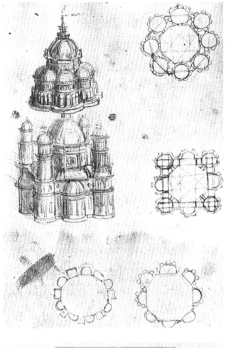

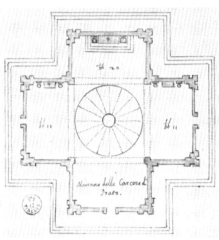

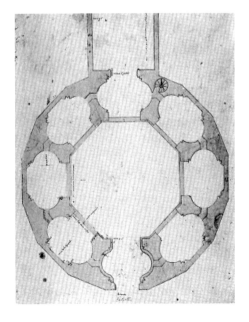

The return to the classical style promoted the forms taken from antiquity such as columns, capitals and entablatures, cupolas, domes and ornament all made up the new vocabulary of the Renaissance style. The orders, at once a system of proportion and of decoration, were the basic structure of the new language.

One of the first achievements of Filippo Brunelleschi was the revival of classical systems of support. Have a look at the façade of the Ospedale degli Innocenti in Piazza SS. Annunziata in Florence which he designed in 1421 with a portico with columns, used to support round arches.

The centralized plan became the standard plan for the votive church being built all over Italy. Giuliano da Sangallo, the architect of the Medici villa in Poggio a Caiano, designed the perfect example of a church based on a Greek cross in Santa Maria delle Carceri in Prato. In the sacristy of San Lorenzo (a Medici funerary chapel) Brunelleschi adopted a square plan covered by a dome, producing a variant of this in the Pazzi Chapel in Santa Croce. His design for Santa Maria degli Angeli (unfortunately never finished) was a rotunda with chapels radiating from it. In smaller buildings he used the centralized plan (that is, a single space that could be enclosed within a circle) which had virtually disappeared since the days of the Romanesque baptistry.

The palace or palazzo is the most important type of civil building. Traditionally, the palace was a block built round a central courtyard, looking very massive from the outside, but with plenty of loggias and balconies opening on to the courtyard.

Florentine palazzi retained their austere exteriors, making extensive use of rusticated stone. The palazzi built at the middle of the 15th century for the most important families of the city, such as Rucellai, Strozzi, Pitti, Tornabuoni, Medici, are intended as monuments to express, through their monumental shape and size, the power and the role of the family. Brunelleschi's project for palazzo Medici called for a building isolated on the piazza, square in design, with nine windows per side and the central door in line with the main door of San Lorenzo church, underscoring the relationship between the church and the family palace. But Cosimo the Elder refused the project, preferring the more conservative one made by Michelozzo in 1444. His design, in spite of its stereometric block and the adoption of classical elements, is really a clearer elaboration of the medieval palace. With palazzo Medici, Michelozzo set a model which was to be widely followed; the most celebrated example being the Strozzi palace, built by Benedetto da Maiano and Simone Pollaiolo in 1489.

Alberti's palazzo Rucellai, built around 1455, differs from Michelozzo's palace: it is the first attempt to apply the classical orders to a palazzo's front with its rows of pilasters and the alternating rhythm of the bays; Palazzo Pitti, which followed Brunelleschi's design in its central part, represents a really innovative example: here the design of the façade is controlled through the application of a modular arch-window scheme. But palazzo Pitti was never used as a reference type.

If the central courtyard is the most typical feature of the palazzo, the first villas built without the reference to a codified model also developed around a courtyard.

We shall now continue to set out a typological-planimetric classification, already attempted by those who have conducted studies on the Tuscan villa from the early years of the 20th century,[11] while remaining aware of the pitfalls of drawing too strict a comparison between the plans and compositional and volumetric results on the basis of considerations already made concerning the complex historical formation of a large number of the buildings. We can therefore state that the chief feature to emerge that is specifically related to the ground-plan is undoubtedly a courtyard, around which stood the main body of the building, usually supplied with an upper-floor loggia on one or more sides. The presence of the courtyard is characteristic of the earliest structures and may be directly derived from urban models.[12] The position of a courtyard with respect to the development of the body of a building tends to repeat itself according to recurring patterns which can be divided, in their simpler forms, into four categories: a) a compact block with the body of the fabric surrounding the courtyard (Palazzo Vecchio is an urban example); b) a building with side-wings (like Palazzo Pitti) and a courtyard closed off on three sides by the body of the building, the fourth side screened or not by a wall which often gives access to a garden (this second type can be considered an elaboration of the *portikus-villa* type, and therefore derived from the Palagio ai Torri layout, and generally developed later than the closed block type, codified in Ammannati's ideal plans, as well as in some exemplary realizations, such as the Collazzi villa in Giogoli); c) an L-shaped building with one wing, usually a service area, annexes and a courtyard enclosed by walls on the other two open sides; d) a courtyard between two separate blocks of building, developed in linear fashion. Alongside these forms, sometimes made more complex by the inclusion of more than one interior courtyard, usually due to an original structure's successive phases of growth, there emerged the

[11] H. D. Eberlein, *Villas of Florence and Tuscany*, New York 1922. Eberlein forms an intriguing, if hard to prove, hypothesis that the Tuscan villa is derived from the Etruscan farmhouse, based on the continuation of characteristic features such as the courtyard and loggia. See also K. W. Forster, *Back to the farm*, in "Architectura. Journal of the History of Architecture" 1, 1974, pp. 86–97.

[12] It is almost a duty here to cite Boccaccio's description in the proem to the first and third days of the *Decameron*, where the courtyard and loggia are used as features for identifying the villa: "*A most beautiful and ornate palace which was situated on a slight eminence above the plain. Entering the palace, they explored it from end to end, and were filled with admiration for its spacious halls, equipped with everything they could possibly need . . . The whole place was decorated and they were seated on a loggia overlooking the central court.*" G. Boccaccio, *The Decameron*, English trans. with an introduction and notes by G. H. McWilliam, London 1972 (1995), p. 189–190.

Below: View of palazzo Medici Riccardi and plan of the ground floor.
Right: From the top villa I Collazzi at Giogoli, villa Petraia, villa Michelozzi at Bellosguardo, Baroncelli, from Giorgio Vasari Jr *Piante di Chiese Palazzi e Ville di Toscana e d'Italia* (Gabinetto Disegni e Stampe Uffizi (G.D.S.U. 4529–4594) Florence).

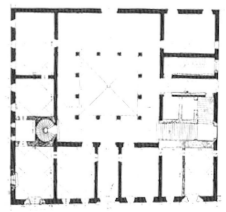

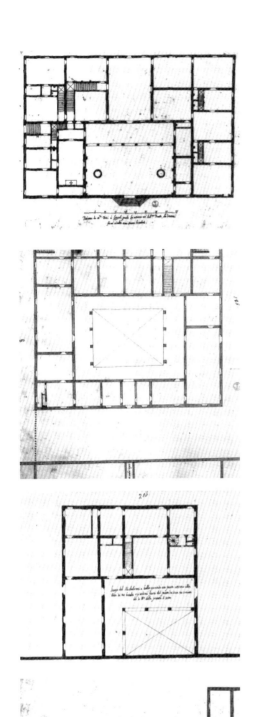

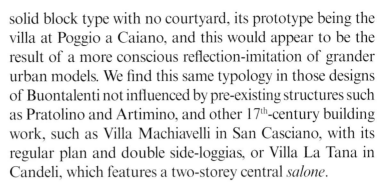

solid block type with no courtyard, its prototype being the villa at Poggio a Caiano, and this would appear to be the result of a more conscious reflection-imitation of grander urban models. We find this same typology in those designs of Buontalenti not influenced by pre-existing structures such as Pratolino and Artimino, and other 17th-century building work, such as Villa Machiavelli in San Casciano, with its regular plan and double side-loggias, or Villa La Tana in Candeli, which features a two-storey central *salone*.

The type of structure with a courtyard closed on all sides includes: the Uguccioni and Capponi villas at Montughi; the Borgherini and the Strozzi villa (known as Lo Strozzino) at Bellosguardo, a stately building with a corner loggia, perhaps the work of Simone del Pollaiolo, owned first by the Pandolfini family and later by the Strozzi; the Salviati villas at Maiano San Cerbone; the Medici Villas Petraia and Castello; the Magia at Tizzana; Villa Corsini at Mezzomonte; Palazzo Bettoni in Montepiano; the Saracino Belvedere, attributed to Baccio d'Agnolo. Types with a courtyard open on the fourth side include: Villa Le Brache and Il Gondo at Castello; Loggia dei Bianchi and the Orsini villa at Quarto; Mula at Quinto; the Medici villa at Lappeggi; Castelletto of the Cavalcanti; Valdimarina of the Salviati family; Il Gioiello in Pian dei Giullari; Villa Palmieri at San Domenico which, after its baroque conversion, has a courtyard closed on the fourth side also, realized by means of a loggia at the upper level of the main body of the building, the central crowning feature of the façade facing the garden. The L-shaped layout is characteristic of structures such as the Pazzi villa (La Vacchia) in Pian dei Giullari, the result of a series of interventions on a 13th-century structure with an incorporated tower, in which the main body of the building with a central great hall is connected to a building at the side, housing a service courtyard and a lemon-house; the Michelozzi villa or Torre di Bellosguardo, a late 16th-century reworking of a medieval building with a tower, with an L-shaped loggia opening onto a courtyard; Villa Pandolfini at Signa, owned by the famous 15th-century merchant and humanist, has a loggia on one side only and a long lateral structure, identified as a "*pollaio*" (hen-house) on Vasari's plan. The Castel Pulci villa, the property of the Riccardi family, is an example of the doubling of an L-shaped layout, in which one L-shaped structure with an arcade and loggia encloses the courtyard, and the other a walled garden.

Lastly, the linear layout, with a courtyard dividing the two main bodies of a building, was the plan of the Marignolle villa and the Antinori villa (known as "Brancolano") outside Porta Romana, while the Torrigiani villa in San Martino alla Palma can be interpreted as a further development of this plan since the central courtyard is surrounded on three sides by arcades.

The first Medici villas were also based on a closed plan round a central courtyard, simpler in the case of the Trebbio and more evolved at Cafaggiolo and Careggi, but still denoted by the building closing around an inner area, and related to a castle's repertoire of forms. The plan of the Trebbio villa consists of an irregular main body round a closed courtyard and an incorporated tower rising from the south-west corner. In the plan drawn by Giorgio Vasari the Younger at the end of the 16th century, although made regular in an arbitrary fashion with respect to the building's true layout, we immediately recognize the typology of the block and closed courtyard, reached through an entranceway with a depressed vault. A loggia on the ground floor is covered by cross vaulting and gives onto a courtyard. On the north side of the courtyard is an exterior staircase, following a layout found in pre-existing structures (for example, the medieval "Torricina" above Falle at Compiobbi, an old villa which later became a farmhouse attached to the Falle palazzo). The crenellated exterior ambulatory encircling the entire block was interrupted by the intrusion of the tower, with the result that the tower appears perfectly embedded in the whole structure. The lunette painted by Giusto Utens, the sole known visual representation of this villa, offers a reliable image of the building, even though only partially corresponding to the actual situation.

At Trebbio, therefore, Michelozzo's intervention, referred to by Vasari ("*at Trebbio likewise he carried out many other improvements which are still to be seen*"[13]) refers to restoration work on a pre-existing structure. This kind of intervention typifies all Michelozzo's work on the Medici villas, because also at Cafaggiolo and Careggi properties Michelozzo was engaged in carrying out works to alter and enlarge pre-existing structures. "*Cosimo de Medici also built, with the advice and design of Michelozzo, the Palace of Cafaggiolo in Mugello, giving it the form of a fortress with ditches round it; and he laid out farms, roads, gardens, fountains with groves round them, fowling places and other appurtenances of a villa, all very splendid and … at a distance of two miles from Florence, also, he built the palatial Villa of Careggi which was very rich and magnificent; and thither Michelozzo brought the water for the fountain that is seen there at the present day*",

Below: Plans of Careggi, Il Trebbio and Cafaggiolo from the book *Piante di Chiese, Palazzi e Ville di Toscana e d'Italia disegnate dal cav. Giorgio Vasari il giovane* (G.D.S.U. Florence). Right: Careggi, Michelozzo's courtyard and plan of the ground floor of the villa.

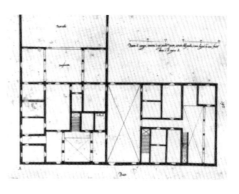

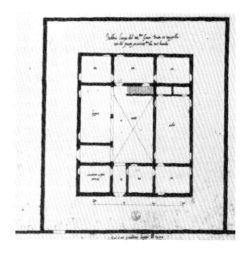

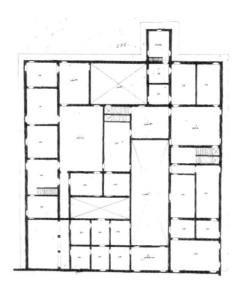

[13] G. Vasari, *Life of Michelozzo Michelozzi*, in *Lives of the Painters Sculptors and Architects*, London 1996, p. 385.

[14] "*Greatly enlarged by Grand Duke Cosimo I and provided with a walled park for festivities, much of which still survives, being built like an old fortress with several towers and a surrounding moat with drawbridges. In the interior is a large chapel, used as a church, dedicated to St Cosmas and St Damian, ancient guardians of the afore-mentioned royal House of Medici. There are fine paved floors, halls and large rooms with several courtyards, loggias and galleries, making it most magnificent and grand (albeit old-fashioned)*". C. Brocchi, *Descrizione della provincia del Mugello*, Florence 1748, p. 50.

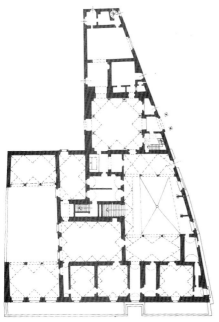

Vasari reports, in a description which corresponds closely to the definition of a *villa-castello*. The estate appears to be unusually grand for a private house of the early 1400s, even discounting the substantial alterations which were already under way by the following century.[14] Vasari the Younger's drawing, though displaying a not quite credible regularity, gives an idea of the grandiose nature of the whole complex, developed around a central L-shaped court which, after Michelozzo's intervention, must presumably have closed the building on the west side with a wall dividing the court-yard from the "secret garden", following a pattern we have already mentioned. The two Medici villas in Mugello are still hovering between the outward appearance of fortified buildings and a new spatial sensibility which is closer to the Renaissance in style, most clearly displayed by the rooms with vaulted ceilings in the interior.

The Careggi villa, where the remodelling in around 1459 of a "*palazzo with courtyard, loggia, well, vault, dovecote, tower and walled garden*", bought by Cosimo from Tommaso Lippi for 800 florins in 1417, displays a similar late-medieval repertoire of enclosed forms and irregular layout, despite the different and more "suburban" nature of this building, being positioned much closer to the city and therefore having the advantage of being easier to visit. The rooms here are given greater regularity, shown by an increasing tendency to align them and by the use of elements such as a tripartite loggia on the ground floor and a smaller loggia above which, later codified by the treatises, were to become part of a common pattern in villa construction. But this does not prevent us from seeing, disregarding the numerous alterations sustained by Michelozzo's complex over subsequent years, the links with examples of late-medieval architecture. At Careggi the towers were removed and two light Renaissance loggias were added to the rear of the building, in a symmetrical manner, to form a small sheltered courtyard. However, these changes appear merely superficial because, although the new additions show a waning of the defensive castle-like character of the more important suburban buildings, they do not belie a lingering taste for traditional architecture and a resistance to the introduction of innovations. In the Medici villa in Fiesole, Michelozzo's project for the: "*magnificent and noble palace at Fiesole, sinking the foundations for the lower part in the brow of the hill, at great expense, but not without great advantage*", according to Vasari's testimony, is more obviously in *rapport* with the landscape. The building is set in a position affording views of the surrounding landscape from determined angles.

Completely open to the exterior, the villa is dramatically dissimilar to its predecessors; it is based on a really innovative layout, in the disappearance of the central courtyard, so that the living space looked outwards, towards the open countryside. The core of the villa is the central salon, connected with two loggias on the west and on the east side. This villa was not an adaptation of a pre-existing building. The site was chosen for the panoramic view and a massive substructure had to be built to support the building and the garden on the steep hillside. It was a cubic block covered in off-white stucco, with arches not moulded and windows unframed "*having in the lower part vaults, cellars, stables, storerooms and other handsome and commodious habitations; and above, beside the chambers, public halls and other rooms, he made some for books, and certain others for music*" (as G. Vasari states in *Life of Michelozzo*).

In the interests of discovering sources and drawing comparisons we are persuaded to make an attempt to reconnect new emerging information to the continuity of the occupation of the countryside, and above all to its agricultural antecedents. But for more elegant extra-urban buildings too, at least until the last quarter of the 15th century, the hypothesis of an evolutionary adaptation is fully and unconditionally confirmed. According to this theory, gradually changing new elements of increasing significance emerged and coexisted around an original nucleus; one should not speak therefore of typological constants but rather of a constant in the manner of formation, in which recurring additions and alterations evolved, drawn from both the rural and urban building traditions. Without entering into the uncertain dating of Michelozzo's interventions on the Medici family's suburban villas,[15] this being a matter, in our opinion, related to a cultural and artistic position of the architect and his *milieu*, we must reconsider in which category to place Michelozzo's work. Similarities to models of the past should probably be understood, not so much as a late legacy of already out-moded designs, but as a revival of structures suited to a society in a period of adjustment, as was the case in Florence during the first half of the 15th century. Thus, the battlements and defensive ramparts of Trebbio and Cafaggiolo should not be read as "*delightful incursions into a medievalism interpreted with ironic detachment*", as interpreted by Tafuri,[16] since the use of such elements had not yet reached the cerebral value of an allusive reference, but still answered a real need. Nor should the presence of the pre-existing building complexes on which Michelozzo was repeatedly called to intervene be

[15] We should recall that for Patzak, work at Trebbio and Cafaggiolo took place in around 1420, while other scholars, starting with Fabriczy, disagree totally with this hypothesis and set the date of Trebbio between 1427 and 1436 and Cafaggiolo later, work being protracted until the middle of the century, while Careggi should be set at around 1457. M. Gori Sassoli, *Michelozzo e l'architettura di villa nel primo Rinascimento*, in "Storia dell'Arte", 23 (1975), pp. 5–49.

[16] M. Tafuri, *L'architettura dell'Umanesimo*, Bari 1972, p. 40.

[17] F. Brunetti, *Le tipologie architettoniche nel trattato albertiano*, in *Omaggio ad Alberti*, "Studi e Documenti di Architettura", Florence, 1 (1972), p. 271.

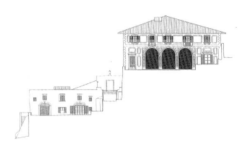

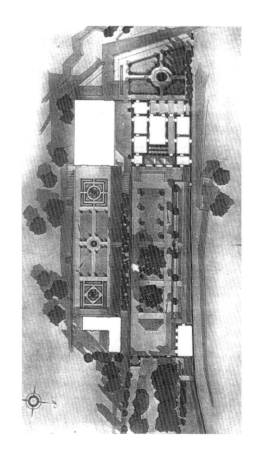

under-estimated, this too being a factor which undoubtedly determined the "traditional" character of his work, more often interpreted as an artistic choice which was dependent, according to some scholars (including Benevolo), on the conservative taste of his patrons. The specialized treatises which appeared in the 15th century, both in what they say and in what they leave unsaid, would seem to share this view on the question of the villa.

Firstly – to examine the treatise writing of the 15th century in relation to the influence that codified models exerted on contemporary building – we find, on the one hand, a notable gap between theory and practical application and, on the other, an uncertain definition, even on a theoretical level, of the type of new villa construction. Moreover, it should be noted that theorists of the early Renaissance confronted the theme of the villa more from a sociological point of view than a strictly typological and architectural one.

We must consider Alberti, architect and philosopher of architecture, to be the most prominent advocate of this opinion, for whom the theme of the villa became the parameter of a "global view", displayed by the indissoluble link between the plan of a building and family life and behaviour. On this aspect, it is chiefly in his *Libri della Famiglia* and in his short treatise on the villa (1438) that Alberti discusses the subject at length, without for that matter detaching himself from the tradition of the *rei rusticae scriptores*. From the *De Re Aedificatoria*, on the other hand, one might expect a more rigorous handling of the subject, and in fact the typological problem is indeed tackled here in greater depth and given more specific consideration. However, as we shall see, what Alberti states in a more general sense on this theme was to find confirmation: "*this type never rises to the level of a plan or model with prescriptive value; it remains rather a conceptual structure*".[17] This view is strengthened, not only by the complete absence of graphic images in the treatise, but also by the way Alberti constantly swings between a collection of building rules and moral preaching, between historical authority and the desire to be middle class and between material datum and social judgement (or prejudice). In *De Re Aedificatoria* Alberti draws on classical sources – Vitruvius above all, but also Pliny the Younger, Varro and Columella – for precepts regarding a whole series of exigencies to be put into effect in planning. In Book V rules concerning the villa are clarified and, starting with the premise already expressed in Book I, of the "*house as a small city*", he proposes the fundamental distinction between the city house and the villa: "*In urban building there are restrictions such as party walls, dripping gutters, public ground, rights of way, and so forth, to prevent one achieving a satisfactory result. In the countryside this does not happen, here everything is more open, whereas the city is restrictive. Here all spaces are free, there they are occupied.*"[18] Here too, a social distinction is drawn: "*with the poor it is necessity that governs the size of the dwelling, whereas the rich are seldom satisfied or able to limit their greed.*"[19] Alberti stipulates precepts concerning sites and evaluates problems connected with hygiene,[20] besides clearly expressing his opinion concerning the most convenient distance from the city.[21]

This possible typological division is based on the difference between the social categories to which the buildings are destined: "*Country houses may be divided into those inhabited by gentlemen and those by workers, the latter being built for financial interests, the former simply for pleasure. Let us now deal with those used for work in the fields. The houses of the workers should not be too far from the master's villa, so that he can check what the former is doing at all times and stipulate the tasks to be carried out. A typical function of this type of building is to prepare, collect and store the produce reaped from the land… the farm manager should live close to the main door to ensure that nobody approaches by night without his knowledge and takes something away; those in charge of livestock should live near the stables, so as to intervene promptly when needed.*"[22] These are precepts to which medieval texts had already made reference, codifying the position and working-links between the various buildings.

In Chapter XVII of Book V the villas of nobles and wealthy landowners are examined in greater depth. Here we find a position which might be defined as "pragmatic" on Alberti's part when he postulates, without too much rigidity, norms on the position of various parts of the building: "*As for the master, some make a distinction between summer and winter villas, and stipulate that the bedrooms for the winter should face the winter sunrise and dining-rooms the sunset at the equinox; whereas for summer the bedrooms should face the midday sun, with the dining-room towards the winter sunrise; they would have the walkways exposed to the midday sun at equinox. We, however, would prefer them to vary from place to place, according to climate and regional characteristics, so as to blend hot with cold, and damp with dry.*"[23]

Here, moreover, he postulates a new relationship between a building and its surroundings in which the villa, while assuming a privileged position with respect to the landscape,

[18] L. B. Alberti, *On the Art of Building in Ten Books*, translated by J. Rykwert, N. Leach, R. Tavernor, M.I.T. Press, Cambridge 1988–97, V, p.140.

[19] Ibid. p. 140.

[20] "*An adverse climate and porous soil are to be avoided; a building site in the middle of the countryside should be chosen, sheltered by hills, rich in water and sunlight, in a healthy region and in a healthy part of that region.*" Ibid., p. 140.

[21] "*In my opinion the site chosen by a proprietor for his country house should be in a part of the country that is most convenient for his town house. Xenophon would have us walk to the villa for exercise and then return on horseback. Therefore it should not be too great a distance from the city, on a good and unobstructed road, easy to travel to on foot or in a vehicle, in both summer and winter, or perhaps even by boat. Better still if the road passes near the city gates which can then be entered in an easy and direct manner, without having to dress up or be gazed at by the public, coming and going as one pleases between city and villa with one's wife and children. Moreover, it would be desirable that the road be in such a position that the morning sun does not bother those arriving, or trouble the eyes of those returning in the evening to the city. A villa should not stand in a deserted, unattractive and unpleasant area. The land should attract people to live there by offering abundant produce, a mild climate, and a pleasant, easy and carefree existence. On the other hand, it should not be in too frequented a place, such as the outskirts of a city, a military road or a port attracting many ships; rather a place that offers the benefits of the above, yet where your family life will not be plagued by visits from acquaintances who are passing by.*" Ibid. p. 141.

[22] Ibid. pp. 141–142.

[23] Ibid. p. 145.

[24] Ibid. p. 145.

[25] Ibid. pp. 146–149.

Right: Bartolomeo Ammannati, drawings for different types of villas (G.D.S.U. 3426A, 3429A, 3425A).

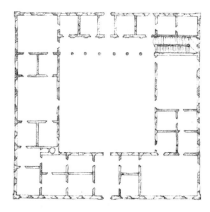

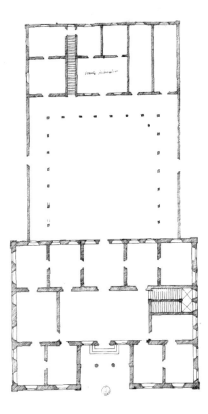

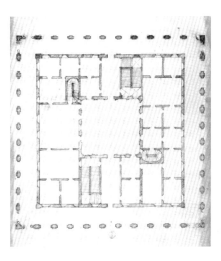

adapts itself to a new spatial sensibility modelled on classical concepts: "*In my opinion the house of the signori should be situated in a part of the countryside that is not particularly fertile, yet notable from other aspects, where it could enjoy all the benefits and delights of fresh breezes, sunshine and view; it should be provided with roads offering easy communication with the owner's farm, and handsome avenues for receiving guests; it should be well in view and offer a vista of a city, town, stretch of coast, fortress, or plain; or it should have within sight the peaks of some notable hills or mountains, delightful gardens, and attractive haunts for fishing and hunting.*"[24]

Alberti then studies the distribution of the interior spaces, starting with what he describes as the "heart of the house" corresponding to Vitruvius's atrium. The "heart of the house" gives access to all other rooms, following a spatial sequence strictly connected with family life and behaviour, earlier theorized in *Libri della Famiglia*. Alberti goes into great detail concerning the distribution of the rooms: "*In the centre of the 'heart of the house' should be the entrance to the corridor; this should be dignified and in no way narrow, tortuous, or poorly lit ... Here it would be convenient to have glass windows, balconies and porticoes, from which it would be possible to look out and, according to the season, appreciate the sun and fresh air ... the dining-rooms should be entered from the 'heart of the house', varying according to their different functions: some for summer, others winter, still others – if we may use the term – for the in-between seasons. The principal requirements of a summer dining-room are water and greenery; of a winter one, the warmth of a hearth; both should be the spacious, welcoming and elegant ... The kitchen should be adjacent to the dining-room, as well as a pantry for storing the leftovers of a meal, tableware and linen. The kitchen should be neither too close to the guests nor so distant that hot dishes cool in transit; it is sufficient that the irksome din of the scullery maids, plates and pans does not reach the ears of the guests. From the dining-rooms we pass to the bedrooms. Grander houses should have different bedrooms for summer and winter ...*"[25] As we see, a seasonal division is recommended for these rooms too, although the conceptions of "*mediocritas*" that inspired Alberti, suggest moderation. He then stipulates the positions of the bedrooms in relation to their occupants: "*As for the mistress of the house, the position most suited to her is one from which she can supervise everything that is going on. A husband and wife should have separate bedrooms, not only to ensure that the husband is not disturbed when his wife is being delivered or is ill, but also to allow both to sleep with greater tranquillity when they so desire, also for the summer. Both rooms should have their own doors and a small common door through which the spouses can communicate without being seen by others. Adjacent to the wife's room should be a dressing-room, to that of the husband's a library. A grandfather, being weary with age and in need of rest and quiet, should have a bedroom that is well heated and set away from any noise coming from inside or outside the house itself; above all he should have the comfort of a good hearth and all other comforts of the body and soul needed by the infirm. Off this should be the strong room; here the boys and youths should pass the night, the young girls in the dressing-room and next to them the nurses. A guest should be given an apartment near the hall, so that he may more freely receive those who visit him without causing disturbance to the rest of the family. Young men should reside opposite the rooms of the guests, or at least in their vicinity, so that they can more easily make acquaintance with them. A guest should dispose of a storeroom communicating with his room where he may conceal the things most precious to him or those he wants to keep hidden, and remove them at his pleasure. The apartment of the young men should communicate with the armoury.*"[26]

And finally, as far as the servants are concerned, with that attitude of aristocratic detachment that is very much his own, already mentioned elsewhere, Alberti prescribes the position of the rooms so that: "*The administrators, domestic staff and servants should be lodged in separate quarters from those of their masters in lodgings befitting to their specific duties. The maids and menservants should be stationed close enough to the areas they serve to enable them to hear calls and hasten solicitously to take orders.*"[27]

The typological distinction, within a single type, is derived from the hierarchical differentiation between social classes. However, the reference models are drawn from the houses of the upper classes. Chapter XVIII of the treatise, in reference to norms to which the buildings of the less wealthy classes must adhere, theorizes thus: "*The residences of less prosperous people should aspire, within the limits of their different financial circumstances, to the elegance of the houses of the wealthier class; such imitation must be tempered so that usefulness is not sacrificed to pleasure . . . The building of farmhouses should provide for the oxen and the sheep as much as for the wife; and to derive profit from them, and not just pleasure, steps should be taken to provide the villa with dovecote, fishponds, etc.*"[28]

In Book IX, returning to the theme of a villa's ornamentation, he emphasizes the greater planning freedom this offers when compared with a town house: "*There is a further differ-*

[26] Ibid. p. 149.

[27] Ibid. p. 149.

[28] Ibid. p. 152.

[29] Ibid. p. 294.

[30] Ibid. pp. 295–296.

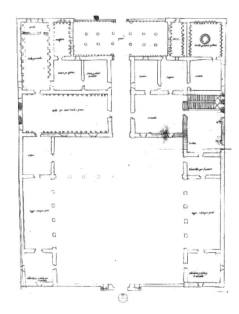

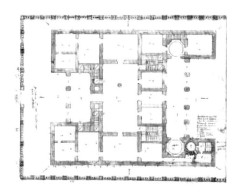

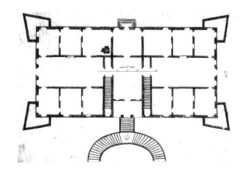

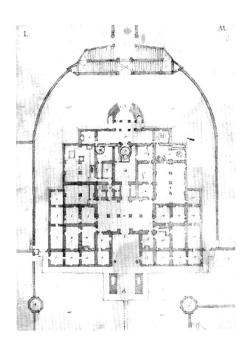

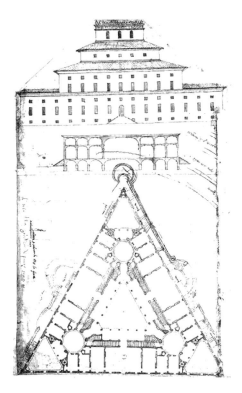

ence between a town house and a villa: the ornament to a town house ought to be more sober in character, whereas in a villa the allures of licence and delight are allowed. Another difference is that with a town house the boundary of the neighbouring property imposes many constraints that may be treated with greater freedom in a villa. Care must be taken that the base is not higher than harmony with the neighbouring buildings requires; while the width of a portico is constrained by the line of an adjoining wall."[29]

Nonetheless, the criteria of compositional freedom to which the planning of a villa was to adhere are stipulated in a rather generic manner, even if Alberti does not fail to include a reference to the geometry of the interior spaces, a subject which was to be developed a great deal more fully and in greater depth, accompanied by schematic drawings, by Francesco di Giorgio in his work on domestic architecture.

"The whole appearance of a building and its mode of presenting itself, a factor which contributes greatly to its appreciation, is improved if it is perfectly clear and in good view from every position. Exposed to a limpid and resplendent sky, it should receive great quantities of light, of sun, of healthy air; nor should there be anything in view that might offend by casting gloomy shadows. Everything should festively welcome the arrival of a guest. The latter, as soon as he crosses the threshold, must wonder whether to stay where he is – from the delight he feels – or to go further, towards other parts that attract him with their pleasing elegance. In this way, a quadrilateral space leads to a circular one, this to a polygonal one, and from this last into another, neither completely circular nor completely bounded by straight lines." [30]

Nonetheless, this criterion of compositional freedom remains at the stage of a theoretical pronouncement. In our opinion Alberti's general discourse remains strongly influenced by the 14th-century model outlined by Pier de' Crescenzi in his treatise on agriculture and rarely offers innovatory indications in respect of contemporary works. Indeed, Alberti adopts the typological characteristics of 15th-century residences in the outlying areas of Florence and codifies the rules for building a villa, while showing himself to be familiar with the norms of Vitruvius's precepts (at times even to the point of transcribing them), in the body of his statements he appears tied to a late-medieval model.

Unlike Alberti's text, the *Treatise* written by Francesco di Giorgio between 1470 and 1480, with a far less philosophical and more pragmatic approach, makes ample recourse to graphic documentation, now *"one of the most pressing demands of the general culture of the last decades of the 1400s, which required a visual illustration of every notion and tended to equate scientific research with the systematic representation of forms and objects."* [31] However, his attention is chiefly directed towards city buildings, for which he follows a social criterion for his typological classification, drawing up five categories to correspond with five classes of inhabitant. As far as the extra-urban villa is concerned, having first made an observation of some interest (*"Firstly I will describe the villa houses because they belonged to farm-labourers before townspeople. And also because they are more necessary to human sustenance"*[32]), Francesco di Giorgio limits himself to discussing only the houses of the "farm workers".

The other leading treatise of the 1400s – that of Filarete[33] – entrusts the ideal impetus for his model-image of a city to a series of imposing new architectural projects, and remains silent on the question of private residences, either urban or extra-urban. However, Filarete includes many fascinating descriptions of gardens, to which we shall turn our attention in the following chapter.

The theories elaborated in 15th-century treatises on the theme of the villa appear in the end to have little relevance to the subject of innovative contributions to the architectural vocabulary, while, as we have seen, contemporary building had adopted a conciliatory position, absorbing many pre-existing elements. It is not until the Medici villa at Poggio a Caiano that we find the first example in the Florentine area of the elaboration of a specific type of villa, produced by a great architect's ability to turn the ambitious programme of a patron of great intellectual gifts into reality, with a design which aimed to take the fullest possible advantage of a strict interpretation of the philosophical content of the new humanist culture. The "Cascine" of Poggio a Caiano, commissioned by Lorenzo, is a most remarkable record of humanist harmony – of an ethical exchange, we might say – between *otium* and *negotium*, between nature and philosophy, the supreme and common ideal of the *gentleman* and the *sage*.[34]

Between 1470 and 1474 Lorenzo the Magnificent purchased a property at Poggio a Caiano from Giovanni Rucellai which included *"a ruined building… called Lambra"*. The contract for building the villa was given to Giuliano da Sangallo, after a form of private competition in which the model submitted by Sangallo seemed, as Vasari relates, *"so completely different in form from the others, and so much to Lorenzo's fancy, that he began straightway to have it carried into execution, as the best of all the models."*[35]

[31] L. Benevolo, *Storia dell'Architettura del Rinascimento*, Bari 1968, I, p. 274.

[32] F. di Giorgio Martini, *Trattati di Architettura, ingegneria e arte militare*, ed. C. Maltese, Milan 1967, p. 342.

[33] Filarete wrote his treatise in Italian between 1451 and 1464, partly in the form of a dialogue between himself, his patron Francesco Sforza and the young Galeazzo Sforza. The treaty was dedicated to Francesco Sforza, but after his return to Florence Filarete dedicated a second copy, furnished with charming drawings of the buildings described in the text, to Piero de' Medici. The work's principal theme is the building of an ideal city, Sforzinda, laid out like a sixteen-sided star, composed of two overlying squares, that constitute: *"an outline pattern of various buildings, where they can be placed without the interference or hindrance of concrete reality"* (L. Benevolo, op. cit., p. 232). In his descriptions of public and private buildings Filarete defines the types in detail, right down to warehouses and workshops. However, he does not write about a villa, although he includes detailed descriptions of gardens and parks, a circus, a basin for naval battles, a zoological garden (drawn from the feudal world of the Sforza court), and a hunting castle.

[34] P. E. Foster, *Lorenzo de' Medici's Cascina at Poggio a Caiano*, in "Mitteilungen des Kunsthistorisches Institutes in Florenz", XIV (1969), pp. 47–52.

[35] G. Vasari, *Life of Giuliano e Antonio da Sangallo*, in *Lives of the Artists*, op. cit., p. 698.

[36] *"I would advise a slightly elevated position; the road leading up should rise so gently that visitors are only aware of having made the climb when they find themselves in a high position with a view over the surrounding countryside."* L. B. Alberti, op. cit., p. 295.

Below: Villa Medici in Poggio a Caiano, an old
drawing of the façade (G.D.S.U. 3246 AV); plan
of the piano nobile; section; under the portico.

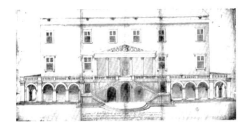

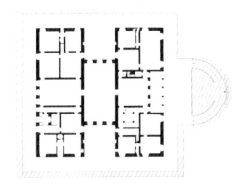

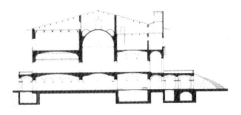

In this case the earlier structure does not appear to have affected the plans for the new building in any way and it appears to be an absolutely independent creation, based on a design with a central plan which obeys the principle of the unification of the parts in all directions, which Sangallo had already attempted to practise in his church architecture.

The villa in Poggio a Caiano represents something that is absolutely new in the architectural domain, an autonomous architectural type not related to the model of the urban palace, nor to the model of the castellated country-house, but deriving from classical forms of antiquity.

Most notably, the entire villa is placed on top of a porticoed level that acts as a podium. This provides a clear gesture of presentation. As opposed to a fluid transition between the architecture and its surrounding, the villa is clearly separated and elevated above its surrounding landscape. This gesture of presentation leads ultimately to the loggia in front of the main entrance to the villa which resembles the façade of a classical temple. Such an addition brings with it many implications beyond simply an architectural quotation. The lack of a central courtyard, replaced instead by a central salon, shifted the focus from interior to exterior, but the building remained structured along very strict rules of geometric harmony. This approach had never been taken before.

The mentality that is intrinsically present in this design is complicated. The focus has been moved to the surrounding land, but the interaction between the interior and exterior is now more rigidly controlled. The view is revered, but removed by the physical distance of the platform and the mental boundaries imposed by the carefully framed scene of the windows.

The villa stands alone on a slight rise, a square block standing on an arcaded base which forms a continuous terrace above. Various openings on this first floor give directly onto the terrace, which acts as an intermediary between the building and the surrounding landscape. Here, the theme of the relationship between an isolated building and the landscape, one of the dominant themes of Renaissance architecture and one which was to be resolved so brilliantly by Palladio half a century later, was perhaps consciously confronted for the first time. The position occupied by the villa answers perfectly to Alberti's dictates on the choice of a site.[36] The villa has a square plan and is perfectly symmetrical with respect to the two right-angle axes, allowing a strictly regular division of the interior spaces. The minor rooms, forming four private apartments, are grouped at the corners, while the more spacious rooms for general use are set together in the centre. The structure's centrality is emphasized by the principal room's bold barrel-vaulted ceiling, occupying two storeys of the villa. To return to Vasari's account: *"Wishing to make a vaulted ceiling for the great hall of that palace in the manner that we call barrel-shaped, Lorenzo could not believe, on account of the great space, that it could be raised. Whereupon Giuliano, who was building a house for himself in Florence, made a ceiling for his hall according to the design of the other, in order to convince the mind of that Magnificent Prince; and Lorenzo therefore gave orders for the ceiling at Poggio a Caiano to be carried out, which was successfully done."*[37] This extremely innovative feature, which, as we see here from Vasari, needed daring technical experimentation is echoed on a smaller scale by the coffered barrel vault of the pronaos-style portico on the main façade, which reaches into the building like an open passageway. We should stress the completely new character of this villa's plan, studied also by Francesco di Giorgio, which Sangallo was to take up again for the palace of the King of Naples.[38] The classical elements which Giuliano Sangallo introduced to the villa include the portico on the ground floor, comparable to the cryptoporticus of Roman villas, and the triangular pediment crowning the pronaos, *"emblem of the neo-Platonic thesis, which places a sacred value on literary pursuits and rural life."*[39] Gustaf Hamberg, in his study of the villa,[40] stresses the originality of the idea of including a classical pediment in a secular building (a feature drawn from the tradition of church architecture), later to become a repeated feature of Palladio's domestic architecture.

The wealth of fresh elements, the free adoption of features from classical antiquity and their harmonious fusion into a remarkable building are the basis of this villa's creation, a *unicum* in the Tuscan world, knowledge of which paved the way towards the major events of the following century. Or, to put it quite simply, the results of Sangallo's ideas proved fruitful in numerous ways to subsequent works and studies. Serlio codified the results of previous research and, drawing largely on the work of his master Peruzzi, published a plan for a villa illustrating an interesting variation of the Poggio a Caiano plan.[42] The studies of buildings with a central plan in Sangallo and Francesco di Giorgio's sketches therefore reconnect, via different routes, with Palladio's design for the Villa Rotonda. The classical references deployed in the villa at Poggio a Caiano were later to be chiefly developed in the Roman area, where there was a conscious effort to reproduce the ancient Roman villa.[43]

[37] G. Vasari, *Life of Giuliano . . .* , op. cit., p. 698.

[38] A. Chastel, op. cit., p. 163.

[39] M. Tafuri, *L'architettura dell'Umanesimo*, op. cit., p.8.

[40] P. G. Hamberg, *The villa of lorenzo il Magnifico at Poggio a Caiano and the origin of Palladianism*, in *Idea and Form. Studies in History of Art*, Stockholm 1959, pp. 76–87.

[41] See also A. Chastel, op. cit., pp. 164–165.

[42] According to Hamberg, Serlio's project can be connected, via Peruzzi, to a plan also studied by Francesco di Giorgio, and thus to the same late 15th-century generation as Sangallo. In Serlio's drawing the arrangement of the rooms preserves the idea of the four private corner apartments, the great hall in the centre and the loggia on four sides, so that the corner apartments do not communicate with the great hall or with each other except via the open loggia. Introduction of the four recessed loggias emphasizes the corner features. See P. G. Hamberg, op. cit.

Above: Poggio a Caiano: A detail of the majolica frieze on the façade representing the Autumn.
Right: The villa Medici at Poggio in the Utens' lunette

[43] In the Rome of the Cinquecento the villa was of considerably less importance than in Florence. This was due to the city's firmly ecclesiastical structure and the absence of a local aristocracy, or a financially powerful class, interested in building in or around the city. It was not until the 16th century that the villa began to appear, more as a reflection of the family fortunes of cardinals and popes than of humanistic interests and country life. Neither did agriculture play a part, the essential ingredients of this type of grandiose villa being particularly magnificent enormous gardens and parks. Particular importance was given to terraces, pools, hippodromes and grottoes, all features drawn from the classical world. Bramante's original project for the Belvedere courtyard, as Ackerman has shown, entailed reviving a Roman villa complex that was thought to have occupied the site. J. S. Ackerman, *The Belvedere as a Classical Villa*, in "Journal of the Warburg and Courtauld Inst.", XIV (1957), p. 70ff. Moreover, the Genazzano nymphaeum, being part of a truly vast villa, the Farnesina, Villa Giulia and the Casino of Pius IV all appear to be attempts to reproduce an ancient villa. In the description of his plan for Villa Madama, Raphael deliberately introduces archaic technical terms, such as "*vestibolo al modo et usanza antica*", "*una bellisima dieta, così la chiamano gli antichi*", "*criptoportico*", "*xysto*", "*teatro*" and "*bagni*", all words which appear, for example, in Pliny's writings. Foster is to be thanked for the copy of Raphael's letter in which he gives a highly detailed description of his project for Villa Madama, an imitation of an ancient Roman villa. P. E. Foster, *Raphael on Villa Madama*, in "Rom, Jahrb. f. Kunstgeschichte", Vienna 1967/68, p. 307.

[44] Behind this pragmatic approach lie some basic health considerations which were resolved during the Renaissance by recourse to astrology, to determine place and orientation according to influences which were beneficial or otherwise. As a man of science, Cardano was first concerned that a building fulfilled its goal, was capable of serving its purpose for some time and, lastly, that it was suitably ornamented. In his treatise, Della Porta describes a house and garden which fulfil the criteria of distribution and orientation according to the seasons. *Villae Jo. Baptistae Portae Neapolitani Libri XII*, Frankfurt 1952. Grapaldi, in his treatise *De Partibus Aedium*, published in Parma in 1494, describes the distribution of the service and residential rooms in a villa, from the cellars to the stables, garden, aviary, drawing-rooms, kitchens, library, chapel etc., on the basis of classical texts and according to a philologically sound method but also from his direct experience. One of the most interesting spokesmen of this "pragmatism", although from outside Tuscan circles, was

On a more general level, the retrieval of relics from archaeological sites which took place with the second generation of 15th-century architects, was to have diverse results, moving in two opposing directions. The first can be recognized in Vignola's treatise which led to the codification of Vitruvius's rules, the other is traceable to the empirical "model-making" of Serlio, whose *Libri* were to be of such fundamental importance to the diffusion of Renaissance ideas in northern Europe.[44]

However, these trends, studies and acquisitions were appearing outside the Florentine area, to which they remained more or less foreign, until finally these very innovations were introduced to build the villa at Poggio a Caiano. The underlying issues that led Tuscan art to a kind of crystallization of its own works has been discussed elsewhere, leaving it, as Benevolo observes, "*with only two possible outlets: jealous and detached personal experience – as with some painters, Pontormo and Bronzino – or intelligent and docile insertion into a ready-made situation... the Grand Duke's artistic production, considered overall, does not have its own system of internal rules, and their place is necessarily taken by external rules: by the precepts of academic culture – already clear in Vasari's painting – from religious morality – which drove the elderly*

Ammannati to write his famous letter to the Accademici del Disegno in '82, in which he repudiates not only the freedom of his previous work but also 'Fiorentinismo', that is, the formal classification of the city's artistic heritage".[45]

This cult of "Florentine nationalism", based on a concept of history as a search for a past to which the present is joined in a pre-established, unbroken and continuous chain, becomes a genuine and real mode of thought as expressed in Vasari's well-known words: *"because the antiquity of things of the past casts more honour, greatness, and admiration on its relics than do modern things."*[46] This view offers an explanation of the overall traits which were characteristic of the building of stately houses, apart from some archaisms with which the architectural vocabulary of the second half of the Florentine Cinquecento occasionally relinked itself to 15th-century models, disregarding Michelangelo's example with this return to the past.

The most gifted interpreter of this school to be engaged on the outlying villas commissioned by the Grand Duke, was Bernardo Buontalenti[47] whose language, unrelated to the

Cardinal Alvise Cornaro who made the following well-known statement: *"I will always praise the modestly beautiful but perfectly comfortable building more highly than the extremely beautiful but less comfortable one, and I therefore advise erring on the side of being too low, because the stairs are more comfortable, than moving upwards, when they are uncomfortable, I would praise dividing some places, for making from one, two which err on the side of being too low, rather than making only one high one, because I speak of rooms for citizens not for Princes."* At the height of the Renaissance, in contrast with adoption of the classical tradition, Cornaro's anti-Vitruvian pragmatism marked the beginning of a new and open-minded attitude which is summed up in the phrase: *"A building may very well be beautiful and comfortable, without being Doric or of any other order."* On this question see also E. Battisti, *L'Antirinascimento*, Milan 1962.

[45] L. Benevolo, op. cit., pp. 676–682.

[46] G. Vasari, *Ragionamenti*, in *Le Opere*, Florence 1823–1838, Giornata I, Ragionamento I, p. 4325.

Poggio a Caiano: the side of the villa

[47] This much talented figure is a perfect illustration of the broad concerns and fields of application of mannerist art: from ingenious machinery and scenic displays for the garden, experiments with special techniques on glass, porcelain and semi-precious stones to the building of fortresses. Buontalenti was born in Florence in 1536 and was thus of a different generation from Vasari and Ammannati, both twenty-five years his senior. Baldinucci called him "Bernardo delle Girandole", referring to his youthful activity as a maker of fireworks. F. Baldinucci, *Notizie dei professori di disegno da Cimabue in qua*, Florence 1681–1728, edited and annotated by P. Barocchi, Florence 1975, Vol. II. See also G. Giovannozzi, *La vita di Bernardo Buontalenti scritta da Gherardo Silvani* in "Rivista d'Arte", 1932, II, IV, p. 505, and, by the same author, *Ricerche su Bernardo Buontalenti*, in "Rivista d'Arte", 1933, II, V, p. 299; L. Gori Montanelli, *Giudizio sul Buontalenti architetto*, in "Quaderni dell'Istituto di Storia dell'Architettura", Rome 1961, VI–VIII, p. 208, and A. Fara, op. cit.; with many largely previously unpublished illustrations.

[48] "*In the year 1569 Prince Francesco bought from Benedetto di Buonaccorso Uguccioni a place called Pratolino, about five miles from Florence in the direction of Monte Senario, with other nearby places, to build the marvellous villa we see today. Bernardo being commissioned for the building, he began work and created the noble villa, devising such a skilful plan without courtyard, loggia or other open space, which every architect makes use of to provide his buildings with the necessary light, yet in raising the building he provided not only every apartment but every room with a good light, and without one obstructing the other, and all the machinery for moving and raising water; the wonderful operations of the latter, activated separately for men and animals, played the organ and other instruments, and similar things, so that I neglected my studies . . . I will only add, that they have surpassed those doing similar things in other parts of Europe.*" F. Baldinucci, op. cit., pp. 496–497. According to Galluzzi the plan of Pratolino was the result of a collaboration between the Grand Duke and Buontalenti: "*The idea and the first drawing of the Pratolino building were his (the Grand Duke's) work, later developed and carried out by Buontalenti, and rendered remarkable chiefly by the great talent of this skilful architect.*" R. Galluzzi, I*storia del Gran Ducato di Toscana*, Florence 1781, Book IV, p. 447. There is a rich bibliography on Pratolino which runs from contemporary accounts to recent critical studies. Among others, see G. Gualterotti, *Vaghezze di Pratolino*, in the 1559 and 1579 editions; F. de' Vieri, *Discorso delle meravigliose opere di Pratolino*, Florence 1586–1587; B. S. Sgrilli, *Descrizione della Regia villa . . . di Pratolino*, Florence 1742, with engravings

works of ancient Rome and classical architecture, goes back to a world of cultural sources and references quite dissimilar from those of his contemporaries. His work on Medici villas, which here concerns us most directly, can be divided between conversions of pre-existing complexes – Petraia, Castello, Magia, Marignolle, Ambrogiana, Seravezza – and entirely new buildings, or instances where the previous structure did not commit the architect to inevitable solutions, as at Pratolino and Artimino.

In the Pratolino villa, commissioned by Francesco I and completed between 1569 and 1575,[48] Sangallo's model at Poggio a Caiano is plainly recognizable: a similar use of a base on which to set the building, here solid and not arched; the planimetric structure, devoid of internal courtyard; the development of the design in three blocks, the central one set back and taller. A recess, spanning the sides in the design of the Poggio villa, was used as the central theme for the main façade of Pratolino, highlighting the entrance. The harmony of the composition is achieved by an increased density at the centre which was to become a feature of Buontalenti's designs. The whole composition, as Utens's view reveals, relies on a subtle counterpoint of volumes and the harmonious pattern of openings which span the masonry, is given horizontal definition by the cornice marking the floor-division.

In his *Life of Buontalenti*, Baldinucci states that "*he gave the villas of Castello and Petraia better form*", and at Castello, the doubling of the planimetric structure, accentuating the longitudinal appearance of the complex, clearly reveals these remodelling operations. Two lower recessed blocks complete the long façade at both ends, punctuated by rows of irregularly spaced openings. At the Petraia villa, the existence of a tower gave Buontalenti the idea of emphasizing the volumes in a simple rectangular structure developed around an interior courtyard, while he raised the tower with an overhanging section supported on corbels in Michelozzo's style. Although the Marignolle villa, rebuilt for Don Antonio de' Medici, shares the kind of intervention earlier carried out at Castello, with emphasis on the simplicity of a structure developed round a central courtyard in an ordered rectangular pattern. The layout of the Ambrogiana villa is more complex, with an interior courtyard and four projecting corner towers with fortified ramparts on the plan's square perimeter. Here again, each façade is marked by the typical grouping of the windows. The idea of setting a building on a base, already tested at Pratolino and, in a more complex and elaborate manner at the Belvedere, appears again at the

Cerreto Guidi villa, where the terracing created by a massive double ramp lends the simple rectangular block of the villa a fortified appearance.

Yet it was with the Artimino villa that Buontalenti's gift found full expression in its most accomplished form, a redeployment of Michelozzo's 15th-century work, both in the treatment of the graceful design of the simple plastered surfaces and the use of detail and elegant creative ideas. The choice of the villa's location already places it in a particular dialectic relationship with its surroundings. It stands on a rise in line with the earlier inhabited nucleus;[49] the land itself acting as a base for the building. The block plan, without an interior courtyard, has corner sections fortified by buttresses which, on the east face, stop short at the level of the lower floor and serve as corner terraces; on the west side they flank either side of the main façade, defining the solidity of its volumes by the depth of their projection, devoid of openings; the "towers" have windows on the interior faces behind the main façade. The openings span the façade rhythmically and are arranged in such a way that they create a frame for the open loggia, the fulcrum of the composition, reached by a flight of steps.

Here, two trends typical of Florentine architecture after the height of the Renaissance seem to fuse. On the one hand

by Stefano della Bella. Also C. da Prato, *Firenze ai Demidoff, da Pratolino a San Donato*, Florence 1886; G. Imbert, *La villa medicea di Pratolino*, Milan 1925, with full bibliography; see also the documented article by W. Smith, *Pratolino*, in "Journal of the Society of Architectural Historians", XX, 4, Dec. 1961, pp. 155–168.

[49] "*They say that when Grand Duke Ferdinand I of Tuscany was hunting one day on Monte Artimino Vecchio (where there is a beautiful broad view of the countryside towards Florence), he was about to sit down on a seat when he called Bernardo and addressed him thus: 'Bernardo, in this very place where you see me, I want a palazzo, large enough for me and the whole court. Now think about it and act quickly.' Buontalenti set immediately to work and built the noble Villa d'Artimino which, although it lacks a good source of water and relies on a cistern, has a wealth of all the delights that a great man could desire for his leisure.*" F. Baldinucci, op. cit., pp. 505–506.

Below: Giuseppe Zocchi, *La Reale Villa d'Artimino*.
Right: A view of the back of the villa at Artimino.

we see the nostalgic reference to a traditional castle, the use of plastered wall surfaces, block design and corner towers, which the drawings reveal to be "added" sections, their inclusion now due to extrinsic rules and to a self-codifying idiom. The second trend is the highly personal, almost self-descriptive, contribution of the sophisticated use of the openings, the thrust of the central exterior stairway on the west façade (erected in recent times according to Buontalenti's design) and the imaginative notion of setting a forest of chimney-pots on the roof without, moreover, disrupting the volumetric compositional rhythm of the whole.

We can perhaps consider the villa of Artimino the last truly creative expression of the great season of Florentine architecture. And though Buontalenti may have sparked off a chain of mannerist works during the 17th century – with Giulio Parigi, Matteo Nigetti, Gherardo Silvani – and into the 18th century – with Foggini, Ruggieri, Zanobi del Rosso, Pellegrini – the limited resources available given the declining economic position of the Grand Duchy of the Medici, or the austerity of the House of Lorraine's rule, allowed only partial expression: interior conversions, modest extensions and fashionable decorations, while the echoes and interpretative reflections of these artistic developments were to have their most active creative hour outside the Florentine area.

CHAPTER FOUR

The Garden: Origin and Development

[1] On this theme see, among others, R.W. Kennedy, *The Renaissance Painter's Garden*, New York 1948, which examines Renaissance painting as an iconographic source for the garden, with a wealth of references. See also C. Acidini Luchinat, *Il giardino fiorentino nello specchio delle arti figurative*, in *Giardini Medicei*, ed. C. Acidini Luchinat, Milan 1996, pp. 16–45.

[2] Pier de' Crescenzi, *Trattato della Agricultura traslato nella favella fiorentina rivisto dallo 'Nferigno Accademico della Crusca'*, Bologna 1784. The quotations are taken from this edition.

[3] "*Every variety of herb is planted, such as rue, sage, basil, marjoram, mint and like things. And in similar fashion flowers from all regions are planted, violets, lilies, roses, irises and other things. Between these plants and low shrubs there is a beautiful tall bush almost like a seat. Again, in the shrubbery, or rather herb garden, which does not like the sun, trees must be planted, or climbing vines, whose foliage will shelter the shrubs and provide pleasant cool shade.*" Pier de' Crescenzi, op. cit., Book VIII, Chap I, p. 137.

Left: The green hut in the garden of the *Hypnerotomachia Poliphili*, Venice 1499.
Following pages: Two details of the berceaux in the same garden.

For all types of villa, from the grandest to the most modest, the presence of a garden was more than a simple addition, it was a fundamental and unifying part of the whole, even if the relationship between a building and its surroundings was established with varying degrees of freedom, linkage and continuity of design. From Villani's account we learn that in the 14th century the outlying residences of Florence's more notable citizens included: "*noble palaces, towers, courtyards and walled gardens*". These gardens were still very simple, of the *hortus conclusus* kind, protected by surrounding walls and remarkable for their regular symmetrical parterres and intersecting paths, a pattern derived from the monastery courtyard that was to spread with little variation all over Europe. Obviously no garden of this period has survived but we can nevertheless gain some idea on the basis of illustrated literary sources[1] and, once again, from essay and treatise writers. We must refer again to the earlier-mentioned *Ruralium Commodorum Libri* by Pier de' Crescenzi,[2] a true codification of the medieval garden. De' Crescenzi displays his impressive knowledge of Latin, Greek and Arab sources, frequently referring to the *rusticus* Palladio and to Avicenna and drawing suggestions from both concerning the site to build a villa: at the foot of a tree-covered hill, far from swamps; a place with beneficial breezes and sources of water. Gardens are divided into three categories, corresponding to the three social categories of their owners. The first garden to be described is the one most commonly shown in medieval illustrations, a "*garden of small herbs*", and its measurements are stated empirically, "*of a size that will suffice those living there*". The treatise specifies the trees to be planted around the garden, to be sown with grass, "*like a green cloth*".[3] The second category includes the "middle" garden, the size being dependent on the "*means and standing of the people*". The difference between this garden and the first lies not so much in the general layout as in the size of the beds and the varieties of plants to be grown, which includes vegetables in the orchard.[4] Finally, the third garden "*for kings and other wealthy lords*", gives us a sumptuous view of a medieval residence on the outskirts of a city. This was the time when magnificent parks and gardens made their first appearance, created by titled families such as the Visconti in Milan, the Scaligeri in Verona and the Este in Ferrara, who held gatherings in their splendid castles and hunting parks. De' Crescenzi codifies this playground of gentlemanly pursuits in his treatise, partly basing himself on what was personally familiar.[5] De' Crescenzi's discourse is supported by a study of contemporary iconographic sources, among which we should mention the *Theatrum Sanitatis* engravings, illuminated manuscripts like *Les Très Riches Heures* produced for Jean du Berry by Paul, Herman and Jean di Limbourg in around 1413, and the frescoes in the Camposanto in Pisa, which generally depict a garden as separate from the building, square in shape, enclosed or walled and crossed by straight paths bordered by hedges and shaded by pergolas. The chief ornament was often a fountain and, according to a garden's grandeur, there would be a flower garden, *herbarium*, orchard and *viridarium*. This kind of organization of space follows the precise demarcations of a monastic cloister and does not appear to rely on any a priori formal design. The pattern and division seem to depend on the particular plants that the beds were intended to grow and on the arrangement of fruit trees, pergolas, supporting structures and hedges. Colour effects and scents also played their part, the former being supplied by the speckled and gaily coloured

[4] De' Crescenzi advises surrounding these gardens with "... *hedges of plum trees, white rose bushes and, above this, a hedge of pomegranates in hot districts, and in cold ones hazelnut, plum or quince trees ... Plant ranks or rows of pear and apple trees and, in hot areas, palms and citrons. Plant also mulberries, cherries, other plums and similar noble trees such as fig, hazelnut, almond, quince, pomegranate and so forth, so that each variety has its row, or rank, and the rows, or ranks, should be at least twenty feet long, or forty at the most, the Lord be willing ... Also, build pergolas in the most suitable and charming places in the form of an arbour,*" ibid., p. 139.

[5] In these gardens de'Crescenzi suggests planting "... *in the northern part ... a wood of mixed trees where the wild animals placed in this wooded area can hide. And in the southern part make a beautiful palazzo where the King, or the Queen, will live when they want to escape from weighty matters and refresh their spirits with joyful pleasures. It is essential that the palace be built in such a way that in summertime there is welcome shade nearby. The windows on the garden side should be sheltered from the burning heat of the sun. There can be also groves of trees in other parts of the garden. A fish-pool should also be made, where many kinds of fish can be raised. Hare, deer, rabbits and similar non-rapacious animals should be included. And among the trees near the palazzo a kind of house can be made, with a roof and sides of closely meshed copper wire, for pheasants, partridges, nightingales, blackbirds, chaffinches, linnets and every variety of song bird. And the rows of trees in the palazzo garden should be at a distance from the woods that makes it possible to watch the movements of the animals put in the garden. In this garden also make a palace with paths and rooms which are simply green arbours, where the King and Queen can live with their barons or ladies in the fair dry weather. This dwelling can be easily made in the following manner. Measure and mark out all the pathways and rooms and, where the walls will be, plant fruit trees, the Lord be willing, trees which will grow easily like cherry and apple. Or it might be better to plant willows or elms for a few years for timber, posts and poles or wickerwork, and make the walls and roof of these. But the house could also easily be made of cut wood with vines planted around it, covering the whole building. A large overhead covering can also be made in the garden of cut wood or trees covered with vines. It is pleasing if a single arbour is made of unusual and mixed varieties of trees, which the skilled cultivator of this garden may well know, like other matters discussed in this book. And it should be said that such a garden is greatly enhanced by trees which do not lose their leaves, such as pines, cypresses, and palms, if they can survive*", ibid., pp. 140–142.

6 "*They were shown into a walled garden alongside the palace, and since it seemed at once to be a thing of wondrous beauty, they began to explore it in detail. The garden was surrounded and criss-crossed by paths of unusual width, all as straight as arrows and overhung by pergolas of vines, which showed every sign of yielding an abundant crop of grapes later in the year. The vines were all in flower, drenching the garden with their aroma, which, mingled with that of many other fragrant plants and herbs, gave them the feeling that they were in the midst of all the spices ever grown in the East. The paths along the edges of the garden, were almost entirely hemmed in by white and red roses and jasmine, so that not only in the morning but even when the sun was at its apex one could walk in pleasant, sweet-smelling shade without ever being touched by the sun's rays. It would take a long time to describe how numerous and varied were the shrubs growing there, or how neatly they were set out, but all the ones that have aught to commend them and flourish in our climate were represented in full measure. In the central part of the garden (not the least, but by far the most admirable of its features), there was a lawn of exceedingly fine grass, of so deep a green as to almost seem black, dotted all over with possibly a thousand different kinds of gaily-coloured flowers, and surrounded by a line of flourishing, bright green orange and lemon trees, which with their mature and immature fruit and lingering shreds of blossom, offered agreeable shade to the eyes and a delightful aroma to the nostrils. In the middle of the lawn stood a fountain of pure white marble covered with marvellous bas-reliefs. From a figure standing on a column in the centre of the fountain, a jet of water, whether natural or artificial I do not know, but sufficiently powerful to drive a mill with ease, gushed high into the sky before cascading downwards and falling with a delectable plash into the crystal-clear pool below. And from this pool, which was lapping the rim of the fountain, the water passed through a hidden culvert and then emerged into finely constructed artificial channels surrounding the lawn on all sides. Thence it flowed along similar channels through almost the whole of the beautiful garden, eventually gathering at a single place from which it issued forth from the garden and descended into the plain as a pure clear stream, furnishing ample power to two separate mills on its downward course, to the no small advantage of the owner of the palace.*

The sight of this garden, and the perfection of its arrangement, with its shrubs, and its streamlets and the fountain from which they originated, gave so much pleasure to each of the ladies and the three young men that they all began to maintain that if Paradise were constructed on earth, it was inconceivable that it would take any other form, nor could they imagine any way in which the garden's beauty could possibly be enhanced. And as they wandered contentedly through it.

plants, and the second by growing a collection of rare sweet-smelling varieties, sometimes for medicinal purposes, among the other plants. As we see, this arrangement was based chiefly on exploration the direct experience of the senses, assembled and juxtaposed in a regular sequence, and never arranged with an eye to the effects of a modelled design. We gain a clearer image of this sensibility, this "atmosphere", from literary sources, including the confirmation provided by Boccaccio's description in the proem to the third day of the *Decameron*,[6] rather than from treatises and iconographic works. While not including any specific descriptions, Dante's work also reveals how important a garden was to the whole image of a medieval villa.

The early gardens of the humanist era differed little from their medieval models. The elements were the same, with perhaps some greater variety of plants. However, in several instances we can see the very first attempts to form a link between a house and garden by installing loggias and porticoes which played an introductory, welcoming or decorative role. In Giovanni Rucellai's *Zibaldone* (notebook) we are given a complete description of the 15th-century garden created at the Rucellai family's villa at Quaracchi (Leon Battista Alberti was commissioned for their famous palazzo in the city). This was the garden of a leading citizen who proudly exhibited it for the admiration of passers-by. There is no one, states Rucellai "*who does not stop for a quarter of an hour to look at the garden which holds many lovely things*".[7] The garden would even seem to have been admired by the villagers of

San Piero a Quaracchi, as a matter of pride to members of the community, since in 1480 *"it seeming to them that the beauty of the garden . . . brought them fame"*, they decided to work at their own expense *"to maintain and preserve the beauty and grandeur of the said garden"*. The Quaracchi garden did not differ greatly from 14th-century examples.[8] On studying the various sections, we find the features of the medieval garden described by de' Crescenzi: fish-ponds, groves, viridarium, pergolas, arbours, flowery hedges and trellised shrubs, rustic seats, mixed vegetable and flower garden, and splashes of colour provided by *"bushes with red, white and pink roses"*. However, we begin to see hints of some newly emerging trends, in particular in the attempt to line up the elements on the same viewing axis as the avenue leading from the villa to the Arno. The introduction of new architectural forms, other than fountains, was still limited to a few isolated instances, such as a small balcony over the door, and some garden furnishings including seats and flower vases. Moreover, certain features now appeared which were to gain great popularity: "secret gardens", works of topiary, frequently described in Rucellai's *Zibaldone*, labyrinths and grassy mounts. Lastly, at Quaracchi, it is interesting to see how much importance was given to the relationship between the position of the garden and the surrounding landscape, something previously ignored, in an attempt to create a visual link between the villa and the river.

making magnificent garlands for themselves from the leaves of the various trees, their ears constantly filled with the sound of some twenty different kinds of birds, all singing as though they were vying with one another, they became aware of yet another delightful feature, which, being so overwhelmed by the others, they had so far failed to notice. For they found that the garden was liberally stocked with as many as a hundred different varieties of perfectly charming animals, to which they all started drawing each other's attention. Here were some rabbits emerging from a warren, over there hares were running, elsewhere they could observe some deer lying on the ground, whilst in yet another place, young fawns were grazing. And apart from these, they saw numerous harmless creatures of many other kinds, roaming about at leisure as though they were quite tame, all of which added greatly to their already considerable delight." Boccaccio, *The Decameron*, op. cit., pp.190–191.

[7] G. Rucellai, *Zibaldone Quaresimale*, ed. A. Perosa, London 1960, p. 21. This is the first philological edition of the text which was edited in part in G. Marcotti, *Un mercante fiorentino e la sua famiglia nel secolo XV*, Florence 1881.

[8] The *Zibaldone* carries a detailed description of the garden at Quaracchi, which included: *"A fish-breeding pool extending twenty yards long and twelve yards wide, all walled around and full of fish. Around this pool are numbers of green pines. The river Arno is nearby . . . A stream, called the 'rio', passes by the door, as clear as timeless amber. The road to Pistoia is there to satisfy every need. A beautiful vaulted pergola with oak arches, eight yards wide and one hundred long. A fine doorway on the road with a loggia at the end of the said pergola. Two box hedges begin on either side of the pergola . . . as long as the pergola, about 1 3/4 high and about a third wide. And above this hedge appear many of the family's coats of arms . . . At the end of the pergola is another doorway leading into the enclosed garden, with a delightful green lawn surrounded by low walls and quantities of box shaped into figures of giants and centaurs, and steps and vases of every kind . . . in such a way that they delight the eye and comfort the body; many blooming Damascene violets, sweet marjoram and basil and many other sweet-smelling herbs to soothe the human senses. Opposite this pergola and the doorways is a road leading to the Arno, eight yards wide and six hundred long, as straight as a die, so that from the table where I dine I can see the boats passing along the Arno . . . the road is lined on either side by tall trees and grape vines. At the end of the road, near the house, is a grove to provide shade and a roof of wooden planks where ball games can be played . . . From the*

road you see the following things: great numbers of beautiful box hedges in various shapes, balls, seats, ships and galleons, shrines, pedestals and pillars, vases, urns, all of impressive size, men and women, lions with the Commune banner, apes, dragons, centaurs, camels, diamonds, sprites with bows, chalices, horses, donkeys, oxen, dogs, deer and birds, bears and wild pigs, dolphins, jousters and bowmen, harpies, philosophers, popes, cardinals, Cicero, and many other things. Around this garden is a great hedge 400 yards long, fashioned of bay, fig and plum trees, vines and dogwood, juniper and mulberries; within the hedge are many seats entwined and covered with bay and vines, and a rose garden; along the hedge is a beautiful pathway: on one side lies the hedge and some of the clipped box I have described, on the other, jujubes, pines and other trees which give great pleasure to the passer-by. Furthermore, there is a circular oratory in the garden, made of bay and lined with benches and a pedestal in the centre with a round stone; the vaulted pathway is covered with damask roses and jasmine and joins the road with the pergola and box hedges. There is also a square arbour of pine and laurel with seats inside, and a small bower of juniper. In the hedge I mentioned are two snares for catching figpeckers and thrushes with rods for raising and lowering the nets. Moreover, there is a hillock, with evergreen pines and shrubs (juniper, strawberry trees, bay, broom and box), eight yards high and it runs a hundred yards below and fifty above, with paths leading around in the centre of the mount. And there is also a high pergola of hazelnut trees, six yards wide and a hundred long, and there is an uncovered path of the same width and length with tall rows of several varieties of sweet grape-vines, and at the ends of these rows are rose bushes (white, red and incarnate roses) grown and trained in the form of a tall bush, which looks very fine in the rose season, while the pen is unable to compete with the pleasure given to the eye. And it is very well laid out and arranged in good proportion. The open spaces, like the paths, are full of fine and desirable trees bearing sweet and flavoursome fruits, wild and domesticated plums, and there are still other trees which are little known here, such as the sycamore." G. Rucellai, op. cit., pp. 20–22.

[9] "Firstly, the villa's landscape has an expansive and paradigmatic influence which makes it an organizational element of the entire surrounding landscape, so that even the worker reproduces a simple outline on his farm" (E. Sereni, *Storia del paesaggio agrario italiano*, Bari 1972, p. 251). In the chapter *Il bel paesaggio della villa all'italiana*, Sereni throws light on the agricultural and utilitarian origins of the villa, recognizing in the directing contact

Left: A hypothetical reconstruction of the garden at Quaracchi.
Below: A circular labyrinth by Baldassarre Peruzzi; a quadrangular labyrinth from Filarete's treatise.

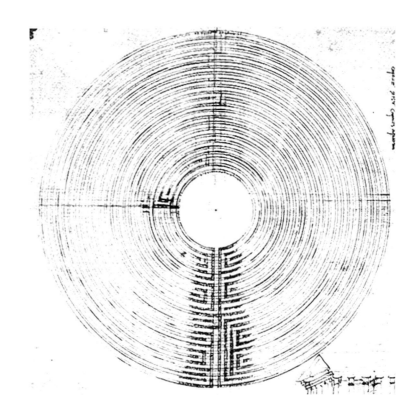

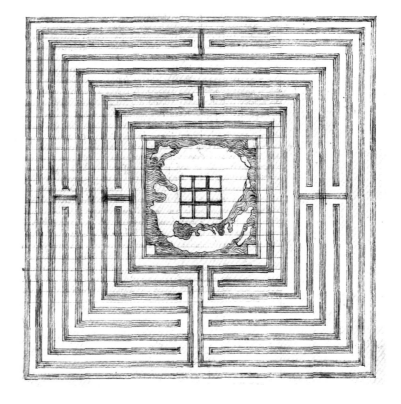

In the 15th century the gardens of the Medici villas – to begin with the most outstanding and impressive examples – still drew on the medieval tradition. At Careggi, the most famous garden in humanist circles, a greater variety and wealth of plants was all that was introduced to the garden, including the famous red carnation imported from the East. Utens's views of the Trebbio and Cafaggiolo villas reveal the simplicity of the layouts of these gardens, with the result that they made little impact on the general landscape. As Sereni observes,[9] the emphasis was not on contrasting effects but on the integration of the elegant part of the villa and garden and the utilitarian farm area, through a standardization of forms involving both the flower-beds and the fields, each bordered in similar manner by evergreen hedges. After all the eulogizing words that the gardens at Poggio a Caiano inspired in literary men at court, in the view that Utens painted a century after its creation the garden is revealed as a series of juxtaposed elements: the walled garden, with a central feature of an octagon of hedges, garden seats and pergolas; orchards on either side and a pine grove behind the villa. It is clear that new ideas in architectural design were not matched by similarly innovative work in landscape gardening. Thus, the novelties and signs of renewal in the description of the Quaracchi garden which we have referred to here do not illustrate a general trend in garden designs of the period.

Alberti's precepts concerning gardens hover between a concept of renewal drawn from the designs of classical writers, and the traditional medieval garden. In fact, while Alberti stresses the importance of the garden and the surrounding landscape[10] or expounds on an "architectural" distribution of trees and plants (*"three circles, semicircles and other geometric figures used in the area near the buildings, bordered by rows of laurel, Lycian cedar and juniper, their branches bent and interlaced"*[11]) drawn from classical precepts (with an occasional, sometimes slavish, reference to Latin sources), his work seems chiefly inspired by literary sources. Indeed, it is not surprising that the reference to a grotto made of *"rough material"* is the only one of which Alberti shows direct experience.[12]

Thus, despite this brandishing of classical sources and instructions concerning the adoption of features drawn from Roman gardens (statues, vases, pergolas and marble columns[13]), Alberti never goes beyond the generic data of literary sources and the absence, moreover, of any overall view of garden design, places his precepts very close to work being carried out at the time, even in the most sophisticated gardens, such as Quaracchi. Alberti was still in a phase of transition as far as the Renaissance concept of a garden was concerned.

that the landowner has with the working of his property, the fusion of the garden and the surrounding countryside, also in a visual sense. The "beautiful" part is thus never in opposition with the "useful" part, since *"the very perfection of its forms remains obviously linked to exigencies arising from the development of new techniques and new agricultural relationships"*, ibid. p. 191.

[10] *"Meadows full of flowers, sunny lawns, cool and shady groves, limpid streams and pools, and whatever else we have described as being essential to a villa, none of these should be missing, for their delight as much as for their utility"*, L. B. Alberti, op. cit., p. 295.

[11] Ibid., p. 806.

[12] *"On the walls of their grottoes and caves the ancients used to apply a deliberately roughened revêtment of tiny pumice chips, or travertine paste, what Ovid called 'living pumice'. We have also seen green ochre used to imitate moss in a grotto. Something we saw in a cave gave us great delight: where a spring gushed out, the surface was covered in a variety of sea and oyster shells, some turned one way, some another, charmingly arranged according to their different colours."* Ibid., p. 299.

[13] *"Phiteon of Agrigentum had in his house three hundred stone vases, each with a capacity of one hundred amphorae; such vases make good garden ornaments when placed beside fountains. As for vines, the ancients would train them over their garden walks, supported on marble columns whose diameter was one-tenth their height, while their ornaments were Corinthian"*. Ibid., p. 300.

[14] M. Recchi, *La villa e il giardino nel concetto della Rinascenza italiana*, in "La Critica d'Arte", II, n. 3, LX, June 1937, p. 12.

[15] *"Then in the garden was a beautiful square [building] built in this form. The bridge and this square were both 20 braccia on one side and 40 on the other. At ground level it was divided into two parts, 16 braccia a side. [There were] halls and rooms with two small towers and an open loggia between each. They were twenty braccia high plus the two small towers on top as is shown here. All these rooms on the bridge and in the angles, or corners, were all vaulted without any wood. There was also a passage on columns from this square at the bridge to the corners. [It was] a double wall built on columns in such a way that one could go under cover at ground level and above in the open. The lower passage had a parapet on the side toward the moat. The upper one ran from one corner to another, in this way it went all around. The garden had four entrances but this entrance was the main one, leading directly into the*

garden. The garden was laid out as described here. First of all a square of 3000 braccia divided into seven parts, one hundred land braccia wide. Each of the paths had a little shelter at the corner 12 braccia square, and leading from one to the other is a garden walk on columns like the one above so that one can move about the whole area either sheltered by one or exposed by the other. They are placed between the two streams of water in such a way that whether one chooses the upper or the lower level of seven ways one can always see the water. One stream runs on the outside and one on the inside, as I have said. To say it was a space of 1000 braccia each way reduced to a circle. This in turn was laid out like a map of the world. All the stream flowed in and flowed out from the centre of this." Antonio di Piero Averlino, known as Filarete, *Trattato di Architettura*, translated with an introduction and notes by J. R. Spencer, Yale Univ. Press, 1965, p. 209.

[16] "*There was another garden built in a new manner, more than 100 braccia high and all on columns. It also enclosed a palace . . .* ", ibid. p. 210.

[17] *Hypnerotomachia Poliphili* was published in Venice in 1499, in Manuzio's edition illustrated with the famous woodcuts. Attributed to the Venetian monk Francesco Colonna, it was described by Temanza as: "*a most mysterious dream, full of knowledge*" (see T. Temanza, *Vita di Fra' Francesco Colonna,*

Below: Baldassarre Peruzzi plan of a garden with portico (G.D.S.U. 580A).

However, there can be little doubt that these developments, aside from the decorative advantages of mixing new plants and objects with traditional ones, contribute greatly to a gradual unfolding of the history of the villa's formal garden, no longer simply a fragmentary succession of parts, but an object in itself, a coherent composition. Here lies the most significant contribution of humanist thought, for which the garden was the very quintessence of natural harmony; [14] nature itself *more geometrico demonstrata*, an area of pure volumes governed by strict relationships, indeed by numerical relationships, rather than by symbolic meanings and situations. Another point to consider here is the mixed effect produced, on the one hand, by contacts between commissioners which led increasingly to the taming of the open countryside and of areas around the buildings, and, on the other, a revival of theoretical critical discourse, including its relationship to classical sources, which would seem to have provided a wealth of suggestions for gardens to serve as models and put into practice.

In Filarete's description of his Ideal City we find a large section devoted to dealing with this question. The gardens are extremely large and most are surrounded by colonnades, with lakes or fountains in the centre. There are frequent proposals for labyrinths in Filarete's text, to be used as a pattern on which to base the entire layout. We find the labyrinth-garden with a palazzo in the centre[15] and the garden-palazzo, divided up like a map of the world,[16] where architectural invention illustrates the world of fable and myth evoked by the text. His preference for the ordered look of geometric designs is

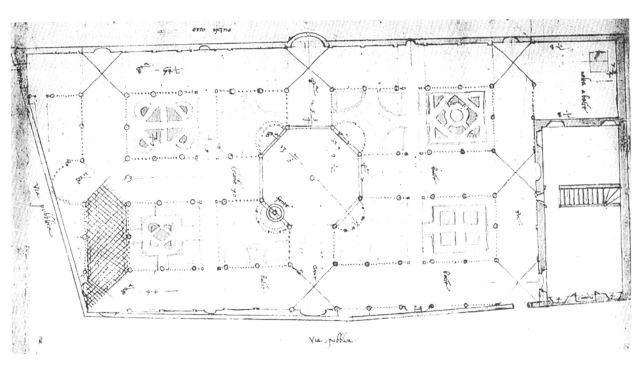

applied by Filarete in a contradictory way, so that the images he presents in his sketched plans accompanying the text appear fanciful and emblematic.

The gardens described in *Hypnerotomachia Poliphili*, the hermetic prose romance whose author, identified as Francesco Colonna, was linked to Filarete when they were both defined as 15th-century Romantics,[17] are again based on geometric shapes. We should recall the garden on the island of Cythera,[18] consisting of a series of concentric circles linked by radiating avenues, crossed by canals and streams and shaded by pergolas, where the relationship between architecture and nature was resolved by subjecting nature to the discipline of geometry. The garden designed by Colonna has much in common with the central radial plan used to illustrate theological systems, as well as with plans for Ideal Cities produced by contemporary theorists, a geometric pattern which is both fable and allegory.[19] The highly fanciful garden designs

Below: The green hut of the garden of Castello in the Utens' lunette.
Right: A labyrinth in the Ferrari's treatise.

sopranominato Polifilo, in *Vite dei più celebri architetti e scultori veneziani che fiorirono nel secolo decimosesto*, Venice 1778, p. 23). *Hypnerotomachia* proposed some hermetic ideas which were to play an important role and influence developments in architectural ornamentation. According to Tafuri's interpretation (*L'architettura dell'umanesimo*, op. cit., p. 91) the setting of *Hypnerotomachia Poliphili* should be shifted to the Roman area; the work being more generally considered a literary expression of 16th-century Venetian romanticism. However, there is still disagreement on the matter. For Casella and Pozzi, the authors of *Francesco Colonna. Biografia e opera*, Padua 1959, with a full bibliography, "*Poliphilo can be easily accepted on the basis of his 16th-century Venetian culture, without having to imagine the author's travels and archaeological excavations in distant lands.*" Vol. II, p. 73.

[18] "*This delightful and pleasant island is shown more clearly here. Its circuit measured three miles around, and it was a mile in diameter, which was divided into three parts. Each third contained 333 paces, one foot, two palms and a little more. The distance from the extreme edge of the shore to the orange-tree enclosure. At this point the field began, proceeding towards the centre and occupying another sixth of the diameter. Thus an entire third of the diameter was taken, leaving another sixth between here and the centre, namely 166 paces, 10 palms. From the peristyle that I have described, some space was eliminated by the contraction of the fields, so as to avoid distorting their squareness. Therefore they ended before completing a third of the diameter. This was deliberate, in order to give the right proportion to the last square formed by the lines drawn to the centre. The space intercalated between the river and the peristyle was all covered with graceful greenery, as has been sufficiently described above.*" Francesco Colonna, *Hypnerotomachia Poliphili, The Strife of Love in Dream*, the complete text has been translated into English for the first time by Jocelyn Godwin, with an introduction and the original woodcut illustrations, New York, 1999, p. 311–312.

[19] "*. . . the intercolumniation was equal to two columns' width plus a quarter; and where the paths met the peristyle, the latter opened with a width equal to theirs, making a gap beneath the peristyle and interrupting the continuity of the enclosure. Thereupon a noble gateway was raised, with its bowed arch resting its ends on the columns on either side. These were made uniform with the other columns as to their shafts and position, but differed in thickness in order to match the superstructure. Above the curved*

beam was a gable or frontispiece, with all its appropriate ornaments finely carved. The epistyle, zophorus and cornice continued in a circle above the columns, marvellously fashioned with all the proper mouldings; they had been hollowed out with admirable effort like a chest, and crammed full of soil in which all sorts of attractive flowers grew. Moreover, box-trees and juniper in topiary work had been planted directly above each column so that a round ball of box, with not a shoot in sight, alternated with a juniper on a foot-high stem, made with four compressed spheres gradually diminishing upward; and there were flowers in between." Ibid., p. 306.

[20] "A mixture of flowering plants grew in this field, which was more beautiful than a painted picture. Again, there were compartments in the corners following the plan already described, except that they were triangular and made of golden-yellow cryselectrum. None like this is collected from the virgin Hesperides; when rubbed it gave off a sweet citric perfume such as is not given by the amber collected on the German island of Citrum; it was more translucent and clear than the tears of Meleagrides. On the lowest level there grew sweet Celtic nard; on the second, mountain germander, on the third, laudanum and cisthos; and on the top one, fragrant ambrosia. The fruit-trees were shaped in a convex hemisphere. In this third range, none exceeded another in height, but all were of a proper stature, various species and many-fruited, there were pistachios, apricots, every sort of balsam-bearing tree, hypomelides, all the Damascene plums, and many other fruits beyond those that are peculiar to our climes, of manifold species and of unknown and unfamiliar colour, shape and delicious taste." Ibid., p. 306.

[21] "Within the circle, around the outlines of the figures, all was planted with mountain hulwort and the bands with laurentiana. The eagle was of groundsel, and the vase of asaron with the opening inside its rim of myrtle. The whole length of the outer bands was of periwinkle, and the other band of aquilegia. The circles that fitted in the corners were filled with wild nard, with foxgloves both in and outside them. The letters were of wild thyme, the spaces of golden-hair. The inside of the loops made by the bands were of wormwood. The rings in the triangles had balls at their centres, two of fragrant aurotano and two of lavender, raised a foot and a half on their stems. In the others were alternately a ball of savin and one of juniper, three feet high. All the herbs had beautiful foliage, freshly green and lovely to behold; it was a wondrous work of accuracy, amenity and delight. Tiny pipes in orderly arrangement irrigated it with a spray of fine droplets." Ibid., p. 323.

in *Hypnerotomachia Poliphili* herald a new trend: the use of plants as architectural materials, a compositional medium in which all items were indiscriminately employed for sculptural purposes: masonry, statues, plants, hedges and shrubs.[20] There is no reason to believe that the matters described in the romance were intended by the author to be pure imaginative whimsy; indeed, the botanical knowledge he displays is so erudite that the wealth of description and terminology used make this a unique work of 15th-century garden literature.[21] Moreover, the planting beds depicted in his highly complex drawings were not simply of symbolic value since by the second half of the 16th century they were already a common feature of contemporary gardens. This is confirmed by Soderini, who lived in Florence from 1501 to 1597, the author of *Trattato sulla cultura degli orti e dei giardini* which discusses making flower-beds in the most varied shapes, such as coats of arms, hour-glasses and even human forms.

71

In Francesco di Giorgio Martini's treatise, written at the close of the 15th century, the revived concept of a garden entirely laid out according to a perfect geometric pattern is discussed in detail.[22] The writer seems to be referring to the organization of an enormous complex with walkways and gymnasiums (in Roman style), used by Martini to establish the garden as a suitably serious creation, which also provided the *"secret places sought by poets and philosophers"*. A further passage in the text describes a garden laid out in front of a broad loggia with pilasters and columns,[23] while in the first book, addressing principles of a general kind, he insists that a garden should be designed according to the same rules of perfect geometry as those used for planning a building.[24]

The notion that a garden's design should be accorded the same importance as the architecture of a building, essentially adopting its value and measure, was to bring an end to the idea of the irreconcilability of the strictly architectural aspect of the building and the natural "random" and living world of nature, now reinterpreted on a miniature scale for the first time.[25] On this same issue, Baccio Bandinelli states that *"things that are built must act as guide and be superior to those that are planted"*.[26] Serlio states, illustrating his treatise with drawings for *"compartments for these gardens"*, that *"they could also serve other purposes"*, and stipulates the geometric rules of abstraction to which nature must be made to conform. Statements of such intransigence, perfectly in accord with Renaissance cultural ideals, gave rise not only to the general principles of composition, but also to the practice of applying architectural techniques to trees, hedges and pathways and even large stretches of garden, all tamed into an abstract perfection of masses and surfaces.

These extreme examples of the mid-16th century obviously concealed an intrinsically contradictory principle, one that was to flower into late mannerism and, in the following century, into the conflict between art and nature, the endless ambiguity perfectly expressed by Claudio Tolomei in a letter to Giovan Battista Grimaldi in which he states: *"mixing art and nature, one cannot discern which is the work of one or the other, what seemed natural artifice is now artificial nature"*[27].

However, while this conflict between art and nature was expressed in inventive designs and sometimes carried to extremes in practice,[28] the treatises, after asserting geometry's role as the supreme master of design, offer no further suggestions for original ideas. In his treatise, Scamozzi presents a traditional garden modelled on existing examples and on pre-established principles. There are few innovations con-

[22] *" . . . since gardens are principally for the enjoyment of those who have them made, and depend also on the amenities of the site, it would seem superfluous to decide on their shape; yet the designer must contrive to reduce it to some perfect form, a circle, square or triangle, and after these more obvious ones come the pentagon, hexagon, octagon etcetera, can be introduced. In a similar fashion, springs and secret places to satisfy the poet and philosopher are sought, walkways covered with greenery to be used as gymnasiums, and all delights that most please the master, as hidden as possible from the eyes of the neighbours."* F. di Giorgio Martini, *Trattati di architettura, ingegneria e arte militare*, ed. C. Maltese, Milan 1967, II, p. 348.

[23] *" . . . a large and delightful garden with beautiful straight paths and a remarkable fount of water, either natural or not . . . There are fish-pools for feeding fish. Around these are trees and green shrubs of the most varied kinds, and many are those that do not lose their leaves for some time. There are other trees and wild and cultivated fruits in separate plots of land places where various birds and animals are kept and fed. And at the very end of the garden is a walled secret place, adorned with plants, which is equipped for lunching or dining in the summertime. Facing this is a holy chapel to be used for prayer or to celebrate mass."* Ibid., I, p. 71.

[24] *"Gardens should be encircled by walls, provided with walkways, greenery and walls . . . And, according to the grandeur of the house, there should be . . . Build a fountain in the centre with natural water or otherwise, shaped like a dish or bowl on a pedestal, as we have said, with many figures and ornamentations. In these water gardens, fishing loggias, covered and uncovered paths, and places half covered and half uncovered, with streams of water and greenery, various animals and birds can be kept. Make ordered straight paths leading between roads and open spaces. Make lawns and groves of mixed trees which can be shaped as shrines, labyrinths, loggias, seats, animals and other fancies. The greater the variety, the greater delight to the eye."* Ibid., pp. 245–246.

[25] The first sign of this trend can be found in Laurana's plan for the hanging gardens of the grand ducal palace in Urbino, where, on a small scale, an overall geometric order was established for the first time. A series of paved paths divide it into square sections, widening to create a circular space at every intersection. L. Dami, *Il giardino italiano*, Milan 1924, p. 11, and G. Masson, *Italian Gardens*, London 1966, p. 64.

[26] See L. Dami, op. cit., p. 13.

27 See E. Battisti, *L'Antirinascimento*, Milan 1962, p. 176.

28 A perfect example of this trend is the Holy Wood of Bomarzo in Lazio, created for a cultured and eccentric gentleman, Vicinio Orsini, who made a startling garden where the visitor is led "*gaping and speechless*" at sights for which art has turned its hand to illusionistic effects. On Bomarzo see the special edition of "Quaderni dell'Istituto di Storia dell'Architettura", Rome, 7–9 (1955), and especially the essays by F. Fasolo, *Analisi statistica del Sacro Bosco*, p. 56, and L. Benevolo, *Saggio d'interpretazione storica del Sacro Bosco*, p. 61; A. Bruschi, *Nuovi dati documentari sulle opere orsiniane di Bomarzo*, in "Quaderni dell'Istituto di Storia dell'Architettura", Rome, 55–60 (1963), p. 13.

29 "*The main forecourt is divided into squares by paths running across and round the edge, so that the greenery is restful to the eyes, the sun beats with less intensity, and there is no glare as there would be with bare earth or paving. In the rear is the garden divided into compartments, with beautiful plants, herbs and sweet-smelling flowers with some paths along the walls which are provided with green shade for walks; in the centre are some fine fountains spraying jets of water. At the top of the garden, facing south, there could be an espalier or pergola of citrus trees, the last vista in the garden, and beyond could be a field planted with vines and fruit trees; some fish-breeding pools, and these are the parts for supplying the master's house.*" The approach would be: "*a very broad long road with elm trees on either side to provide shade and to give those travelling along it a view of the fountain and the buildings from afar.*" V. Scamozzi, *L'idea della architettura universale*, Venice 1615, Part I, Book III, Chaps. XIII and XXII.

30 "*Choose a shape for the Garden that is in accord with the site, whether large or small, choose whatever shape you please, figures and squares, or strips, circles or multi-sided forms. It should be noted that since the garden will be surrounded by hedges or walls, the length will run from East to West . . . thus the larger part will be less shaded and more exposed to the sun . . . The compartments . . . should not be so large that the centre cannot easily be reached from the surrounding paths to gather flowers, pick herbs or cut . . . no paths should measure less than two palms, for walking without intruding or stepping on the plants. However, there should be some broader paths, the ones which cross in the centre, and then those by the hedge that surrounds the garden. The shapes of Meanders or Labyrinths, usually employed on floors or ceilings can also be used with graceful and amusing effect in Gardens.*" G. B. Ferrari, *Flora ouero cultura dei fiori*, Rome 1638, Book I, Chap. III, p. 14ff.

cerning questions of detail apart from a more inventive use of water, and greater variety of trees and shrubs for building trellises, niches, vaults and loggias which, moreover, had already been fully illustrated over a century earlier by Colonna in his *Hypnerotomachia Poliphili*.29 It is hardly surprising that later works on gardening are more concerned with botany than with garden architecture, turning interest in science and aesthetic novelty chiefly towards the rare varieties imported from foreign lands. Explorers and travellers were opening markets in the West and East Indies and this encouraged the fashion for growing exotic plants and rare and precious varieties began to be popular not only in the botanical gardens which had been created a century earlier but also in the gardens of private houses. A treatise of this period, *Flora ovvero cultura di fiori* by the Jesuit father Giovanni Battista Ferrari, printed in Rome in 1638, is a mine of information on the current fashions for ornamenting gardens. In discussing the site for a garden Ferrari does not diverge from the edicts of 15th-century treatises, often with traditional comments,

A design for a green parterre in Ferrari's treatise

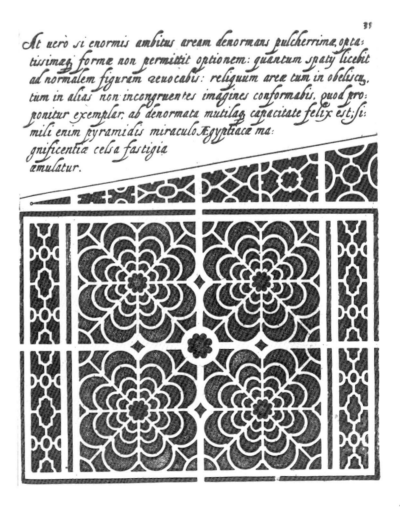

73

and in discussing geometric form he would seem to draw directly from Francesco di Giorgio.[30] Nevertheless, Ferrari offers us a series of interesting examples of the design of parterres and flower-beds and from these we can see how the inner divisions had become freer, along the lines of schema earlier illustrated by Serlio and by Vasari the Younger who, in *Città Ideale*, created highly fanciful designs for gardens to grace princely residences.[31]

By the middle of the 16th century, the landscaping of the gardens for the grander villas in the Florentine area followed the principles stipulated in treatises more closely than on the architectural side. It is our belief that this phenomenon is explained by the interval in time between the high point in the state's economy and the ripening of the theoretical designs produced by the art of the Renaissance. Thus, the capital invested in this sector was not employed to alter the more costly buildings but was, instead, invested in the garden, a feature that ornamented and embellished the villa. We should also recall that Florence was no longer the hub of artistic life (one sign of this being the continual migration of Florentine artists) and gardens created at this time, even the grandest, had a slightly traditional and old-fashioned air, especially when compared with contemporary works in Rome (we need only compare Bramante's revolutionary creation of the Belvedere courtyard with the gardens of the Castello villa, designed some decades later). Moreover, a distinction must be drawn between the gardens of the Medici family and those of private citizens during the course of the 16th century. In fact, the former, apart from being created with abundant funds, reflect the celebratory establishment of grand ducal power and are completely different in character to more modest and restrained designs for private gardens. The latter more clearly reflect the lingering of tradition in the layout of the garden parterre: an exterior lengthening of the house, more or less of the same width as the building, and basically two-dimensional in development. The third dimension first appeared in gardens in Rome, when archaeological finds began to form part of the architectural repertoire. But this was virtually unknown in contemporary Florentine gardens and even the move towards different levels was very cautious, with the introduction of steps and terracing only in late 17th-century landscaping.

The garden at Castello was still based on the notion of an elongation of the building, although conceived on a grander scale if we consider the scale, richness of the layout and the originality of its component parts. Even Vasari, who was

[31] G. Vasari the Younger, *La città ideale*, ed. V. Stefanelli, Rome 1970, p. 109.

[32] G. Vasari, *Life of Tribolo*, in *Lives*, op. cit., p. 234.

[33] "*The villa of Castello stands at the foot of Monte Morello, below the Villa della Topaia, which is halfway up the slope, before it is a plain that descends little by little for the space of a mile and a half down to the River Arno and, exactly where the hill begins, stands the palace, built in past times by Pier Francesco de' Medici, according to a very good design. The principal façade faces directly south, overlooking a vast lawn with two enormous fish-ponds full of running water which comes from an ancient aqueduct built by the Romans to carry water from Valdimarina to Florence, provided with an underground vaulted cistern; and so it has a very beautiful and charming view. The fish-ponds are divided in the middle by a bridge twelve braccia wide which leads to an avenue of the same width, bounded at the sides and covered by an unbroken vault of mulberry trees, ten braccia in height, thus making a covered avenue three hundred braccia in length, delightful for its shade, which leads to the highroad to Prato through a gate placed between two fountains that serve to give water to travellers and animals. On the east side the palace has a very beautiful block of stable buildings, and on the west side is a private garden which is entered from the courtyard of the stables, passing straight through the ground floor of the palace by way of the loggias, halls, and chambers on the ground level. From this private garden one can enter, by a door on the west side, into another garden, very large and filled with fruit trees and bounded by a wilderness of fir trees which conceals the houses of the labourers and others who live there, engaged in the service of the palace and the gardens. The part of the palace that faces north towards the mountain has a lawn in front of it as long as the palace, the stables and the private garden together, and from this lawn one climbs by steps to the principal garden, surrounded by the customary walls. This slopes gently upwards, extending beyond the palace, so that the midday sun fills it and bathes it with its rays, as if there were no palace in front; and at the upper end it rises so high that it commands a view not only of the whole palace, but also of the plain that surrounds it and the city. In the middle of the garden is a wilderness of very tall and thickly-planted cypresses, laurels and myrtles which are laid out in circles in the form of a labyrinth, all surrounded by box hedges two and a half braccia high, so even and grown with such beautiful order that they appear to have been painted with a brush. At the centre of this labyrinth, at the desire of the Duke, Tribolo made a very beautiful marble fountain, as shall be described below. At the principal entrance, with the above-mentioned lawn and two fish-ponds and the avenue lined with mulberry trees, Tribolo*

wanted to extend the avenue so that it reached as far as the River Arno and the waters running off the fountains would flow gently along graceful channels down the sides of the avenue, and be filled with various kinds of fish and shrimp, accompanying it down to the river. As for the palace – to describe what has still to be done as well as what has been completed – he wished to make a loggia in front which, passing through an open courtyard, would lead on the stable side to another building, as large as the old one, with the same number of apartments, loggias, a private garden and all the rest, which addition would have made a vast palace, with a most beautiful façade. After passing through the court leading to the large garden with the labyrinth, at the first entrance where there is a spacious lawn, steps lead up to the labyrinth and an open space thirty braccia square, to be occupied by a enormous fountain of white marble, spouting water above ornaments fourteen braccia in height, while from the mouth of a statue at the highest point was to issue a jet of water rising to the height of six braccia. At either end of the lawn two loggias, facing each other, each thirty braccia in length and fifteen in width, in the middle of each loggia a marble table twelve braccia in length and on the outside a basin of eight braccia to receive water from a vase held by two figures. In the centre of this labyrinth Tribolo had thought to achieve the most decorative effect by means of jets of water and a very beautiful seat round the fountain, the marble basin of which was to be, and was thus made, much smaller than that of the large principal fountain; at the top was to be a bronze figure spouting water. In the centre, at the end this garden, was to be a gateway with marble children spouting water on either side, fountains on either side, and in the corners double niches to hold statues, as in the others in the walls at the sides, at the opposite ends of the avenue crossing the garden, all covered with greenery arranged in various ways. Through the above-mentioned gateway at the upper end of this garden, above some steps, one enters into another garden, as wide as the first but of no great length . . . In this garden were to be two other loggias, one on either side, and in the wall opposite the gateway, made to support the soil of the mountain, was to be a central grotto with three basins and water playing into them in imitation of rain. The grotto was to be between two fountains set in the same wall and opposite these, in the lower part of the garden, two more, one on either side of the gateway; so that the fountains of this garden would be equal in number to those of the other which lies below and receives its water from the first, higher one. And this garden was to be full of orange trees which will have, whenever that may be, a most favourable situation, being protected by the walls and the mountain from the north and other harmful winds. From this garden two stone staircases, one on either side, lead to a wilderness of cypresses, fir trees, holm oaks, laurels, and other evergreen

not unfamiliar with Roman gardens, states that, had it been completed, it would have emerged as "*the most sumptuous, most magnificent and most ornate garden in Europe*",[32] and in his *Life of Tribolo*, the artist chosen by Cosimo I to create the garden, Vasari gives a detailed description of the original project.[33] The importance of the design, pointed out by his contemporaries and reiterated by numerous scholars as the perfect example of a 16th-century Tuscan garden, lies less in its general plan than in the introduction of elements and of garden forms that were for the first time to be employed in a definitive layout. Furthermore, we should recall that Tribolo's project was not carried out according to his original plan, the grandeur of which we can only imagine from Vasari's description, particularly the sweep of the avenue stretching

Bernardo Sgrilli, Plan of the Fattoria di Castello in 1747 (A.S.F. Piante Scrittoio RR Possessioni, p. 91)

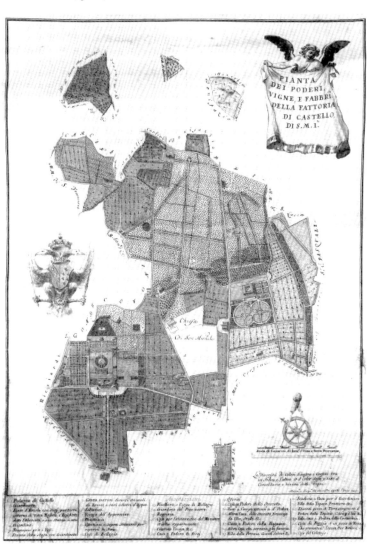

75

from the front of the villa to the river Arno, a precursor of triumphal baroque examples.[34] We can gain some idea of the part that was actually completed from Utens's lunette depicting the Castello villa, although unhappily already missing the famous *berceaux* that Montaigne so admired during his visit in the autumn of 1580.[35] The lunette represents villa and garden in an idealized image where the main axis of the garden corresponds to the centre of the building; in reality it is shifted sideways. The whole complex was composed of two secret gardens flanking the villa, a meadow in the rear and a main garden containing a boxwood labyrinth – the central point of the composition – set on a slight slope and bordered by cypresses, with an end wall housing a central doorway flanked by two fountains. An orchard was planted to the left, surrounded by a "wilderness" of pine trees. Beyond the labyrinth-garden was a narrow band of orange trees

Castello, the façade towards the garden.
Villa and gardens in a 18th-century map (A.S.F. Piante Scrittoio RR Possessioni, Vol. II, c.10)

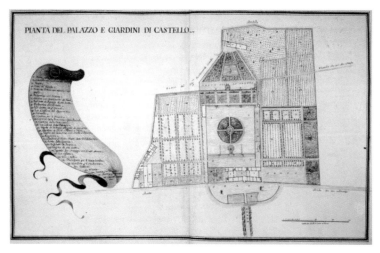

trees, distributed in beautiful order, in the middle of which, according to Tribolo's design, was to be a lovely fish-pond, which has since been made. And because this part gradually narrowed to form an angle it was to be blunted by the width of a loggia from which, after climbing some steps, there would be seen the palace, gardens, fountains, and all the plain below and around as far as the ducal Villa of Poggio a Caiano, Florence, Prato, Siena, and all that is around for miles." Ibid., pp. 235–237.

[34] Among numerous publications we should mention (in alphabetical order): A. Aldrich, J. Walker, *A Guide to Villas and Gardens for the American Academy in Rome*, Rome 1938; W. Arntz, *Die Gardenkunst*, Frankfurt 1910; A. J. Cartwright, *Italian Gardens of the Renaissance*, London 1914; M. T. Cruciani Boriosi, *La realizzazione barocca del giardino italiano e la sua parziale discendenza dalla contemporanea scenografia* in "Antichità Viva", 4 (1963), pp. 15–28; L. Einstein, *The Tuscan Garden*, London 1927; G. S. Elgood, *Italian Gardens*, London 1907; F. Fariello, *Architettura dei giardini*, Rome 1967; M. L. Gothein, A *History of Garden Art*, London 1928; G. Gromort, *L'art des jardins*, Paris 1953; L. Hautecoeur, *Les jardins des dieux et des hommes*, Paris 1959; E. Le Blond, *The Old Gardens of Italy*, London 1905; E. March Phillips, A. T. Bolton, *The Gardens of Italy*, London 1919; R. Standish Nichols, *Italian Pleasure Gardens*, New York 1928; M. Pasolini Ponti, *Il giardino italiano*, Rome 1915; C. A. Platt, *Italian Gardens*, New York 1894; A. Scotti, *Giardini fiorentini e torinesi fra '500 e '600. Loro struttura e significato*, in "L'Arte", 6 (1969), pp. 36–55; J. Sheperd, G. A. Jellicoe, *Italian Gardens of the Renaissance*, London 1953; H. Inigo Triggs, *The Art of Garden Design in Italy*, London 1906; E. Wharton, *Italian Villas and their Gardens*, New York 1904. And the previously quoted L. Dami and G. Masson.

[35] "There are many thick glades of intertwined fragrant trees of every kind, such as juniper, cypress, orange, lemon and olive, their branches so closely interlaced that one realises that the sun cannot penetrate them even at the height of summer; and the cypresses and other trees along the avenues are set so close together along the avenues that only three or four can walk side by side." *Journal de voyage de Michel de Montaigne*, ed. F. Rigolot, Paris 1992, p. 83. The French naturalist Belon visited the villa between 1546 and 1549 and admired what was planted there, including the exotic trees and the secret garden of "simples". L. Berti, *Il principe dello studiolo*, Firenze 1967, p. 86.

[36] "Nor will I omit to tell what was the intention of Tribolo in regard to the statues that were to

ornament the great garden of the new labyrinth, in the niches that can be seen regularly distributed in various places. He proposed – acting on the judicious advice of Benedetto Varchi, a most excellent poet, orator and philosopher of our time – that at the upper and lower ends should be placed the Four Seasons of the year, Spring, Summer, Autumn and Winter, and that each should be set in the part where the particular season is most felt. At the entrance on the right hand, beside Winter, and in the part of the wall which reaches upwards, were to stand six figures demonstrating the greatness and goodness of the House of Medici, and all the virtues of Grand Duke Cosimo: Justice, Compassion, Valour, Nobility, Wisdom and Liberality, which have always dwelt in the House of Medici, and are all united today in the most excellent Lord Duke, in that he is compassionate, valorous, noble, wise and liberal. And because these qualities have made the city of Florence, as they still do, strong in law, peace, arms, science, wisdom, tongues and arts, and also because the Lord Duke is just in the laws, compassionate in peace, valorous in arms, noble through the sciences, wise in his encouragement of tongues and other culture, and liberal to the arts, Tribolo wished that on the other side from the Justice, Compassion, Valour, Nobility and Liberality, on the left hand, as will be seen below, there should be other figures: Laws, Peace, Arms, Sciences, Tongues and Arts. And it was most appropriately arranged that in this manner these statues and images should be placed, as they would have been, above the Arno and the Mugnone, to signify that they pay honour to Florence. It was also proposed that on the pediments there should be portrait-busts of men of the House of Medici, one on each. For example, above Justice, the portrait of his Excellency, that being his particular virtue, above Compassion, that of the Magnificent Giuliano, above Valour, Signor Giovanni, above Nobility, Lorenzo the Elder, above Wisdom, Cosimo the Elder or Clement VII, and above Liberality, Pope Leo. And on the pediments on the other side it was suggested placing other heads of the House of Medici, or of persons of the city connected with the house. But since these names make the matter somewhat confused, they are placed here in the following order:

Summer - the Mugnone - Gate - the Arno - Spring

ARTS	LIBERALITY
TONGUES	WISDOM
SCIENCES	NOBILITY
ARMS	VALOUR
PEACE	COMPASSION
LAWS	JUSTICE
LOGGIA	LOGGIA

Autumn - Gate - Loggia - Gate - Winter

G. Vasari, op. cit., pp. 243–244.

and the wall holding the entrance to a central grotto. This wall served to form a terrace for the upper part of the garden with its wilderness of cypress, pine, ilex and laurel surrounding a fish-pond crowned with a bronze figure crouched on a rock. However, it should be stressed that this was the first time a garden was the subject of a comprehensive design, in which the fact that the villa was set on a slight slope allowed water to be used in elaborate ways. The statuary, grottoes and other features were included by Tribolo in a unitary plan, an allegorical image of Tuscany and, at the same time, as Benedetto Varchi has suggested, a celebratory depiction of the virtues of the House of Medici.[36]

According to what Vasari tells us, to install the ingenious system of water-works that he had devised, Tribolo was obliged to channel and carry water from the gardens of the Petraia villa above. In the upper grotto were statues in niches, on one side Monte Asinaio, who, "*wringing out his beard,*

The garden of the labyrinth at Castello today

spouted water from his mouth into a basin set before him; the water drained from this basin in some unseen manner to pass the wall and reach the fountain which is today beyond the slope of the labyrinth garden, filling the pitcher on the shoulder of the River Mugnone; this stands in a large niche of greyish stone, beautifully ornamented and all covered with porous rock. Had this work all been completed, as it was in part, it would have appeared most life-like, the birth of the Mugnone on Monte Asinaio."[37] In the corresponding niche Monte Falterona fed water into a spring portraying the Arno. In the fountain in the centre of the "labyrinth" garden, gathering water from the sources of the Arno and the Mugnone, stood Giambologna's bronze Venus,[38] later moved to Petraia, adding to the illusionistic-magical effects by using her hands to wring water from her hair. The waters of Castellina and Petraia then parted once more, one flowing into a secret garden of medicinal herbs and feeding a fountain with a statue of Aesculapius, the other into a secret garden in which the surprise feature was an evergreen oak,[39] described by Montaigne with amazement: "*There is even an arbour among the branches of an evergreen tree, but much more solid than those previously met with because it is made entirely of the living and leafy branches of the tree itself, and so enclosed on all sides by foliage that nothing can be glimpsed except through special openings made by prising aside the branches; in the middle is some invisible piping through which water passes and reaches the arbour, gushing out of the centre of a marble table. Here too, music can be produced with water.*"[40]

One reason why this garden can be taken as an example of a fully mannerist conception is the use of the labyrinth, the central theme of the main garden. The image of the labyrinth was often deployed as a decorative feature for ceilings and gardens and in the Renaissance world it assumed several symbolic meanings, expressing – in a reversal of the traditional Christian message – a basic scepticism regarding man's ability to fully comprehend existence.[41] "*The course of the labyrinth*", as Battisti says, "*which prevents any view beyond the imposed path, not only perplexes man but removes all his confidence in reality.*"[42]

Natural elements were employed with the same aim, to create wonder and suspense, to shake the assurance of the viewer by means of a whole series of illusionistic effects created by devices which sometimes made it difficult to distinguish between the deliberate intentions of the artificer and the suggestions offered by nature itself. The water gushing from the ground, pouring from statues and springing from secret foun-

[37] "*The above-mentioned Maestro Piero da San Casciano, having carried work on the aqueduct as far as Castello, and having fed into it all the waters of Castellina, was overtaken by a violent fever and died within a few days. Whereupon Tribolo, taking charge of building operations himself, perceived that though the waters brought to Castello were very abundant, nevertheless they were not sufficient for all that he wanted to do; not to mention that, coming from Castellina, they did not attain the height that he required for his purposes. Having therefore obtained from the Lord Duke a commission to conduct thither the waters of Petraia, a place more than a hundred and fifty braccia above Castello, which were good and very plentiful, he caused a conduit to be built, similar to the other, and so high that one can enter inside it, so that the Petraia waters could reach the fish-pond along another aqueduct with enough fall for the fish-pond and the main fountain.*" Ibid., p. 238.

[38] "*In Florence he cast a woman combing her hair for the Castello villa of his Lordship.*" F. Baldinucci, "Vita del Giambologna", in *Notizie*, op. cit., pp. 128–129.

[39] "*On the east side, on a lawn outside the garden, Tribolo arranged an oak tree in a most ingenious way, for besides being thickly covered above and around by ivy intertwined among the branches so that it seems like a thicket, one climbs up a comfortable wooden staircase, similarly covered with ivy, and at the top, in the middle of the oak, is a square chamber lined with seats, the backs of which are living verdure, and in the centre is a small marble table with a vase of variegated marble in the middle, from which a strong jet of water flows and spurts into the air through a pipe, and after falling runs away through another pipe. These pipes climb upwards from the foot of the oak, so well hidden by the ivy that nothing of them is seen, and the water can be turned on and off at will by means of certain keys; nor is it possible to fully describe in how many ways the water of the oak is used, for various copper instruments for drenching someone, or using the same instruments to produce various sounds and whistlings.*" G. Vasari, op. cit., p. 242.

[40] M. de Montaigne, op. cit., p.84.

[41] The garden "inventions", like the similar and contemporary works for feast days, scenic apparatus or the creation of places of fantasy, the best-known example being the Orsini wood at Bomarzo, all had something in common: "*to freeze what moves, to confuse the mind in a way that suspends rational behaviour, overwhelm the emotions with sights, noise, sound, climatic and environmental conditions . . .*" E. Battisti, op. cit., p. 135.

[42] Ibid.

[43] "*They were now able to experience with pleasure what I have mentioned above. While they walked in the garden looking at particular features, the gardener – having left them for this purpose while they were gazing at some marble statues – released jets of water through countless little holes beneath their feet and between their legs, so fine as to be almost invisible and the spray of light rain was wonderfully stimulating, not soaking them at all, and all by means of some hidden valves that the gardener had operated over two hundred paces away, and with such skill that even from afar he managed to raise and lower the jets, directing them at will; and similar amusements are found in various places.*" Montaigne, op. cit., pp. 83–84.

[44] "*. . . the great fountain with eight sides which was to receive all the above-mentioned waters into the lower basin – those from the waterworks of the labyrinth and also those from the main conduit…. The outline of the fountain has the shape of a vase, and the body, holding the water, is round. The base has eight faces and there are eight seats almost reaching the tazza, upon which are seated eight life-size children's figures in various positions and in the round; linked together by their arms and legs, they make a rich adornment and a most beautiful effect. Since the tazza, which is round, projects to the extent of six* braccia, *the water of the whole fountain pours evenly over the edge all around fountain, sending a lovely spray, like the drippings from a roof, into the octagonal basin mentioned above, and the children on the shaft of the tazza are not wetted at all and seem to be where they are to avoid being wetted, almost like real children, full of delight and playing as they shelter under the lip of the tazza, which could not be equalled in its simplicity and beauty. Opposite the four paths that intersect the garden are four bronze figures of children, playing in various attitudes, which though produced by others were designed by Tribolo. Above this tazza is another shaft with marble children in the round on projections at its base, squeezing the necks of geese which spout water from their mouths; and this water comes from the principal conduit coming from the labyrinth and rises to exactly this height. Above these children the shaft of the pedestal continues and is made of scrolls which spurt forth water in a most bizarre manner, and then, returning to its quadrangular form, it rises above some very well-fashioned masks. Above this is a smaller tazza with the heads of four capricorns attached by their horns to the rim, making a square. They spurt water from their mouths into the large tazza below, together with the children, in order to make the spray which falls, as we have said, into the first basin with eight sides. Still higher rises another shaft, adorned with other ornaments and with children in half-relief who, projecting outwards, form a round space at the top that serves as the base for the sculpture of Hercules crushing*

tains was a fundamental ingredient of this garden, deployed in particular ways to involve the viewer in an impromptu spectacle of the elements.[43] Tribolo developed the motif of the double-bowled fountain for the villa at Castello, paying particular attention to the ornamentation of the fountain of Hercules.[44] Ammannati's statue of the Apennines, envisaged as a hoary old man dripping water, would seem to make a

The garden of the labyrinth at Castello in the Utens lunette

complete break with the traditional notion of a fountain.[45] The grotto too, another important feature of the mannerist garden,[46] made its first appearance at Castello,[47] in a form that was still static with three fountains ornamented with groups of exotic and fantastic animals – including a unicorn – in stone, white and coloured marbles and bronze, probably sculpted by Fancelli.

This was the pattern followed by Buontalenti when he produced the scenic decoration for his famous grotto in the Boboli Gardens, employing the experience he had gained in the field of theatrical scenery and urban decorations. After Castello, the second most remarkable achievement during the 16th century was the Boboli gardens. Buontalenti continued the work begun by Tribolo, who passed on the general plans in 1550,[48] which envisaged the main highlight as a large grotto in the courtyard, designed at Francesco I's wishes to hold Michelangelo's *Prisoners*. The stage was set as a porous

Below: The grotto of the animals at Castello.
Right: The Apennine by Ammannati at the top of the garden at Castello.

Antaeus, designed by Tribolo and later executed by others, as will be related in the proper place. He intended that from the mouth of Antaeus, instead of his spirit, there should gush out quantities of piped water, as indeed it does. The water is that of the large conduit at Petraia, which flows with much force and rises sixteen braccia above the level with the steps, making a wonderful effect as it falls back into the large tazza." G. Vasari, op. cit., pp. 240–241.

[45] We have news of this statue from Ammannati himself. In a letter of 3 February 1563 to Cosimo I, he recounts: "*I have supplied the wax figure of the Apennine for the Castello, and because of bad winter conditions I had not made the mould, but I will now pursue and complete it. I myself will take care of the necessary experience for the giant, so there will be no delay. However, if your Lordship thinks that people should not come to my room every day just to gossip to others . . .*" (G. Gaye, Carteggio Inedito d'Artisti, Florence 1840, Vol. III, p. 90); and again, "*. . . I had the Apennine figure taken to the foundry, when the metal arrives they will cast it at once*", in a letter of 6 November 1563 (p. 21).

[46] According to Battisti, the 16th-century grotto is the opposite of the dome: "*The late 16th century introduced a contrasting theme to the cupola, unusual in the Christian West and with all the drama of the Antique: the natural or artificial grotto. In a sense the grotto is, like Dante's inferno, a dome turned upside down, pointing to earth instead of towards the heavens. But, even more, it is an inverted spire. Its area of greatest interest is less the most luminous part than the darkest; the darkness we must move towards, while knowing this is not the road to knowledge but to mystery. Moreover, the grotto, especially if artificial, has the ability to transport and immerse us in the heart of nature. Indeed, its decoration is not abstract like that of the dome, but naturalistic: its walls are faced with tufa and shells; famous sculptors hurry to produce likenesses of every animal on earth; makers of mechanical devices reproduce the songs of birds, and figures of Orpheus taming the beasts . . . The grotto has something static about it, timeless. The grotto leads man back to himself, isolates him from distracting appearances, immerses him in the very heart of reality.*" E. Battisti, op. cit., p. 182.

[47] "*Here too there is a beautiful grotto where one sees life-size representations of animals of all kinds which spray the water of the fountains from their beaks, wings, talons, ears or nose.*" Montaigne, op. cit., p. 139. On the Castello grotto see L. Chatelet Lange, *The Grotto of the Unicorn in the garden of the villa of Castello*, in "Art Bulletin", 50 (1968), pp. 51–58.

[48] The lunette by Utens gives a view of the garden at the end of the 16th century. The amphitheatre appears to be completed, made entirely of greenery, and thus unlike the actual outline; half way up the slope of the hill beyond the courtyard is the fish-pool, without Stoldo Lorenzi's statue of Neptune; on the terrace we see Ammannati's fountain, first installed at Pratolino, then at Pitti before being replaced by Susini's work. This is a geometric garden, where greenery plays a leading role as an accompaniment to the architecture and statuary which includes, apart from Ammannati's statues and Giambologna's fountain of the Ocean, Bandinelli's rustic grotto, ornamented with cherubs, baby goats and stalactites. Among the accounts of numerous visitors, the one by de Brosses is interesting for his romantic description of the garden, seen as a collection of " . . . *hills, valleys, woods, meadows and forests, scattered freely without order or rule . . .* ". C. de Brosses, *Viaggio in Italia*, Bari 1973, p. 205.

[49] F. Baldinucci, op. cit., p. 25.

[50] Ibid.

rocky cave and the ceiling was painted by Poccetti with fanciful illusionistic effects. "*This grotto has a large opening in the very centre of the ceiling, similar to the Rotunda in Rome. Buontalenti employed this opening to realise a fresh idea, using it to hold several large pieces of crystal which, covering it all over, forms a basin to hold water and fish, which can be seen from below, and all without depriving the grotto of the necessary light*".[49] The overhead lighting gave the chamber its particular atmosphere, and the theme of metamorphosis was further reiterated by a succession of chambers like "*a sequence of differentiated and subtly linked environmental descriptions*"[50] – the side entrance-hall and small grotto in the rear, also frescoed by Poccetti.

The search for the wondrous and the amazing was enhanced by the connection between the figures of animals, carved in the porous rock of the cave, and the real live fish circling overhead in the crystal ball, together with the natural element – water – gushing through a network of pipes installed in the carved trees. But nature, once the ideal of humanist thought, now

becomes envisaged in a scene of infinite variations: reality itself is destabilized by it, everything is alive and as such may change, may suddenly assume new and unexpected forms, the most idyllic scene may be transformed into a vile and monstrous sight. The artist could no longer reflect the universal reality but must suspend all belief and certainty, and nothing remained for him to do but surmount this obstacle and follow the laws of the infinite permutations of materials, playing the disenchanted inventor while he attempted elaborate operations verging on magic and invocation.[51]

But Buontalenti's most outstanding contribution in this direction was the garden at Pratolino, alas now destroyed.[52] There, the artist had the task of overcoming the obstacles that nature set in his path, creating an ingenious and amazing fusion of artifice and nature in which, moreover, the play between the two never slackens. This is well described in Gualterotti's courtly words in his poetic paean to the villa: "*l'arte avanzarsi e la natura a prouva, / l'una sempre rinnova le sue bellezze e l'altra e quelle unisce / e delle unite poi mill'altre ordisce.*"[53]

The lunette painted by Utens shows the layout of the garden which, in this instance, extended equally in front and behind the villa and was linked by terraces and steps. We see a garden geometrically divided in the "Italian" style surrounded by an extensive area of parkland, dissected by avenues which introduce geometry even to this freer area, starting from the large main avenue which forms a central axis to the whole complex. The park stretches behind the villa, ornamented with a large fountain and Giambologna's colossal statue personifying the Apennines, so dominant a work that it carried the development of the traditional idea of a fountain to extremes, replacing it with a mountain giant: "*so large that the head can serve as a chamber, with the eyes for windows, where the Grand Duke Francesco sometimes fishes, since this huge figure is set above a great pool of water.*"[54]

Below the south terrace were six grottoes faced with pumice stone and encrusted with shells and sea creatures. These grottoes (known as *Diluvio, Galatea, Stufa, Spugna, Europa* and *Samaritana*) were among the most amazing sights of the gardens and park because of the use of the highly elaborate machinery which had been recently introduced, in simplified form, in the Castello gardens. Besides the decorative apparatus for festivals and ceremonial occasions, it was the scenic and theatrical experience of this period which provided the model that guided and influenced garden design in the principal late 16th-century examples in Florence, through the talent of a gifted artist like Buontalenti and his contact

[51] M. Tafuri, *Il mito naturalistico nell'architettura del '500*, in "L'Arte", V (1968), pp. 25–26.

[52] "*A palace which the Duke of Florence has been building for twelve years, making it appeal to all the five senses. It seems that he deliberately chose a place without resources, arid and steep, completely without springs; proud of the fact that he had to travel five miles to find water, and another five to collect the necessary sand and lime. This is a place where there is no level ground, where one can enjoy the view of the numerous hills which form the usual panorama of this region.*" Montaigne, op. cit., pp. 132–133.

[53] F. Gualterotti, *Vaghezze sopra Pratolino, dedicate al Serenissimo Don Francesco Medici, secondo Gran Duca di Toscana*, Giunti, Florence 1579.

[54] F. Zuccaro, *L'idea de' pittori, scultori e architetti*, ed. D. Heikamp, Florence 1961, p. 260. On this Montaigne states: "*the figure of a giant has been built which has an eye cavity measuring three gomiti [circa a yard and a half], and the rest in proportion.*" M. Montaigne, op. cit., p. 80.

[55] Buontalenti and his relationship with Francesco I is well presented by Battisti in *L'antirinascimento* (esp. Chap. IV). On Francesco I's role as a patron see L. Berti, *Il principe dello studiolo*, Florence 1967. Montaigne speaks of Francesco I as "*a lover of alchemy and the mechanical arts, and above all a great architect*". Indeed, one of his more unusual sides was being a creator, or at least promoter, of magical hydraulically powered apparatus and machinery. Borghini states: (Buontalenti and the Duke have discovered) "*…what has never been seen before, and what many thought could never be found, that is, an instrument in perpetual motion, containing the four elements, an instrument which, once it is assembled, moves on its own for ever.*" R. Borghini, *Il Riposo*, Florence 1584, p. 613.

[56] M. Tafuri, *Il mito naturalistico*, op. cit., p. 15.

[57] "*Among the remarkable sights is a grotto with many niches and chambers which surpasses anything we have seen elsewhere; it is encrusted and covered all over with a material they say comes from certain mountains, held together with hidden nails. The movement of the water not only produces music and harmonies, but also activates statues and doors, producing various movements, such as animals stooping to drink, and similar things. By means of a single mechanism the grotto fills completely with water, the seats spray water up to your thighs and if, fleeing from the grotto, you try to climb the castle stairs, every second*

step sprays – for anyone who wants to enjoy such pleasures – a thousand jets to soak you before you reach the top." M. Montaigne, op. cit., p. 79. The Pratolino villa and garden were a must for travellers coming to Italy. Among the numerous descriptions of visitors, there follows one by a contemporary of Montaigne, the Scotsman Fynes Moryson, who visited the villa in 1594: "*W . . . came to Pratolino, the Duke's famous garden . . . . If a man well consider he may justly say of the gardens of Italy, as Mounster saith of the towns of Valesia, that their water costs them more than their wine . . . and there is a cave under the earth leading three miles to the Fountaine of water, from whence by many pipes the waters are brought to serve the workes of these gardens*". *The Itinerary of Fynes Moryson*, Glasgow University Press 1907, I, p. 327.

John Evelyn's diary, written in the 17th century, is also very informative: "*The house is a square of 4 pavilions, with a faire platform about it, balustred with stone, situate in a large meadow, ascending like an amphitheatre, having at the bottom a huge rock with water running in a small channell like a cascade; on the other side are the gardens. The whole place seems consecrated to pleasure and summer retirement. The inside of the palace may compare with any in Italy for furniture of tapistry, beds, &c., and the gardens are delicious and full of fountaines. In the grove sits Pan feeding his flock, the water making a melodious sound through his pipe; and an Hercules whose club yields a shower of water which falling into a grate shell has a naked woman riding on the backs of dolphins. In another grotto is Vulcan and his family, the walls richly compos'd of corals, shells, coper and marble figures with the hunting of severall beasts, moving by the force of water. Here having ben well washed for our curiosity, we went down a large walke, at the sides whereof several slender streams of water gush out of pipes concealed underneath that interchangeably fall into each other channells, making a lofty and perfect arch, so that a man on horseback may ride under it and not receive one drop of water. This canopy or arch of water, I thought one of the most surprising magnificencies I had ever seene, and very refreshing in the heate of the sum'er. At the end of this very long walk stands a woman in white marble, in the posture of a laundress wringing water out of a piece of linen, very naturally formed, into a vast lavor, the work and invention of M. Angelo Buonarotti. Hence we ascended Mount Parnassus, where the muses plaied to us on hydraulic organs. Neere this is a great aviarie. All these waters came from the rock in the garden, on which is the statue of a gyant representing the Apennines, at the foote of wich stands this villa. Last of all we came to the labyrinth in which a huge colosse of Jupiter throws out a streame over the garden. This is 50 foote in height, having in his body a square chamber, his eyes and mouth*

with an artist-patron such as the Grand Duke Francesco.[55] According to Tafuri, "*This development was one of the most important to an evaluation of the meaning of that basic component of 16th-century naturalism which blossomed in imagery, irony and play.*"[56]

The wealth of invention in Galatea's grotto made it the most spell-binding. The spectacular nature of the work is clear from Montaigne's amazed description.[57] The grotto was presented in a crumbling state and displayed a marine scene with walls faced with mother-of-pearl and reefs covered with coral and seashells. From an entrance on the left, the nymph arrived on a shell drawn by dolphins, while her retinue of companions appeared from various other positions. "*The machinery*", observes Battisti, "*has won independent and general acclaim as a wonder of ingenuity, an imitation of nature stretched to the extreme limits of human endeavour, and also a path to learning about new concepts of reality. The fairytale imagery and the biomorphic flavour naturally prevail.*" This domination of nature by artifice became triumphant showmanship, creating results which aroused the wonder and admiration of an enquiring and open-minded intellectual like Montaigne. As Tafuri rightly observes: "*The 16th-century garden was a real theatre – sometimes created for didactic purposes and sometimes to reflect the cosmic order (and disorder) – allegories, mechanistic myths and rites paying homage to the magic of the elements with plays of water, mechanical movements and the artificial reproduction of natural sounds, all concrete examples of man's urge to overcome nature, the dominant theme of all creative 16th-century writings.*"[58]

A sketch by Bernardo Buontalenti for a grotto at Pratolino (G.D.S.U. 2323A)

The gardens we have described were the exceptional ones, not only in the general ambit of Florentine villas, but also among those created by the Medici family. The Castello villa was rebuilt by Cosimo I at the high point of his rise to power, making it a visual symbol of wealth and importance. The Boboli gardens formed the background to the official residence when Eleanor of Toledo bought the Pitti Palace in 1549 and the Grand Duke's apartments were transferred from Palazzo Vecchio. Pratolino was the creation of Francesco I, artist, prince and patron, built at a time when the state's economy was still flourishing. Other Medici villas were provided with considerably more modest gardens in terms of both conception and layout and more obviously displayed "conservative" taste. However, from time to time one would become the favourite residence of one or other of the Grand Dukes or be ceded to a cadet branch of the family, and then the gardens would be embellished with rare and precious flowers and plants, or the design of the planting-beds would be altered to accord with the prevailing style and taste of subsequent centuries. The lunettes painted by the Flemish artist Utens at the close of the 16th century rival engravings in the accuracy of their painting and give us a clear image of these gardens, still tied to traditional notions.

The lingering of the "Tuscan" flavour remains more obvious in the gardens of grand private villas and some notable examples include the grounds of Villa Capponi in Arcetri, laid out in a series of three gardens (a terraced stretch of grass next to the villa overlooking a view of the city, a garden holding tubs of lemon trees and a small walled private garden), and the Villa Gamberaia at Settignano, where the garden's contemporary reconstruction faithfully followed the principles of the Tuscan tradition in its skilful spatial layout, organized along an axis in line with the villa, leading to a wood on one side and on the other to a formal garden spanned by great water basins and ending in a semicircle of greenery.

Between 1600 and 1700 work on the gardens of the villas around Florence appears to have been largely confined to refurbishing and replenishing existing layouts to meet new criteria. Rather than the actual garden itself, these innovations involved the surrounding land which was provided with hunting-parks and netting-groves – thickly planted with the trees used for snaring birds – and great tree-lined avenues, all designed to create a scene in which the villa was the fulcrum of a landscaped composition in accordance with the rules of perspective governing baroque architecture. The most remarkable example of this latter effect remains the avenue

serving as windows and dore." J. Evelyn, *Diary*, Oxford 1955, II, pp. 418–419.

[58] M. Tafuri, *Il mito naturalistico*, op. cit., p. 23; see also G. Gobbi Sica, *I giardini medicei del Cinquecento: natura e arte nel Journal de Voyage di Michel de Montaigne*, in "Firenze Architettura"1&2 2005, pp. 118–127.

[59] G. Gobbi, *Strutture storiche nel territorio fiorentino: la villa del Casale*, in "Bollettino degli Ingegneri", 6, Florence 1975, p. 10.

[60] According to the discovery of unknown letters in the Corsini Archives, the 18th-century transformations of the villa and the garden have to be ascribed to Giovan Battista Foggini and not to Antonio Ferri, as supposed before. See M. Visonà, *Giovan Battista Foggini e gli altri artisti nella villa Corsini a Castello*, in "Rivista d'Arte" XLII, 1990, serie IV, vol VI, pp. 147–211 and L. Zangheri, *La villa Corsini a Castello e l'intervento di Antonio Maria Ferri*, in "Bollettino degli Ingegneri", 11, Florence 1969, p. 1.

[61] G. Guicciadini Corsi Salviati, *La villa Corsi a Sesto*, Florence 1937.

[62] A. Targioni Tozzetti, *Cenni storici sulla introduzione di varie piante nell'agricoltura e orticultura toscana*, Florence 1867. On this subject see G. Masson, *Italian flower collectors' gardens in seventeenth-century Italy*, in *The Italian Garden*, Washington D.C. 1972.

Right: The garden of Villa Capponi at Arcetri; the cypresses avenue at La Pietra; the Isolotto fountain at Boboli.

leading to Poggio Imperiale which, in Giulio Parigi's 17th-century design, began from the vast forecourt, delimited by the wings of the building and the semicircular balustrade in front which held three openings, one being positioned at the beginning of the leafy avenue. The whole being further ornamented by four fish-basins with colossal tufa statues personifying the Arno and Arbia rivers.

The use of the avenue as an axis, which at Poggio Imperiale was linked to the urban notion of a perspective axis, was introduced in the Boboli gardens as an organizational feature by the broad path running crosswise to the 16th-century avenue linking the first garden area with the roundabout at the end, facing the exit by Porta Romana, and having as its focal point, as designed by Alfonso Parigi the Younger, the open area of the *Isolotto* and Giambologna's fountain. Around this central axis were bird-netting areas and labyrinths of greenery, the first instance of the concept of the "natural" garden, causing Pindemonte, among others, to claim that the "English" romantic garden was derived from the Boboli gardens.

Interesting examples of perspectived avenues can still be seen at Villa La Pietra on Via Bolognese; at the Casale villa, north-west of the city on the slopes of Monte Morello, where woods running down the steeply sloping hill are to be seen, tall banks of ilex intersected by paths and glades spaces ornamented with statuary and garden pavilions;[59] and the 17th-century layout of Villa Orsini, between Quarto and Castello, where an avenue of now largely destroyed cypresses formed a perspectived vista of the entrance to the villa, and extended as far as Via Sestese. Among other works of 17th-century garden landscaping we should mention Villa Palmieri at San Domenico, with a spectacular terraced garden; Villa Campi at Signa; Villa di Poggio Torselli; Villa Corsini at Castello, an 18th-century operation by G. B. Foggini, where an interesting garden, now in a sorry condition, was the result of a series of successive operations;[60] and Villa Corsi Salviati at Sesto, an example of a garden laid out on flat terrain and the outcome of a series of alterations, culminating in the 18th century in the addition of large fish-ponds, groves of trees and exotic plants.[61] During the 18th century the Medici villas of Lappeggi and Ambrogiana reached their point of greatest splendour when Cardinal Francesco Maria was given the right to use the former and Grand Duke Cosimo III the latter. This is recorded by the lavish design of their gardens, shown by illustrated material of the period, as well as by the variety of plants imported from distant countries,[62] such as double jasmine known as "*mogherina del Granduca di Toscana*", brought from Goa in 1689 to ornament the grand ducal gardens.

And here we come to the end of the various stages of development of the garden-park that were particularly Florentine in character. This did not, of course, bring a halt to the continued adaptation of large and small gardens in the area. But changes which appear innovatory break with the Tuscan "tradition" (still faithfully reproduced and defended in a whole range of instances), alterations to accord with the new tastes in garden design and landscaping that became widely adopted in the general climate of renewal that was sweeping Europe. New practices, with complete disregard to the example of large-scale French parks, unrealizable given Florence's economic and geographic position, were to lead to the fashion for English gardens, the result of the pioneering work of W. Kent, B. Langley and L. Brown, to name but a few. France provided some informative works on the subject: *Essai sur les jardins*, C. H. Watelet (1774); the fundamental *Sur la formation des jardins*, A. N. Duchesne (1775); *Théorie des jardins*, J. M. Morel (1776). The first works by Italian authors were produced by travel writers and by theorists, such as F. Algarotti and his high paean to the English villa in *Saggio sopra l'opera in musica*, 1762. Indeed, the attempt to claim artistic primacy, while historically unfounded, is interesting since it involved Italian essayists and theorists, already engaged in the contradictory activity of both promoting and defending the principle of a national identity in the wake of the universality of the Enlightenment.[63] Here, we should mention *Dissertazione su I giardini inglesi e sul merito in ciò dell'Italia*, which Pindemonte delivered to the Academy of Science, Letters and Arts in Padua in 1790;

[63] In one of his *Lettere familiari e critiche* of 1758 Martinelli, in describing Lord Temple's famous garden at Stow, states that the English had adopted "*that rural, cultured and thoughtful elegance that is more generally admired in foreigners*". Together with Baretti, Martinelli maintains that the idea of the natural garden developed by the English was derived from the Boboli gardens, while Cesarotti, full of patriotic zeal, goes so far as to say: "*. . . is it not a shameful scandal that the Italians themselves use the term English garden for what was created as an Italian garden?*". On this question see A. Graf, *L'anglomania e l'influsso inglese in Italia nel secolo XVIII*, Turin 1911, the chapter *La melancolia e i giardini inglesi*, pp. 341–351, from which we have drawn the quotations.

[64] M. Dezzi Bardeschi, *Le macchine desideranti, in Il giardino romantico*, Florence 1986, pp. 29–45.

[65] D. Mignani Galli, *Un'idea di giardino moderno per un giardino prospettico*, ibid., pp. 46–55.

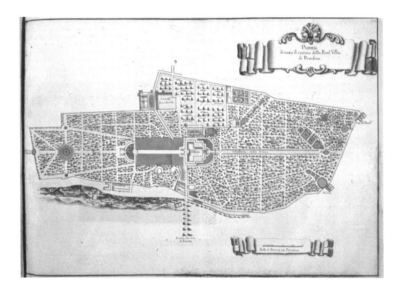

Left: Pratolino.
Right: Careggi Vecchio, Careggi Nuovo, Castello, Petraia, from the manuscript by Giuseppe Ruggieri "Piante de' Palazzi, Giardini, Ville et altre fabbriche dell'Altezza Reale del Serenissimo Gran Duca di Toscana" (B.N.C.F. Pal 3.B.1.5 GF 181).

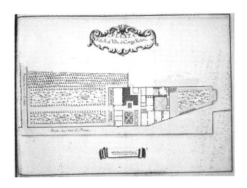

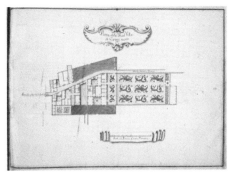

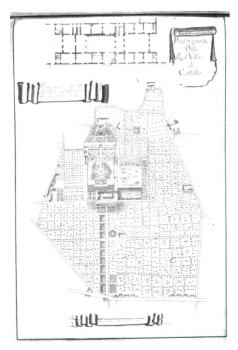

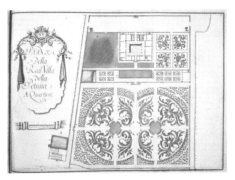

Saggio sopra l'indole dei giardini moderni, read to the same Academy by Luigi Mabil in 1796; followed by subsequent works by Mabil (*Teoria dell'arte dei giardini*, 1801), and by Ercole Silva (*Dell'arte dei giardini inglesi*, published in Milan in 1801), who concentrates more on the theoretical side and on the codification of material.

The fashion for the English garden became increasingly widespread in Florence, drawing the leading families, first and foremost the Grand Duke's, into a kind of aristocratic competition. Between 1811 and 1813 Giuseppe Manetti designed gardens for Poggio a Caiano and Poggio Imperiale and, although never realized, these were the prototypes that inspired the creation of every subsequent landscaped garden in the Florentine area.

At Poggio a Caiano, the plan to build a bridge across the river Ombrone (not built until 1833, by Alessandro Manetti, Giuseppe's son) suggested the idea of creating a small lake and an island with a temple dedicated to Diana. The introduction of mythological figures recalling rites of initiation fulfilled a twofold purpose: a celebration of post-revolutionary French culture on one hand, and of pagan ritual on the other, forging a link with the great season of mannerism. The romantic garden and its accompanying features lent itself easily to the notion of paths of initiation[64] (later, for Stibbert, with Masonic connections). In 1811 the plan for the Poggio Imperiale villa was also to create a romantic garden, conceived as an extension of the villa's existing Italian garden. The layout included an avenue leading from a flowery parterre with a fountain to a temple dedicated to Victory built on a steep rocky outcrop, symbolizing how hard is the path to victory, surrounded by a thickly planted wood of oaks and bay trees dotted with statues and monuments. The path to initiation and mythology, given here a romantic interpretation, provided the main inspiration for the visual composition which, according to Manetti himself, was emphasized by the scenic effect given to the landscaping around the villa: "*All these objects create various viewing-points between each other, as described, so that the most beautiful views of the fine nearby hills, a large part of the Florentine plain and the more distant peaks can be enjoyed from each place*".[65]

The theme of the initiatory path became an allusion to a journey through a garden as an irrational world removed from the laws of change, represented by nature's yearly cycles. Florence and the rest of Tuscany were affected by the radical changes in taste. The neo-classical and romantic climate, in relation to the Enlightenment at least, changed the balance between the immutable forces of nature and the dynamics of existence. This change influenced the forms of the garden. Controversy concerning the "modern" gardens in Florence led to heated debate, exemplified in 1831 by Giuseppe Del Rosso who writes of "*the barbaric manner of uprooting gardens which have no lack of beauty and stripping them to suit the latest fashion for the new, or so-called English, style.*" Ruins, esoteric objects and islands with a romantic or mythological theme became all the rage, gardens of fantasy and mystery.

Ercole Silva's work *Dell'arte dei giardini inglesi* (1813 edition) contains a long list of the symbols used in a garden, including: "*The harpy symbolises valour; the phoenix hope and the eternal nature of the empire; the sphinx prudence; Cerberus vice... In the English romantic gardens of Florence the sphinx watches over gateways, stairs, founts, islands of myth... We find neo-Egyptian hieroglyphics and decorations in the Cascine pyramid and in the one Manetti dedicated to the virtue of the ancients, for the modern garden at Poggio Imperiale.... The Egyptian sphinx watches over the islands of death, the labyrinths of green and the cemeteries of stone, often contemplating the horizon of the rising sun; it watches over the confines of eternity, the memory of the past and the future; it is the guardian of forbidden doors and simulacra; it listens to the music of the spheres; it is protective and implacable and has the expressive power of a 'sun god'; an enigma which embodies the agony of doubt or the silence of absolute truth. It is imperturbable and betrays no disquiet...*".[66]

In the romantic garden created by Frederick Stibbert for his villa at Montughi the Egyptian temple with sphinxes looms mysteriously over the lake while other elements, such as the rustic fountain, grotto, and the ruins, reconstructed from ancient remains, the "Swiss chalet", lemon-house and *tempietto*, all play their part in a scene of elegant originals and clever reproductions. This evocation of past eras and of the exotic, nostalgic in mood and searching for what was rare and wondrous, which drew inspiration from re-creating objects from familiar places (a kind of 19th-century Hadrian's Villa), was organized by its eccentric commissioner and supervized by Giuseppe Poggi, assisted by the engineer Gerolamo Passeri.

The Anglicization of gardens in Florence and the replacement of farming land by romantic parks took place in the climate of fashionable "updating" which swept the area and was supplanted early in the following century by a new trend, one which owed much to the presence of foreign residents. This was the revival of the formal garden which reintroduced geometrically organized spaces with a new sensibility, leading to an Anglo-Saxon reinterpretation of the Renaissance and mannerist garden.

[66] A. Vezzosi, *Pitture di macchia e di sfinge, isole romantiche e simulacri, vaghezze in giardini d'esperidi*, ibid., pp. 92–116.

[67] D. Ottewill, *Outdoor rooms: houses into gardens in Britain at the turn of the century*, in *Cecil Pinsent and his Gardens in Tuscany*, Florence 1996, p.2.

[68] G. Grahame, *In a Tuscan Garden*, London 1902.

Right: Lappeggi, Poggio a Caiano, Cerreto Guidi, Topaia, Ambrogiana from Ruggieri's manuscript.

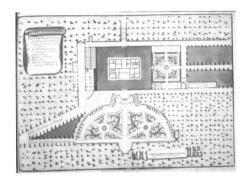

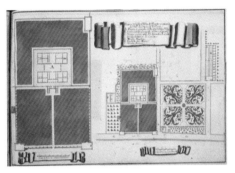

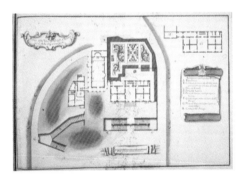

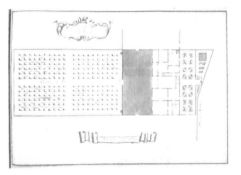

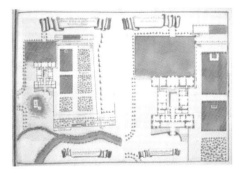

In Britain, the revival of the Renaissance tradition in architecture and garden design took place in around 1880, the formal garden being based on a particular interpretation of the Italian Renaissance garden. The reasons for this revival seem to lie in the new sense of freedom felt by the urban middle classes, now inspired by an Arcadian dream of rural life, a movement which swept England during the years between 1880 and the First World War. Outdoor life became a cult and gardening a national pastime *"The effect of this on design was an opening up of the house which overflowed into the garden, forming a succession of outdoor rooms. These not only provided shelter from the wind and a sense of enclosure, they also allowed a wide variety of themes, such as rose gardens, herb gardens, secret gardens. The elements of anticipation, discovery and surprise were important. Instead of the whole garden being revealed at once, you were led in succession from one compartment to another".*[67] These same elements formed the basis of the first Renaissance garden at Quaracchi, and later, the one theorized by Pier de' Crescenzi in his agricultural treatise. This change of attitude led to many so-called English gardens being given a "new" traditional design. The Italian Renaissance garden was revived and given a fresh interpretation.

Many visitors to Florence, especially English and American ones, fell in love with the villas and wanted to buy them. At the turn of the century many were still available, some of immense splendour like the Villa Medici, and some small and unremarkable, but almost all with land which included woods, gardens full of ilexes, cypresses, stone pines, olive trees, oleanders and bougainvillea, exotic to northern eyes more accustomed to oaks and herbaceous borders. *"Almost every house had a lemon store, where orange and lemon trees, camellias and delicate shrubs were kept in winter. And because it was largely the English who colonized the Florentine hillsides, it was the English who imposed their taste and their fashions on the gardens they took over. Very often, olives and vineyards were replaced with lawns and deciduous shade trees, herbaceous borders were planted with irises, crocuses, peonies and daffodils, wood and scrub were cleared, and dry-stone-walled terraces were covered with roses: Banksia, 'Irene Watts' and 'Madame Metral'. These English residents knew and cared about their gardens: they ordered bulbs from England, and they never went away at planting time."* Often, like Georgina Grahame,[68] they wrote books describing them. In the early years of the century Georgina Grahame published a book about her life in Florence called *In a Tuscan Garden* which became a textbook for new foreign residents.

In reaction to the enduring fashion for the picturesque which had flourished for almost a century, there now emerged a taste for the formal, more clearly integrated relationship of indoor and outdoor space, of house and garden. Numerous writers wrote essays on the subject of the Italian garden. Among these, we must include a quotation from Charles Adams Platt whose book *Italian Gardens*, first published in 1893, was a turning-point in the history of the Italian garden in the United States. His goal was to revive the garden of the Italian villa in its entirety and to adapt it to American soil. In his book Platt writes:

"The evident harmony of arrangement between the house and the surrounding landscape is what first strikes one in Italian landscape architecture – the design as a whole, including gardens, terraces, groves, and their necessary surroundings and embellishments, it being clear that no one of these component parts was ever considered independently, the architect of the house being also the architect of the garden and the rest of the villa. The problem being to take a piece of land and make it habitable, the architect proceeded with the idea that not only was the house to be lived in, but that one still wished to be at home when out of doors; so that the garden was designed as another apartment, the terraces and groves still others, where one might walk about and find a place suitable to the hour of the day and feeling of the moment, and still be in that sacred corner of the globe dedicated to one's self."[69] This idea came from the Renaissance treatises derived from the letters of Pliny. Platt's concept concerning *"all the formal parts of the garden (are) arranged in direct relation to the house, the house itself being as much part of it as the garden or the grove"* comes from his direct experience of numerous visits to villas and gardens, especially in Tuscany and Lazio. At the Medici villa at Castello, the flower garden was what appeared to him the really *"interesting feature"*, being *"one of the most beautiful in Italy"*, and he describes it at length:

"... the arrangement of the flower beds (which) are very full in regard to the plantation, and very remarkable as to bloom, for so large a garden. One is conscious only of the principal paths, so well concealed it the necessary net-work of small ones by which the gardener reaches his plants. The arrangement of the vines on the high stucco wall is an exceedingly good one – the lower part of it covered with climbing roses, which are fastened to it with slender bamboo sticks attached to the wall, and the upper part for grape-vines, which having grown up to a point above the roses, are made to grow laterally in lines one above the other, forming a sort of frieze".[70]

[69] C. A. Platt, *Italian Gardens*, New York 1984, pp. 6–7.

[70] Ibid., pp. 137–138.

[71] C. W. Earle, *More Pot-Pourri from a Surrey Garden*, London 1899, p. 348, *"Here were cypresses taller and straighter than I had ever seen; long green alleys ending in small temples; high walls over which Oleanders tossed themselves, their branches heavy with the bloom of their exquisite pink flowers"*, writes this British follower of Robinson and Gertrude Jekyll. During the late 1890s and early 1900s more and more articles on the gardens of Italian villas appeared in British and American periodicals. Janet Ross, an English writer who settled in Poggio Gherardo, near Settignano, wrote a book entitled *Florentine Villas*, published in 1901, including Giuseppe Zocchi's 18th-century views. Charles Latham wrote *The Gardens of Italy* (1905); Sir George Sitwell, *On the Making of Gardens* (1909). Sitwell began studying Italian gardens in the early 1890s and his essay emphasizes the aesthetic appreciation of their qualities by all the senses, as well as their relationship with the surrounding landscape.

[72] V. Lee, *Old Italian Gardens*, in *Hortus Vitae and Limbo*, London 1897, p. 260–269.

Right: Topaia (Archivio di Stato Firenze (A.S.F.) Piante Scrittoio delle RR Possessioni Vol. II, c. 4); Petraia (ibid., c.7/2); three projets for the garden of villa Petraia (ibid., c. 2/4, 2/3, 2/2).

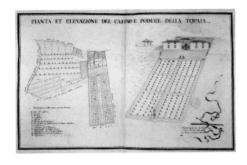

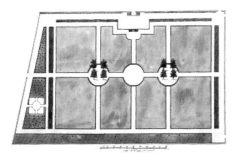

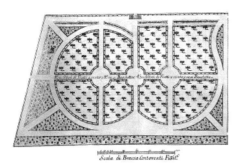

Platt comments only briefly on the grotto and fountain as *"very remarkable and dignified in character"*, evidently without fully grasping either the great artistic achievement of Tribolo, Ammannati and Buontalenti, admired by centuries of cultured visitors, or its deep iconographic significance.

Widespread appreciation of the Italian garden, to which Platt greatly contributed, soon demanded a more detailed critical study than his brief, unsatisfying notes could provide. Information on the subject began to appear here and there, such as C.W. Earle's description of the small Villa Gamberaia at Settignano, just outside Florence, which she judged *"the most wonderful of all as regards its surroundings and views"*.[71]

The architectural garden of the Edwardian era used the same basic vocabulary as the traditional Italian garden: compartments, geometric patterns, vistas, enclosing borders and pergolas, rows of pleached trees and topiary. What then are the distinguishing features? There is perhaps greater variety in the British garden because of the desire and need to respond to the widely varying regional characteristics, including local materials.

Edith Wharton, on the wave of the great success of her *Decoration of Houses* (1897), was asked to write a series of articles on Italian villas. These appeared in 1903 and 1904 in the "Century Magazine" and were soon collected in the well-known book *Italian Villas and their Gardens*. The book is dedicated to Vernon Lee, a British writer and critic who lived in Villa Il Palmerino in Settignano, near Florence, the perceptive author of *Studies in Eighteenth-Century Italy* and other essays, among which is the interesting "Old Italian Gardens", published in her Limbo (1897). The following excerpts from this essay by Vernon Lee display the keenness of her observations:

"Gardens have nothing to do with nature, or not much. Save the Garden of Eden, which was perhaps no more a garden than certain London streets so called, gardens are primarily the work of man. I say primarily, for these outdoor habitations, where man weaves himself carpets of grass and gravel, cuts himself walls out of ilex or hornbeam, and fits on a roof, so much of blue sky or of starspecked, moonsilvered night, are never perfect until Time has furnished it all with his weather stains and mosses, and Fancy, having given notice to the original inhabitants, has handed it into the charge of little owls and fur-gloved bats, and of other tenants, human in shape, but as shy and solitary as they",[72] and again: *"The shift from this orchard-garden, this orto of the old Italian novelists and painters, to the architectural garden of the sixteenth and seventeenth centuries, is indicated in some of the descriptions and illustration of the*

Hypnerotomachia Poliphili, a sort of handbook of antiquities in the shape of a novel, written by Francesco Colonna and printed in Venice in about 1480. Here we find trees and hedges treated as stone and brick work; walls, niches, colonnades, cut out of ilex and laurel, statues, vases, peacocks, clipped in box and yew; moreover, antiquities, busts, inscriptions, broken altars and triumphal arches, temples to the graces and Venus, stuck about the place very much as we find them in the Roman villas of the late sixteenth and seventeenth centuries. But I doubt whether the Hypnerotomachia can be taken as evidence of the gardens of Colonna's own days. I think his descriptions are rather of what his archaeological lore made him long for, and what came in time, when antiques were more plentiful than in the early Renaissance, and the monuments of the ancients could be incorporated freely into the gardens. For the classic Italian garden is essentially Roman in origin; it could have arisen only on the top of ancient walls and baths, its shape suggested by the ruins below, its ornaments dug up in the planting of trees; and until the time of Julius II and Leo X, Rome was still a medieval city, feudal and turbulent, in whose outskirts, overrun by baronial squabbles, no sane man would have built himself a garden; and in whose ancient monuments castles were more to be expected than belvederes and orangeries. Indeed, by the side of quaint arches and temples, and labyrinths which look like designs for a box of toys, we find among the illustrations of Poliphilo various charming woodcuts showing bits of vine trellis, of tank and fountain, on the small scale, and in the domestic, quite unclassic style of the Italian burgher's garden. . . . The real Italian garden brings in a new element – that of perspective, architecture, decoration; the trees used as building material, the lie of the land as theatre arrangements, the water as the most docile and multiform stage property . . .".

In her book *Italian Villas and their Gardens* Edith Wharton indicates the lessons to be learnt by Americans and warns against superficial imitation: *"There is, nonetheless, much to be learnt from the old Italian gardens, and the first lesson is that, if they are to be a real inspiration, they must be copied, not in the letter but in the spirit. That is, a marble sarcophagus and a dozen twisted columns will not make an Italian garden; but a piece of land laid out and planted on the principles of the old gardencraft will be, not indeed an Italian garden in the literal sense, but, what is far better, a garden as well adapted to its surroundings as were the models which inspired it."*[73]

The aim of the book was to educate American taste by conveying the essence of the Italian garden, which, in Wharton's view, had been previously misunderstood. She insisted that

[73] E. Wharton, *Italian Villas and their Gardens*, revised ed., New York 1988, p. 12.

[74] Ibid., p. 41.

[75] H. D. Eberlein, *Villas of Florence and Tuscany*, Philadelphia and London 1922, p. 67.

[76] G. Sitwell, *On the Making of Gardens*, London 1909, p. VIII.

[77] *Cecil Pinsent and his Gardens in Tuscany*, ed. M. Fantoni, H. Flores, J. Pfordresher, Florence 1996, and particularly, V. Shacklock, *Pinsent's work for C. A. Strong at Villa Le Balze Fiesole*, ibid., pp. 71–90, G. Galletti, *Cecil Pinsent, architetto dell'Umanesimo*, in *Il giardino europeo del Novecento 1900–1940*, ed. A. Tagliolini, Florence 1993, pp. 184–200.

"*The garden must be studied in relation to the house, and both in relation to the landscape.*" In fact the title of the book stresses the link between architecture and outdoor space. Wharton paid special attention to Villa Gamberaia which "*... stands nobly on a ridge overlooking the village of Settignano and the wide-spread valley of the Arno*", a late building, of around 1610, that was "*distinctly Tuscan*" and "*even in Italy where small and irregular pieces of ground were so often utilized with marvellous skill, it was probably the most perfect example of the art of producing a great effect on a small scale.*"[74]

The great interest of English and American scholars in Italian gardens at the turn of the century also influenced the English-speaking colony in Florence, and by restoring their own houses and gardens they contributed to the reintroduction of the formal style.

In his book *Villas of Florence and Tuscany*, published in London in 1922, Harold D. Eberlein suggests the possibility of restoring gardens to their original splendour by using literary descriptions and sources, early images, general knowledge of the garden and, finally, the remains of old gardens still *in situ*.[75] And George Sitwell writes: "*If the world is to make great gardens again we must both discover and apply in the changed circumstances of modern life the principles which guided the garden-makers of the Renaissance, and must be ready to learn all that science can teach us concerning the laws of artistic presentment.*"[76]

In 1908 Cecil Pinsent,[77] a young British architect, lived in Florence and worked for Harvard art collector Charles Loeser, a friend of the famous art historian and collector Bernard Berenson. In the summer of 1909 he began building a lodge at Villa Gattaia, work continuing in 1910, and produced a plan for a loggia and extension. At Villa

Left: Gamberaia, the villa from a green arch of the garden.
Above: The water parterres.
Below: Perspective view, front, section and plan in J. C. Sheperd, G. A. Jellicoe, *Italian Gardens of the Renaissance*.

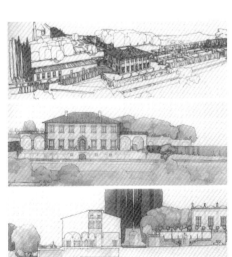

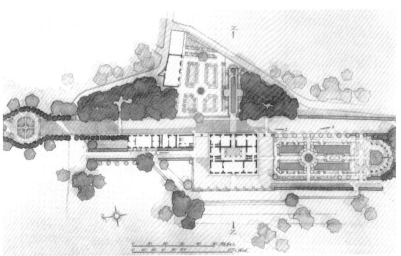

Gamberaia he made a drawing of the water-parterre, probably a gift for the interior designer Elsie de Wolffe. In 1911 Pinsent and Geoffrey Scott established a formal partnership and in April 1912 Pinsent produced his drawings for the villa and garden at Le Balze. Pinsent and Scott were commissioned by Lady Sybil Cutting for alterations and additions to the Villa Medici in Fiesole. But Pinsent's first major commission, more directly concerned with landscape architecture, was for Villa I Tatti for Berenson's wife Mary. In around 1911 Pinsent and Scott, Mary Berenson's protégé, began to transform the fifty acres around the villa (then largely olive groves and vineyards) into an Italian garden. The garden was conceived as an outdoor extension of the house, an unfolding sequence, designed with the open intention of reviving the Italian style.[78] Villa I Tatti is the concrete expression of an ideal shared by many intellectuals in the cultured and sophisticated British colony living in the villas around Florence at the turn of the century. A long cypress avenue leading from the Vincigliata road provided the original approach to the villa; at the end, a small elegant stairway, adorned with a niche, leads to a small garden with an entrance to the villa. On the west side is a secret garden ornamented with box topiary work. On the south side is the large terraced garden, designed as a series of open-air rooms on the slope of the hill. The garden's main axis crosses the centre of the lemon-house, the arched entrance of which frames a spectacular view. The terraces are closed on both sides by walls of cypresses and by parallel paths shaded by rows of ilexes. Another path lined with ilexes and surrounded by groves of trees leads to the pavilion at the end of the garden, near the Mensola stream. "*A garden such as I Tatti, with its geometric patterns precisely defined by wide box borders and its gigantic enclosing cypress hedge recalls the monumental forms of late Victorian and Edwardian formal gardens*", as E. Neubauer writes.[79]

The research work of the Fellows of the American Academy in Rome has made a major contribution to the study and knowledge of the Italian garden. The American Academy was established in 1894 and in 1915 began to offer three-year fellowships in landscape architecture. The programme involved the Fellows in producing a detailed survey of Italian garden design, still today an indispensable source for the study of Italian gardens and one which has influenced the work of many landscape architects in the United States.[80]

[78] The villa was designed as a place for study as well as social gatherings, and so it was described by one of its earliest and most faithful visitors, Edith Wharton, "*a bookworm's heaven: the fulfilment of all he has dreamed that a great working library should be this 'great good place' [was] used not only as a library but as a living room.*" E. Wharton, *A Backward Glance*, New York 1964, p. 327.
Villa I Tatti "*although alluding to the Renaissance architectural style in its chosen idiom, was an evocation of or invocation to cultural values, not an imitation of Renaissance forms…. It was neither a restoration nor a re-creation of a Renaissance residence. With its stately libraries and its picture gallery, its model was as much the English country house as the Tuscan villa.*" P. Rubin, Bernard Berenson, *Villa I Tatti and the visualization of the Italian Renaissance,* in *Gli Anglo-Americani a Firenze. Idea e costruzione del Rinascimento,* ed. M. Fantoni, Rome 2000, p. 210.

[79] E. Neubauer, *The garden architecture of Cecil Pinsent,* in *Journal of Garden History*, 3, 1, 1983.

[80] M. Azzi Visentini, *The Italian garden in America: 1890s–1920s,* in *The Italian Presence in American Art 1860–1920*, ed. I. B. Jaffe, Fordham Univ. Press and Istituto della Enciclopedia Italiana, 1992, pp. 240–265.

Right: Villa I Tatti from the garden.

CHAPTER FIVE

Villas in the Nineteenth Century

[1] The court's liberal attitude allowed even "problem" elements such as members of Napoleon's family a gilded and trouble-free exile and hence several members of the Bonaparte family settled in Florence. See A. Corsini, *I Bonaparte a Firenze*, Florence 1961.

After reaching its peak in terms of quality, size and number during the Cinquecento, the villa assumed a generally stable pattern over the ensuing centuries, with a marked slowing down and reduction in operations, leaving us with the image of the same unchanging, almost static, situation in the outlying areas that prevailed in the city. The weakening of the dynamic impetus of the Florentine entrepreneurial classes in both relative and absolute terms, and the economic crisis that struck the Grand Duchy, made more acute by the unification of Italy in 1861, and then when the capital was shifted to Rome in 1870, meant that reliance was chiefly placed on the legacy of the great achievements of the past four centuries. Operations became limited to renovations to satisfy changing tastes and the emergent middle-class's demands for a new dignity and social position.

However, during the course of the 19th century events of a new kind emerged in this pattern of stability which are of interest in terms of forms of expression, from the architectural point of view of a building and its site, its regional context, and for the nature of the commissioners since these points throw light on the last if not truly final chapter concerning the impact that villas made on the Florentine area.

A study of commissioners immediately reveals the "extraordinary" nature of the ensuing developments, which were encouraged by the fact that Florence had a reasonably liberal and cosmopolitan court, so that even for the normally closed circles of the local nobility, the presence of foreigners in the city was in no way unusual.[1] The events we refer to were obviously limited to a certain élite and not, or only rarely, connected with local agricultural production. In fact in almost all instances the incentive of agricultural investment, although encouraged by the Duke of Lorraine, was of decidedly secondary importance to the character and social significance of these newly developed buildings.

To analyse all the varied aspects of the story of the Florentine villa during the 19th century we shall examine the different forms and styles that were adopted, grouping them into

Left: John Singer Sargent, *Villa Torre Galli: the Loggia*, 1910, private collection.

different "categories" within which we can identify common features. However, it should be mentioned that the rebuilding or restructuring of early pre-existing buildings, whether radical or not, concerned less the architecture than the new role that a villa was to assume in the surrounding area. During the 19th century the villa was no longer the centre of agricultural production it had been at the height of its development in the late Middle Ages, when the class emerging from a rich trading and manufacturing city invested its money in the purchase and use of lands and property.[2] It is clear that such a change of position, while confirming that the recreational side of villa life prevailed over the productive one, is also firm evidence of the dwindling importance of farming which, in perpetuating share-cropping agreements as its means of production, was becoming increasingly a task of mere subsistence.

To emphasise the nature of this shift we should mention the changing face of the surrounding terrain which, along with the buildings, was transformed to suit the prevailing taste, agricultural lands being turned into romantic parks, according to the latest fashion.[3]

The 19th century marked the last great season of the Florentine villa. Many still survive today, on the outskirts of a city vulgarized by mass tourism, evidence of a time when Florence was the city *par excellence* of the Renaissance legacy, the seat of cosmopolitan culture,[4] a city loved and lauded by countless foreigners as the "*città felix*", the garden of Europe, a showplace of fine taste and style where nature, art and life were perfectly combined. In the mid-19th century many foreigners, especially those from England and America, settled in Florence, the cradle of that magic dream of art, history and beauty which fuelled their emotions and inspired their lives, where the views were still those of Renaissance paintings. As Edith Wharton says: "*In Florence [you] may go forth from the Riccardi Chapel and see the Castle of Vincigliata towering on its cypress-clad hill precisely as Gozzoli depicted it in his fresco.*"[5] The *vita in villa* is re-evoked in countless literary and poetic works.[6] Hillside villas were perfectly placed for gazing at distant vistas, in accordance with the 19th-century taste for a secluded position in the countryside, and ideal for the comforts to which the foreign upper classes were accustomed.[7]

The hillside villas became the chosen residences of a sizeable foreign colony which elected to live in this city of art, an artistic workshop where people lived cheek by jowl with masterpieces of the past and where the existential mirage of a possible balance between life and art proved a reality for many scholars

[2] Thus, the very existence of the *casa da signore* was due to particular economic circumstances, and it consolidated the life-style of an emerging bourgeoisie which received produce from their properties as well as an improved social status. (See Chapter Two.)

[3] Among the numerous examples of this change of use are the Petraia, Quarto, Ventaglio and Boschetto villas.

[4] Among the many accounts we could choose from we will quote the poet Leigh Hunt who wrote, describing his visit to Florence in 1837, "*I loved Florence, and saw nothing in it but cheerfulness and elegance. I loved the name; I loved the fine arts and the old palaces; I loved the memories of Pulci and Lorenzo de' Medici....*" Leigh Hunt, *Autobiography*, London 1860, p. 337.

[5] E. Wharton, *Italian Backgrounds*, New York 1905, p. 181.

[6] We should not under-estimate the contribution to the appreciation and quality of the *vita in villa* made by foreigners who chose to settle in Florence, or preferably in the surrounding hills.

[7] "*The villa stood on the top of a hill. From the terrace in front of it you had a magnificent view of Florence; behind was an old garden, with few flowers but with fine trees, hedges of cut box, grass walks and an artificial grotto in which water cascaded with a cool, silvery sound from a cornucopia. The house had been built in the sixteenth century by a noble Florentine, whose impoverished descendants had sold it to some English people....*" S. Maugham, *Up at the Villa*, London 1941, p. 1.

[8] L. Dentler, *Famous Foreigners in Florence*, Florence 1964, pp. 64–65. The Strozzino villa became the home of the Pre-Raphaelite painter Spencer Stanhope between 1880 and 1908, the year of his death. The painter's niece, A. M. Wilhelmina Stirling, recalled it as follows: "*The villa was a spacious medieval building, encircling a courtyard where grew massive creepers, and orange and lemon trees laden with fruit. From the terrace, amid the roses, one looked out over Florence, drowsing in the sunlight, cut by the silver line of the shining Arno. In the loggia, which my uncle fashioned into a delightful room, the wide windows commanded a panorama of the Vallombrosian hills, where in the winter evenings, Monte Morello showed purple against a flaming sky. Dotted about on the hillside below were blue-grey olive trees, orchards powdered in springtime with fairy-like blossoms, melancholy cypress-groves, and, here and there, other villas, embowered in exquisite Italian gardens and breathing an atmosphere of old-time romance.... In the winter months my*

uncle and aunt occupied the upper part of the house; with the coming of spring, they, with their pictures, furniture and all belongings, migrated to the terreno for coolness. Both upstairs and down, however, the height and structural beauty of the rooms made a perfect setting to the loveliness of the decoration. Stencilling by Bodley, rich brocaded hangings, fine needlework, medieval treasures in art and furniture, presented a wealth of exquisite design and colour. And everywhere little Loves looked out amid the tones of pink and rose or gold and amethyst which he loved. Of rare beauty, too, was some of the furniture designed by himself, and executed by Italian workmen under his directions: tall graceful clocks, richly embossed cassoni, and a cabinet in a lovely shade of egg-shell blue patterned in raised gold and enhanced by panels of radiant dancing figures in variations of the same entrancing colour-schemes." A. M. W. Stirling, *Life's Little Day*, London 1924, pp. 145–146. Spencer Stanhope was also the uncle of the Pre-Raphaelite painter Evelyn Pickering, later the wife of the potter William de Morgan who collaborated with Ulisse Cantagalli. During his stay in Florence, Stanhope decorated the Holy Trinity Church in Via Lamarmora and St Mark's Church in Via Maggio.

[9] *"The God who made the hills of Florence was goldsmith, metal engraver, sculptor, caster in bronze and painter; he was a Florentine"*, says Miss Bell, the literary incarnation of Vernon Lee, in *Le Lys Rouge* by Anatole France, It. ed. Milan 1970, p. 362. See F. Baldry, *Abitare e collezionare: note sul collezionismo fiorentino fra la fine dell'Ottocento e gli inizi del Novecento*, in *Herbert Percy Horne e il suo tempo*, ed. E. Nardinocchi, Florence 2005, pp. 103–126.

and art lovers. Their image of what was truly "Florentine" was realized in their art collections, sometimes embroidered by new settings aimed at recreating the atmosphere of the past by idealizing it. Frederick Hervey, Earl of Bristol, collected the masterpieces of Cimabue, Giotto and other early painters, showing that his taste was well in advance of contemporary trends.[8]

The villas and castles on the surrounding hills became fairy-tale residences, images of long ago, restored, furnished and decorated to evoke the atmosphere of past eras, now relived with a contemporary and fresh sensibility which proposed to re-invent the "spirit of place".[9]

At the turn of the century the Florentine experiences of two unusual figures, Sloane and Spence, were closely bound up

Top: Phillipp Hackert, the villa Medici at Careggi from San Piero, 1805 oil on canvas, Bonn Bundespräsidialamt.
Bottom: The western façade of the villa with the loggia.

with the most famous 15th-century Medici villas, the first at Careggi and the latter at Fiesole.

Frances Joseph Sloane was a geologist, wealthy business man and lover of Tuscan art and history. He went to Florence in 1824 as librarian to the Russian, Count Demetrius Bouturlin, and grew affluent working as an expert for the grand ducal copper mines in Volterra, of which he later became a share-holder. In 1848 he moved to the Villa Medici at Careggi where he created a museum of Medici paintings, drawings and prints. In 1853 Sloane began to enlarge the building, focusing his attention on the Tuscan atrium, the first-floor *salone* and the old great hall, at the same time redesigning the grounds to keep pace with contemporary taste and introducing numerous exotic plants. When remodelling the building he obviously installed modern conveniences, while making every attempt to respect the villa's original style, and in his subsequent renovation of the adjoining villa, Il Belvedere, he made even greater efforts to recapture the 15th-century character of the rooms (once occupied by Marsilio Ficino). The dream of reviving the Renaissance and medieval "ideal" led Sloane to search for original furnishings and period reproductions, such as the Della Robbia-style glazed terracotta lunette, made by the Ginori firm of Doccia, for the ground-floor chapel. "*He collected furniture of the Medici period and portraits of all the friends of Lorenzo the Magnificent; he employed the best Italian artists to portray on the walls the chief events that had transpired there . . . At a later period he became the owner of Villa Le Fontanelle, Villa Le Lepricine and others, all of which he greatly transformed.*"[10]

Another famous villa at the gates of the city, the Villa Medici at Fiesole, had a long line of British residents from the 18th century onwards and in 1862 it became the home of William Blundell Spence, art lover, collector, painter and dealer as well as author of the famous guidebook, *The Lions of Florence*.[11] The descriptions he sent his son are full of enthusiasm and the works he carried out did not affect the original structure, involving only decoration and refurnishing.[12] The villa provided Blundell Spence with a setting for society occasions and an extremely active social life and it gave him an *entrée*, moreover, into a world of highly influential people, helping him to gain international standing as an art dealer. In 1866 the discovery of the remains of an Etruscan wall on his property, at the entrance to the upper garden, caused Spence's name to become even better known, as we see from the correspondence in the magazine "The Athenaeum".[13]

[10] Dentler, op. cit., p. 221. In 1853 Sloane engaged Antonio Puccinelli to paint "*Plato's family celebrations*" and, the following year "*Cosimo the Elder surrounded by famous men of his time*". Lord Holland, the proprietor until 1847, had already made a move in this direction by having the loggia painted by a young guest, George Frederick Watts, with "*Doctor Leoni being thrown down the well when suspected of the death of Lorenzo il Magnifico*", a work completed in 1845. G. Carocci, *La villa medicea di Careggi*, Florence 1888.

[11] In the first edition of Lions (1847), Blundell Spence describes the Villa Medici as having been "*built by Cosimo il vecchio, the very place where, in 1478, the Pazzi conspiracy was to have taken place, which, from its elevated position, commands a splendid view of Florence*".

[12] "*The graved approach is magnificent, gravelled and vased, the summer house all done in mosaic as in front of Medici arms bust of Cosimo. Villino lovely, grand iron gate and all furnished with pictures*"; and again, "*I have had the doors and windows shutten, and in the green room painted to match the furniture, it looks very well, had all the doors scraped in the passage upstairs, they are of fine stone which was plastered over, and is much better. I have taken up carpet in small room where large picture was and put it in the passage upstairs and all is getting splendid – we have lots of visitors*". From two of Blundell Spence's letters to his son William Campbell, known as Mino, presumably from the early 1860s, quoted by D. Levi, *William Blundell Spence in Florence*, in *Studi e Ricerche di collezionismo e museografia, Firenze 1820–1920*, Quaderni del Seminario di Storia della Critica d'Arte 2, Scuola Normale Superiore di Pisa 1985, pp. 87–149. In 1866, a year before the death of his wife Fanny Waugh Hunt, the Pre-Raphaelite painter William Holman Hunt lived in the Villa Medici with Spence, with a studio above the carriage-house. Dentler, op. cit., p. 125.

[13] "*These discoveries are of such importance that Mr. Spence purposes continuing the excavations in hope of finding further relics of the past*". "The Athenaeum" n. 2203, 17 March 1866, 367–368, quoted by D. Levi, op. cit., p. 147.

[14] H. James, *Florence, Italy Revisited*, New York 1878, p. 325.

Right: Baccio del Bianco, a view of the Villa Imperiale after 1624; G. Zocchi the Villa around 1744; plan after the transformation of the 19th century; a view of the Villa around 1820 by an anonymous artist (G.D.S.U.); the façade of the villa today.

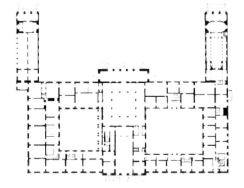

The hillside villas were places for social occasions and intellectual gatherings and, as we can easily imagine, the changes in social structure also involved some notable changes in interiors, furnishings and gardens. We will leave it to the more masterly and sensitive pen of Henry James to express how attractive, if open to ridicule, was this changing social scene and the different ways in which the multifarious colony of foreign residents used their old Florentine villas.

"The villas are innumerable and if you're an aching alien half the talk is about villas. This one has a story; that one has another; they all look as if they had stories – none in truth predominantly gay. Most of them are offered to rent (many of them are for sale) at prices unnaturally low; you may have a tower and a garden, a chapel and an expanse of thirty windows, for five hundred dollars a year. In imagination you hire three or four; you take possession and settle and stay. Your sense of the finest is something very grave and stately; your sense of the bravery at two or three of the best something quite tragic and sinister. From what does this latter impression come? You gather it as you stand there in the early dusk, with your eyes on the long, pale-brown façade, the enormous windows, the iron cages fastened to the lower ones. Part of the brooding expression of these great houses comes, even when they have not fallen into decay, from their look of having outlived their original use. Their extraordinary largeness and massiveness are a satire on their present fate. They weren't built with such a thickness of wall and depth of embrasure, such a solidity of staircases and superfluity of doorways, simply to afford an economical winter residence to English and American families. I don't know whether it was the appearance of these stony old villas, which seemed so dumbly conscious of a change of manners, that threw a tinge of melancholy over the general prospect; certain it is that, having always found this note as of a myriad old sadnesses in solution in the view of Florence, it seemed to me now particularly strong. 'Lovely, lovely, but it makes me "blue"', the sensitive stranger couldn't but help murmuring to himself as, in the late afternoon, he looked at the landscape from over one of the low parapets, and then, with his hands in his pockets, turned away indoors to candles and dinner."[14]

Thus, as we have said, during the 19th century the villa became chiefly a place for the holidays or, if close to the city, the settled residence of a frequently foreign, aristocratic or upper-class élite. As Sir Harold Acton, the last Anglo-Florentine, states in his memoirs: *"Nearly all the old Florentine villas had Anglo-Saxon ramifications, and a large proportion of Florentine palaces and villas were inhabited by English-*

men half the year round. That the Englishman's home is his castle was especially true of the Villa Medici at Fiesole, of Vincigliata, Villa Palmieri (and countless other country seats whose romantic records were published by Mrs Janet Ross) .... Queen Victoria set the seal of royal approval on this tradition by staying twice at Villa Palmieri.... they wrote, they painted, they composed, they collected works of art and cultivated their gardens; Myron Taylor's Schifanoia, the Franchetti and Huntington villas at Bellosguardo; Charles Loeser's La Gattaia, Berenson at I Tatti, Vernon Lee at Maiano, Lady Sybil Lubbock at Fiesole, held gatherings where literary and aesthetic problems were debated as earnestly as at the Platonic Academy of the Medici. Janet Ross wrote on Florentine history and supervised her farm at Poggio Gherardo, Edward Hutton produced his invaluable guide-books at the neighbouring Casa Boccaccio, Mabel Dodge presided over Bohemia at the Villa Curonia...."[15]

Ouida, an English writer who had a certain reputation in her day lived in Florence for some years around the end of the 19th and early 20th centuries and wrote a vivid description of a villa in her novel *Pascarel*, based on the Villa Farinola where she lived. *"The villa was high up on the mountain side – vast, dusky, crumbling, desolate without, as all such places are, and within full of that harmless charm of freedom, space, antiquity, and stillness that does no less perpetually belong to them. Where these old villas stand on their pale olive slopes, those who are strange to them see only the peeling plaster, the discoloured stones, the desolate courts, the grass-grown flags, broken statues, the straying vines, the look of loneliness and decay. But those who know them well, love them and learn otherwise; learn the infinite charm of those vast silent halls, of those endless echoing corridors and cloisters, of those wide wind-swept sunbathed chambers, of those shadowy loggie, where the rose-flow of the oleander burns in the dimness of the arches ... of that sense of infinite solitude, of infinite light, and stillness, and calm..."*[16]

In order to study the character of 19th-century extra-urban villas, we must first divide them into two categories: those which emerged from the remodelling of pre-existing buildings and those that were newly built. Within these two groups we shall be able to make further classifications on the basis of their prevailing styles. Those belonging to the first category, the many pre-existing villas which were "up-dated" to suit the latest fashion, are certainly

[15] H. Acton, *More Memoirs of an Aesthete*, London 1970, pp. 363–364.

[16] Ouida, *Pascarel*, Melbourne 1873.

[17] Giuseppe Cacialli showed great ability in his arrangement of the interior spaces. Apart from being engaged for the chapel and loggia at Poggio Imperiale, as an architect of the "Reali Fabbriche" he had carried out some work on Palazzo Pitti and the palazzo of the Conti della Gherardesca.

[18] The peristyle on the first floor was ornamented with stucco decorations by Spedulo and Marinelli and with painted allegories of the Seasons, attributed to Giuseppe Gherardi. The landscape decorations in one room are attributable to Giorgio Angiolini. During the period when Florence was the capital city, the villa was ceded to the girls' boarding-school of the Santissima Annunziata, a school for well-born young ladies.

Right: The Galleria of the "piano nobile"; a salotto at the ground floor with frescoes by Tommaso Gherardini in Pompeian style (1741); plan of the Villa Poggio Imperiale and the gardens.

102

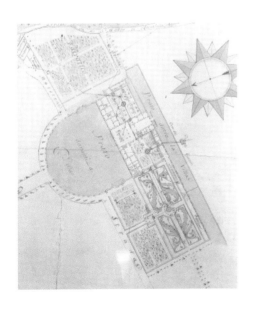

the more numerous. Early in the century the neo-classical style made its mark on several of the grand ducal villas, particularly Poggio Imperiale (1807–1828). The work of converting this famous complex, during the 17th century the chosen residence of Grand Duchess Maddalena of Austria, was begun by Pasquale Poccianti in around 1806, during the period of French domination. Poccianti's work on the project was interrupted the following year when Marie Louise of Bourbon, Queen of Etruria, was obliged to quit the throne. He had already built the portico on the ground floor of the central body but the general volumetric and planimetric layout was later completed by Cacialli.[17] Cacialli's intervention broke away from his predecessor's design, being more decidedly classical in inspiration. This is displayed in the elevation of the floor above the entrance portico and in the glassed-in loggia, crowned by a frontispiece ornamented with a clock and two winged Victories. The arrangement and ornamentation of the interior spaces was also altered.[18]

On the hilly slopes to the west of the city the Villa Borghese, or Villa Paolina, offers another example of the neo-classical transformation of a pre-existing building. Bought by Prince Camillo Borghese in 1820, it was restored and lavishly re-modelled between 1826 and 1831 by Antonio Carcopino and turned into a princely out-of-town residence, a *pendant* of the family's city palazzo in Via Ghibellina, renovated by Baccani, which the prince had inherited from his mother's side, the Dukes of Salviati. The remodelling works on the villa were based on new aesthetic canons, most clearly displayed on the south façade. The villa follows the line of Via di Castello and has a symmetrical plan with rooms leading off two corridors on the ground and first floors. The traditional "block" pattern of the Florentine villa was modified with a design which counterposes a ground floor with alternating volumes and spaces with an upper floor more markedly chiaroscuro in tone, spanned by simple windows with underlying decorative panels and lateral recesses with stucco decorations holding statues. There are some very fine ornamentations in the interior including a series of stucco bas-reliefs on the walls of the gallery, the work of Costoli who was also responsible for the statues on the façade. The latter is further enhanced by handsome frescoes portraying an allegory of Triumph, the work of Bezzuoli, who was also engaged on the decoration of the city palazzo. There is an unusual arrangement on the exterior where an iron suspension bridge stretches from the first floor of the villa to the park in the rear, designed and landscaped during the same period as a romantic park, full of statues, pools and rare plants encircling a green amphitheatre. The latter marks the heart of the park, connected to the entrance by an avenue of cypresses on one side and, on the other, by way of the bridge, to the round drawing-room on the first floor. This unusual bridge was a miniature version of more ambitious examples which were beginning to appear in Europe following the enthusiasm of the time for technical innovations and was probably inspired by a similar iron bridge installed at the same period in the park of the villa at Poggio a Caiano.[19]

Villa Il Ventaglio, in Via delle Forbici, was built for the Milanese Count Archinto in 1839 and was the first commission to be received by the young Giuseppe Poggi. The irregular plan appears to have been conditioned by a pre-existing building, not completely absorbed into the strict new design, while the classically inspired façades rise above a base which echoes Sangallo's work at the Medici villa at Poggio a Caiano and forms a continuous terrace circling the first floor.

In order to create the park, laid out in sections divided by winding avenues, the old farm was "sacrificed" and transformed into a mixture of woods and meadows, a clever blend of landscaped views and vistas to suit the now widespread taste for the romantic English garden.

The Strozzi villa at Boschetto was also the work of Giuseppe Poggi, now commissioned from a well-known and established architect who satisfied the needs of the Florentine aristocracy. The original building, the property of the noble Strozzi family, was in very poor condition and in 1855 it was rebuilt. The building's compact plan is developed around a central stucco-ornamented two-storey rotunda providing access to the rooms. The ceilings of the ground-floor rooms were lowered, leaving only the large room to the south-west at its original height. The only feature projecting from the building's compact block is the entrance hall with overhead terrace.

The murals in the interior were entrusted to the leading Florentine exponents of narrative painting, Antonio Marini, Carlo Brini, Cesare Mussini and Antonio Puccinelli, while Rinaldo Barbetti, son of the more famous sculptor and cabinet-maker Angelo, produced the stamped leather decorations lining the small drawing-room, a revival of a local 16th-century tradition. Poggi was also responsible for renovating the buildings around the villa.[20] When the stables were rebuilt they encompassed the old chapel, frescoed by Bernardino Poccetti with *Scenes from the*

[19] G. Gobbi Sica, *Alcuni interventi ottocenteschi nel territorio fiorentino*, in "Bollettino degli Ingegneri", 10, Florence 1974, pp. 15–21.

[20] "*Boschetto's improvements were not limited to the villa, but extended to the annexes, which really gave the place the importance it deserved. Thus, the building standing above the villa was remodelled, containing the gardener's house, stables, various quarters and a chapel painted by Poccetti which is a real little jewel.*" G. Poggi, *Ricordi della vita e documenti d'arte*, Florence 1909, p. 62.

[21] G. Gobbi Sica, op cit..

Life of St John the Baptist and *Virtues*. The layout of the romantic gardens crosses the land south of the villa with an avenue, winding to follow the gentler slopes through a succession of clearings and thick woods. Where the old and new woods meet stands an elegant conservatory, inspired by Palladian models.

The Quarto villa, the ancient seat of the Pasquali family to the north-west of the city, is a further example of the alterations which affected many pre-existing buildings over the course of the 19th century, changes being introduced to both buildings and land. The villa was bought by the ex-king of Westphalia, Jerome de Montfort, who fled to Florence after the collapse of the Empire, later coming into the possession of another foreign resident, Anatol Demidoff, an enormously rich Russian who, as we shall see, also made his mark on other buildings during his stay in Tuscany. After marrying Jerome's daughter, Matilde Bonaparte, Demidoff bought the villa from his father-in-law in 1843 for 200,000 francs and over the course of five years he carried out the work of remodelling the building and, especially, the surrounding land. He bought a farm from the Conservatorio degli Angiolini and other pieces of adjoining land, transforming the whole into a romantic park, full of rare plants and trees and embellished with statues, pavilions and small lakes. During this same period work was being carried out in the gardens of the adjacent Villa Petraia, also realized on the site of an existing farm, and contemporaries praised them both for their grandeur and beauty.[21]

Not far from the Quarto villa, in the Quinto area, is another example which is notable for the scale of the alterations and the "new" character given to a pre-existing villa, no longer serving to manage an agricultural estate, now entirely transformed into a park. This is the Villa Torrigiani at Quinto, where the original residential-farm complex was transformed into a grandiose residence. After the remodelling alterations the villa became an alternative summer home to the well-known Torrigiani family who held a particularly important position among the Florentine nobility of the time due to the fact that Pietro, a cosmopolitan nobleman, was politically linked to the circles of Napoleon and his successors, active among the supporters of unification with the realm of Piedmont. His grandson, also called Pietro, was to be mayor of the city when Florence became the capital. Works on the original building, today unhappily changed in both use and appearance, once reproduced traditional Renaissance features, even in the choice of materials – plaster and *pietra serena*, a grey stone. The vast English park surrounding the villa lies on a slight slope and is a mixture of thick woods, meadows and clearings, with a lemon-house, greenhouses and a small lake hollowed out of an Etruscan tumulus, discovered in the course of operations. The only park to exceed it in scale is that of the Petraia, the splendours of which it must once have rivalled.

Villa Favard at Rovezzano, an ancient medieval building, was transformed into a villa in the Cinquecento for Bartolini Salimbeni by Baccio d'Agnolo, who also built the family palazzo in the city, and in 1829 both this and the farm were bought by Prince Stanislao Poniatowski.[22] Aside from the neo-classical façade, produced by an unknown architect, further alterations were carried out between 1830 and 1840 by Giuseppe Poggi, while he was working for the same commissioner on his city palazzo at Porta al Prato. Poggi was again engaged for some interior alterations commissioned by Fiorella Favard d'Anglade, who bought the property in around the mid-1850s. Poggi, now well-established in his career, worked on both the exterior and interior,[23] creating a ballroom on the ground floor by roofing over the original courtyard, an idea probably drawn from a similar operation carried out at the Petraia villa and in general influenced by the technical experiments conducted at this time using materials such as iron and glass.[24] The introduction of these new materials during the 1860s had led to an original and bold transformation of the central courtyard at the Petraia villa, turning it into a ballroom with iron and glass roofing designed by the architects to the Royal House, Fabio Nuti and Giuseppe Giardi.[25]

The villa's rich interior ornamentation includes the intaglio work for the ballroom ceiling, carried out by Francesco Morini, and paintings by Orazio Pucci and Annibale Gatti and stuccoes by Bernardo and Nicola Ramelli. Poggi also took part in redesigning the park to the west of the villa, bringing it into line with the new prevailing taste for romantic gardens. A chapel in neo-classical style was now added, built with the collaboration of Pietro Comparini Rossi and consecrated in 1877. The chapel is shaped like a Greek cross and crowned with a hemispherical dome with an Ionic tetrastyle pronaos, inspired by the Renaissance eclecticism which marks Poggi's mature works. In the chapel is the Baroness's evocative tomb, a work by Giovanni Duprè.

[22] In a subsequent contract of sale for the property, the date of Poniatoski's purchase is given as 10 July 1823. L. Zangheri, *Ville della provincia di Firenze*, Milan 1989, p. 189.

[23] "... *a new room, new stables, a new avenue with a large entrance gate in Via Aretina ... an elegant chapel*', G. Trotta's entry on the villa in L. Zangheri, op. cit., p. 187.

[24] Beneath the iron and glass structure of the roofing, Poggi made a second self-supporting wooden structure with curved side sections. The lower structure with panels set at different angles, converging towards the central peak of the framework. The structure and ornamentations were coloured and fashioned in a manner normally used for metal constructions, so that the wood resembled cast iron, ibid.

[25] C. Acidini Luchinat, G. Galletti, *La villa e il giardino della Petraia a Firenze*, Florence 1995, p. 46.

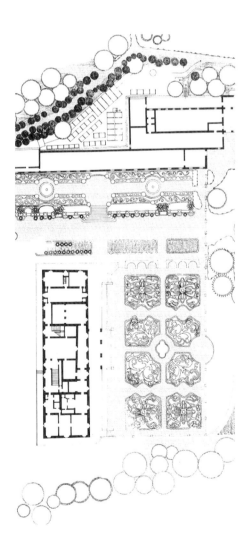

Left: Plan of the Quarto Villa.
Below: A view of the villa Favard in the frescoed salone of the ground floor; Bacco and Arianna, painted in the vault decoration of the orchestra room; the old courtyard transformed into a ballroom by Giusppe Poggi in 1860; the main façade of the villa.

The villa at Montalto, the area near Maiano, shows the result of the unusual combination of a foreign commissioner, Count Hochberg, who bought the property in 1885, and his Swedish architect, Alfred F. E. Grenander. During the 19th century the villa had already been the property of northern Europeans, the German bankers Kleiber and Holle. The building goes back to late-medieval times and originally consisted of two main bodies, still identifiable in the layout. The design is asymmetrical and unfolds from the central entrance-way for carriages. The building's architectural design, clearly northern in inspiration, includes quite disparate elements: a polygonal tower with a domed copper roof, cornices, overhangs, balconies, turrets and loggias, a mixed bag drawn from the neo-18th-century style so popular in northern European countries during the second half of the 19th century. The architect was better-known in Germany, having worked on several buildings in Frankfurt and Berlin, while the Montalto villa, his only known work in Italy, remains a fairly isolated instance of a foreign contribution

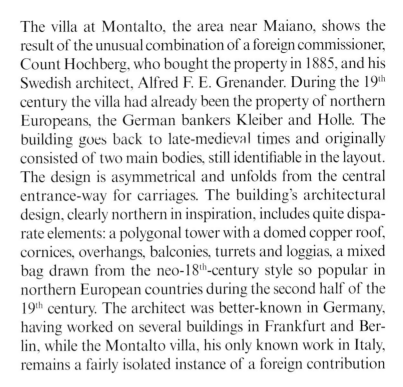

in the Florence area. During the late 1920s the villa became the property of the Neapolitan bibliophile Tommaso De Marinis who gave the furnishings a more markedly neo-Renaissance flavour.

A typical example of this occupation by a succession of foreign residents during the 19th century is offered by the Villa dell'Ombrellino at Bellosguardo. This very early villa was occupied during the 17th century by Galileo, and during the early decades of the 19th century the owner, Countess Teresa Albizzi, had the building remodelled and enlarged by adding two side-wings; in the middle of the century it became the home of the De Rast de Fall family and then of Baron Marcel Desboutin. In 1874 the villa was bought by Maria Zubow who annexed the adjacent Torricella villa, where Ugo Foscolo had stayed. The gardens of the two villas were turned into a single park and planted with numerous exotic plants and trees, while the building, as Carocci states: "*was almost entirely rebuilt by the present owner, who turned it into a fine modern dwelling*". Further alterations were made in the early decades of the 20th century when the estate became the property of the unconventional Englishwoman Alice Keppel. She had some parts rebuilt, such as the loggia for musical occasions, demolishing the Torricella to improve the view of the city. The park was also changed and turned into an Italian garden, an Anglo-Saxon reinterpretation of Renaissance classicism, landscaped by Cecil Pinsent.

Among countless other villas which belonged to northern Europeans during the course of the 19th century we must not forget Villa Palmieri in Via Boccaccio. From the first decades of the 19th century it housed many famous figures, including Lord Cooper, before being bought by Miss Mary Fairhill who bequeathed it to Maria Antonia di Toscana. In 1873 it was bought by Sir Alexander Crawford who was responsible for radical changes to the whole complex, including the new course of Via Boccaccio, skirting the edge of the property, and an enormous English-style park full of rare varieties, palms and sequoias. Not far from Villa Palmieri lies Villa Schifanoia where, according to tradition, Boccaccio stayed. This was owned by the Young Norwood family and, during the 20th century, by Myron Taylor, American Ambassador to the Holy See. Villa Palmerino at Camerata, a 15th-century complex, was for many years the home of the English writer Violet Paget who, writing under the pseudonym Vernon Lee, described the *fin de siècle* cultural scene in her many works on art, literature and aesthetics, under the influence of Walter Pater's new ideas on aesthetics.[26]

[26] On Vernon Lee and the Villa Palmerino, Mario Praz's writings give a perspicacious and stylish account of the atmosphere in which this writer lived and worked. M. Praz, *Vernon Lee, Musica udita dalla stanza accanto, Fantasmi culturali*, now in the anthology of Praz's work *Bellezza e Bizzaria*, ed. G. Cane, Milan 2002, pp. 1071–1100.

Above: Villa Montalto.
Right: Villa Temple-Leader at Maiano; villa Palmieri; villa Ombrellino at Bellosguardo; villa Fabbricotti.

Another building belonging to this category and involving the transformation of a pre-existing structure is Villa Curonia in Via Suor Maria Celeste at Poggio Imperiale. The villa, probably rebuilt during the 1500s by Baccio d'Agnolo, was bought in the 20th century by the wealthy and eccentric American, Mabel Dodge, who with the aid of her architect husband, Edwin, made major changes to the villa where the couple lived a busy social life surrounded by foreign artists and writers. The loggia, the flight of steps to the south-west, the belvedere to the east, the glass covering of the courtyard, and the music-room were among their remodelling operations, together with new landscaping for the garden.

The Villa Gattaia at Monte alle Croci, originally a 15th-century building, was bought at the end of the 19th century by the American collector and art lover Charles Loeser who enlarged the existing structure, building annexes for entertaining musicians (he supported the Lehener Quartet) and housing his painting collection.

Among the pre-existing structures to be almost totally rebuilt we should include Villa Fabbricotti, remodelled in around 1864 in Roman and Venetian neo-Renaissance style by Vincenzo Micheli. He also built the family villas in Livorno and Carrara. The original villa which Giuseppe Fabbricotti bought had been owned by the Strozzi family from the 16th century until the 1820s, then by Marchese Zambeccari who sold it, in 1864, to this wealthy member of the Fabbricotti family from Carrara, which had made its fortune from the marble quarries. In 1880 Giuseppe Fabbricotti was honoured by being made a count and deservedly became one of the city's élite, advancing his social position to such a point that in 1894 he played host to Queen Victoria and members of her retinue when the British queen visited Florence. Some photographs in the Alinari Archives record the appearance of the villa at the end of the 19th century, topped with a crenellated tower and fronted by a loggia with broad arched openings supporting a large terrace above. The structural framework was deeper in tone, emphasizing the neo-Renaissance character of the new complex, derived from Giuseppe Poggi's work. The Neapolitan architect Antonio Cipolla was called upon to landscape the impressive hillside park; he was also responsible for important buildings in the city of Florence, including the head office of the Banca d'Italia. Cipolla's design, illustrated in *Ricordi d'Architettura* in 1878, was based on a series of semi-elliptical ramps leading half way up the slope and meeting on a terrace constructed on the roof of a large loggia, to then continue in a further series of terraces and ramps to the garden in front of the villa. However, Cipolla's plan was abandoned and it would seem that the park should be attributed to Vincenzo Micheli. The design of the park, full of rare plants and trees and ornamented with a tholus-style *tempietto* and a chapel with a Doric tetrastyle pronaos, was based on a great scenic stairway linking the top of the hill on which the villa stands with the entrance on Via Vittorio Emanuele, following a pattern inspired by the contemporary work carried out by Poggi in the area adjoining Piazzale Michelangelo.

The interior was richly decorated with allegorical paintings by local artists, including Annibale Gatti, and in the main drawing-room with an *Outdoor Serenade* (1882), in the style of Antoine Watteau, very similar to the one the artist frescoed in a room in the Favard villa at Rovezzano. Sumptuous furnishings were produced by the Barbetti workshop, but little trace of them remains today.

The Fabbricotti park adjoined the grounds of the Villa Stibbert, on the Montughi hillside. Here again, this former property of the Davanzati family was enlarged and transformed into a sort of medieval castle in a startling mixture of styles. Some suggestions were offered by Giuseppe Poggi but Gaetano Fortini was given overall charge of the works. Several artists were engaged on the decoration of the interior (the painter Gaetano Bianchi, the sculptor Augusto Passaglia, Michele Piovano and Frederick Stibbert himself). The assorted styles and features include a Renaissance loggia and a Gothic tower, the result being a bizarre mixture which re-evoked various earlier periods considered suitable for housing the numerous antiques that Stibbert had collected (including a Venetian loggia, dismantled and reassembled to form a small courtyard). One surprising mixture of decorative elements is presented by the smoking-room on the first floor, entirely decorated with tiles from Ulisse Cantagalli's workshop, a good example of the prevailing eclecticism of the day. Even the park surrounding the villa proved something quite unique in Florentine landscape gardening: a romantic park dotted with some surprising items such as a neo-classical Greek shrine, the *Tempietto* designed by Telemaco Bonaiuti, a Renaissance lemon-house and, by the lake, an Egyptian temple (designed by Poggi) connected with a Masonic initiation ceremony, built at the wishes of Stibbert, a member of the oldest and most influential Italian Masonic Lodge, La Concordia, originally founded in England.

[27] This is how John Ruskin described the countryside around Vincigliata in 1854: "*The traveller passes the Fiesolan ridge, and all is changed. The country is suddenly lonely. Here, and there indeed are seen the scattered houses of a farm gracefully set upon the hillside, here and there the fragment of a tower upon a distant rock; but neither gardens, nor flowers, nor glittering palace walls, only a grey extent of mountain ground tufted irregularly with ilex and olive: a scene not sublime, for its forms are subdued and low, not desolate, for its valleys are full of sown fields and tended pastures; not rich nor lovely, but sun-burnt and sorrowful; becoming wilder every instant as the road winds into recesses, ascending still, until reaching the higher woods, now partly pine, and partly oak, dropping back from the central crest of the Apennine.*" Quoted by F. Baldry, *John Temple Leader e il castello di Vincigliata*, Florence 1997, p. 99.

Left: Villa Fabbricotti, plan for the garden by Antonio Cipolla; Villa Stibbert.
Above: Vincigliata, the courtyard and the tower.
Below: The lake in the park of Vincigliata.

In the countryside in the hills between Vincigliata and Maiano[27] (then deserted) there is an unusual example of the neo-Gothic reconstruction of what was virtually a ruin which affects the contours of a large area of surrounding hills. Once again this was carried out for an Englishman living in Florence, where he settled permanently in 1848 and in 1850 bought the Pazzi Tolomei villa at Maiano. John Temple Leader, a member of a wealthy English family and an informed art lover, realized his dream of the medieval world in stone. He made the past live again – a background to historical events – by rebuilding the Vincigliata castle, of which nothing remained but ruins. The whole amazing operation involved 280 hectares of land, 120 of them being turned into woodland. Within the outer walls, trapezoidal in shape and with a perimeter of almost 400 metres, he built a central tower, a second look-out tower, courtyard, loggia and cloister, quite freely reproduced in a manner that combined the desire to create the true likeness of a feudal dwelling with an ideal reconstruction of a whole way of life. Temple Leader's dream of recreating the atmosphere and surroundings of an era he had studied and loved, was realized in his work of creating and reconstructing buildings, ornamentations, furnishings, original masterpieces and faithful copies. Giuseppe Fancelli was the architect of this re-creation, while interior decorations were carried out by Gaetano Bianchi and the stone-carvers, Davide and Attilio Giustini and Angiolo Marucelli.

Giuseppe Fancelli had earlier designed an English-style wood for the Querceto villa at San Martino a Mensola for Marchese Riccardo Strozzi, and with his assistance and that of his friend the engineer Alessandro Papini, an expert on hydraulics and outdoor installations, Temple Leader installed a plantation of clumps of cypresses mixed with pines and ilexes and combined with the existing deciduous trees, creating a new landscape by mixing northern varieties with local ones. In 1867 Temple Leader bought an old quarry and converted it into a swimming-pool, taking the water from the Mensola stream which flows past on its course down to the valley. Stone walls and natural grottoes alternated with trees and plants to meet the requirements of an English garden; rocks were carefully positioned to "lend movement to the scene". In 1888 and 1893 Queen Victoria visited the Vincigliata park at Maiano as Temple Leader's guest.[28]

Other examples of neo-medieval conversions in the nearby hills, albeit on a much smaller scale, include Torre del Gallo on the Arcetri hill, a late reconstruction carried out by the restorer and antiquarian Stefano Bardini who in embarked on this twenty-year complete rebuilding operation in 1902, eventually transforming the building into a neo-Gothic castle. Bardini was responsible for similar changes at the Castello di Marignolle. Among other examples which should be included in this pot-pourri of different styles is Castel del Poggio, restored at the close of the 19th century by Giuseppe Castellucci, *"a happy fusion of the architectural remains of a confused aesthetic and war-like medievalism and the decorative pomp of a deliberately dark Renaissance"*.[29] Similar instances include Montauto, Villa di Torre Galli, Villa Franceschi and Villa Roti Michelozzi, before arriving at Coppedè's inventive reconstructions for the villas of the Pagani and the Contri di Mezzaratta. These outcomes reveal, like the town houses, the fashion for the simulated revival of a period that was both historically and stylistically admired in a contradictory way, according to a notion of what was "Florentine". The *Florentinitas* derived from the cultural myth of what the city embodied, or inspired by a belated sense of guilt, fuelled by the heavily critical reaction of the foreign press when the city destroyed its earliest, truly medieval building, the old market.[30]

Much less numerous, though representative of a certain taste and culture, are the newly built villas on the outskirts of the city, and here too the majority were due to the arrival of foreigners.

The Villa Demidoff in San Donato in Polverosa was one of the most interesting examples of a complete rebuilding operation, alas now destroyed. The San Donato villa provided an unusual break from the typical pattern of the grand residence, both in the character of its commissioner and in the extent of the work and its situation. The estate of San Donato in Polverosa, the property of the monks of Santa Croce, was bought between 1825 and 1827 by Nicholas Demidoff, an enormously rich Russian who had first settled in Paris but moved to Florence in search of a milder climate. The land where the villa was to stand was flat and damp, highly suited to cure the owner's ill heath, and the building work was speedily carried out, on Giovan Battista Silvestri's designs, a vast complex which included a villa, stables, stalls, open loggia and an outdoor theatre, all surrounded by spacious grounds. After Nicholas's death in 1828, his son Anatolio, a restless and lively cosmopolitan

[28] F. Baldry, op. cit., p. 99.

[29] G. Morolli, *Firenze degli stranieri. Architetture dell'Ottocento immaginate per un contesto europeo*, in *L'idea di Firenze*, ed. M. Bossi and L. Tonini, Florence 1989, p. 295.

[30] The destruction of the city's oldest quarter provoked heavy criticism, particularly from the foreign residents in Florence, for whom Vernon Lee was a spokesman. She was a sophisticated writer, living in the Villa Palmerino at Maiano, who wrote impassioned reports for *The Times* newspaper. In Augustus J. C. Hare's widely distributed guide to Florence (by 1907 it was in its seventh edition) we read: "*This most interesting part of Florence was destroyed by its ignorant and short sighted Municipality in 1889 . . . the ancient quarter of the Mercato Vecchio, when cleaned, restored and put in order, would have offered the faithful image of a medieval town, as Rome and Pompei are samples of the Latin towns. Visitors could have walked in the old genuine Florentine city, in those very streets which Dante trod, in that city where the Guelph and Ghibelline factions fought against each other for centuries, the birthplace of many Florentines illustrious in science, letters, arms; where so many conspiracies were plotted and where one might say, without exaggeration, that every wall, every stone, recorded a page of Florentine history,*" adding that "*Piazza Vittorio Emanuele, which has replaced it, would be second-rate in Birmingham*". A. J. C. Hare, *Florence*, London 1907. See D. Lamberini, *Herbert Horne, architetto restauratore e membro dell'Associazione per la difesa di Firenze antica*, in *Herbert Percy Horne*, op. cit., pp. 49–85.

[31] F. Bisogni, *I Demidoff in Toscana*, in *L'idea di Firenze*, op. cit., pp. 67–84.

Left: View of the Villa di San Donato in an engraving by G. B. Silvestri around 1830; the villa after the alterations made by Anatolio and Paolo Demidoff; the Odeon of San Donato by G.B. Silvestri; a salon of the villa San Donato; the villa after the Second World War.

figure, collector and philanthropist, honoured by the Grand Duke with the title of Prince of San Donato, turned part of the villa into a silk-weaving factory to provide work for the many poor of the area. Extremely large sums of money were invested and lost in this charitable venture and in 1846 the building was reconverted into a handsome villa to house the owner's highly valuable art collections. We can thus divide the villa's history into three stages: initial building, conversion into a factory and reconversion into a villa. In fact, during the dismantling of the silk factory, Anatolio Demidoff had fresh work carried out on the house with the help of Luigi del Moro, Giuseppe Martelli and Niccolò Matas. Only a few traces of this interesting complex remain today (the triumphal arch at the entrance and the *Tempietto* with a hemispherical dome), having been engulfed by the building speculation that hit the Novoli area during the 1960s. The villa had a long façade spanned, on the first floor, by Ionic pillars flanking large arched windows, blind at the top, above which stood a triangular pediment dominated by the great dome rising behind it, gleaming with gold and decorated with paintings by Carlo Morelli of scenes with Cupid and Psyche. The interior held a series of unexpectedly varied rooms in French and oriental styles, ornamented by finely wrought works from the Barbetti workshop, wood carvings, leather decorations and a wealth of ornamentation of the most varied kind. The land was developed into a park: gardens full of rare plants, zoological gardens containing all kinds of animals and enormous greenhouses for exotic plants.[31]

Half villa, half city palazzo and surrounded by gardens, Villa Favard was built on the banks of the Arno in 1857 and proved one of Giuseppe Poggi's most exacting works, a crossroads between the old city and the new Cascine quarter. The work appears to have been inspired by 16th-century models, interpreted in an accomplished manner in its ordered planimetric layout and the design of the façades. The face overlooking the Arno has a central loggia formed by a double row of columns holding arched windows flanked by windows with pediments; the opposite face has a projecting covered entranceway to shelter arriving carriages. The sumptuous interior was decorated with a great variety and profusion of stucco ornamentations and paintings by the most fashionable artists of the day, including Gatti and Bandinelli (frescoes), Mussini (encaustic work), Pucci, Mazzoli and Ramelli for the mouldings and Barbetti and Morini for the furnishings.

A similar situation is presented by a building once owned by Adriano Righi on the confines of the old and newly-built area of the city. This house was built not in the true sense of the villa, apart from its "isolated" position in respect of the surrounding buildings and its altered character, due to the ring roads that now circle the city. This house was built between 1869 and 1870 on the corner of Via Manzoni and Via Leopardi, and in 1877 it became the property of Giuseppina Augusta Garner Graham. The villa-palazzo is surrounded by a garden and a series of large arched windows on the main façade resemble Poggi's style, but it suffered an inappropriate work of renovation which entirely altered its character. Another late 19th-century example on the ring road is Villa Strozzi, formerly Villa Vittoria, opposite the Fortezza da Basso, designed by Girolamo Passeri between 1886 and 1891 and transformed in the mid-1960s into a conference and exhibition centre.

The opening of the hillside avenue, built by Poggi between 1864 and 1865, was a decisive steps towards the expansion of Florence as a capital city, introducing the idea of a panoramic route climbing to a large square with a belvedere. In 1906 Guido Carocci described its course as follows: "*many buildings stand on the first stretch of the splendid avenue of the Colli. We are in the midst of the truly modern, as we see from the villas, small houses and numbers of elegant buildings embellished with charming gardens which almost form a new quarter in this delightful area, occupied particularly by numerous foreign families.*"[32]

The opening of this avenue was to have encouraged the emergence of a new luxury quarter, suitable for building houses for court dignitaries, the new political classes, or internationally renowned artists, foreign representatives and legations. However, the brevity of Florence's position as capital city had the effect of drastically reducing building programmes.

Among the more interesting buildings in the "hillside quarter", between Viale di Poggio Imperiale, Viale Machiavelli and Viale Torricelli, also known as the Tivoli[33] area, is the Villa Oppenheim. The villa was built between 1870 and 1871 and designed by Pietro Comparini Rossi, Poggi's pupil and collaborator. The building is in the form of a compact cube, the layout revolving around a central rotunda which gives access to the main rooms on the ground floor. A row of giant Ionic half-columns and pilasters appears on the principal façades, slightly projecting and clearly derived

[32] G. P. Trotta, *Ville fiorentine dell'Ottocento*, Florence 1994. The stretch of land between Viale dei Colli and the two side roads leading to Viale del Poggio Imperiale, part of the old farm "delle Monache", was bought by the Gelazio Lazzeri and Riccardo Ciampi company, contracted for the work along the whole hillside avenue, later ceded to the city on the understanding that the company could construct the necessary roads and build new houses. The land was divided into building lots between Viale Michelangelo, Via Dante da Castiglione and Via Farinata, at the junction with Viale di Poggio Imperiale. The original group were to become the homes and studios of English and American artists and among the earliest purchasers were some leading American sculptors. Hiram Powers had a house at number 10, and extended his property to include the adjoining lot, later occupied by his heirs. In 1868 Thomas Ball lived in a villa that was probably built by the same company, with a large studio, use of which he offered to visitors; among these were the American sculptors William Couper and Daniel Chester French, who lived at number 6 Via Farinata.

[33] The area takes its name from the Tivoli, a restaurant and beer-garden and a place for socialite gatherings, the concession for which was given to the Messeri brothers. The building was designed by Giuseppe Poggi with garden structures by Giacomo Roster, and opened in 1869.

Right: Villa Strozzi, opposite the Fortezza da basso; Villa Oppenheim; the rotunda of Villa Oppenheim.

from Poggi, while the opulent interior was the work of Edoardo Gioia of Turin who took over from Comparini in 1871, introducing lavish decorations in different styles for each room, an example of the more exuberant eclectic French style.

Among those late examples, which overstep the confines of the 19th century, while maintaining a conceptual continuity that fully justifies their inclusion in a chapter devoted to the development of the 19th-century Florentine villa, we cannot possibly omit Villa I Tatti and Villa Le Balze, whose gardens we have mentioned in Chapter Four.

The most interesting aspect of the evolution of the ideology of the villa is the residential role it began to assume during the 19th century, a symbol of the emergent bourgeoisie and aristocratic or privileged townspeople. In these instances, it should be noted that any relationship with the surrounding land was limited to a garden or park, an ornament to the place of residence.

This accentuation of the "residential" and recreational nature of these new hillside villas, where a lively society followed its own pursuits, became the prevailing if not invariable pattern and this also explains the transformation of agricultural land into gardens and parks to ornament the handsome villas. This process, as we have seen, took place in concomitance with the transformation of pre-existing buildings and is, in our view, one of the most distinctive aspects of the impact that the institution of the villa had on the land during the course of the 19th century. It may be true that stylistic innovations in architectural designs were reduced to questions of prevailing "taste", sometimes favouring traditional neo-16th-century features, as in Poggi's work, neo-medieval ones for rebuilding castles, or a patchwork of many, but it is the transformation of the land which must be considered the most significant outcome of these events. The creation of romantic parks and gardens covering large expanses of land was the final stage in the evolution of the traditional rural structure, still bound by financial conditions established in the Florentine countryside four centuries earlier. These changes, while varying as regards both commissioners and their reference models, did not yet create a break in the continuity of the pattern of settlement and use of land which revolved around the villa. This break was to come later and particularly during the second half of the 20th century with, on the one hand, the decline in agriculture and, on the other, the increasing pressure of the city.

A view from villa Topaia

PART TWO

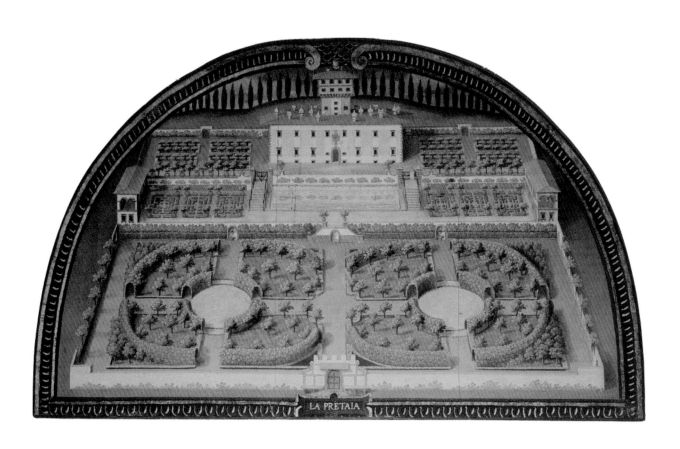

CHAPTER SIX

The Shape of the Landscape

This area comprises the land lying between Florence and Sesto which rises from the plain and climbs up the wooded slopes of Monte Morello, bounded on two sides by the Terzolle and Zambra streams. A first strip of land runs along the plain to an average depth of about 200 metres, bordered to the south by the road linking the two towns; this is followed by a strip of low hillside (climbing increasingly steeply) which stretches from Via di Castello to the edge of the woods, on average about 1200 metres wide, rising from a height of 75 metres to 300 metres above sea level. This strip is followed by a further band of higher hillside which at 600 metres meets the mountain slopes.

The use of the soil on these stretches of land varies according to altitude. The first strip is under cultivation; the land in the second strip is also cultivated, with some encroachments of woodland; the third is woodland. This hillside position could rely on the supplies of water carried by the numerous streams flowing down from the peaks of Monte Morello, the principal ones being the Zambra, the Termini and the Terzolle, and their offshoots, which once fed the many water-mills in the area.

The present road system retraces the old paths in the foothills: a principal road running lengthwise, and a secondary system forking off at intervals towards the hillside. The roads follow the hillside at various levels, largely retracing the often tortuous course of roads used in Roman times, as we see from the place-names, Quarto, Quinto, Sesto (named after the various milestones). The network has remained little changed, as we see from a study of the old system of roads in a valuable series of maps drawn up by the Magistratura dei Capitani di Parte Guelfa in the late 16th century. What changes have occurred chiefly involved developing the major longitudinal roads (links between urban centres and routes for the area's recreational opportunities) while letting the majority of the secondary access roads fall into disuse, now impassable or used only as farm tracks.

The longitudinal roads include, aside from Via Pratese and Via di Castello bordering the strip of plain, Via della Castellina

Giusto Utens, *Petraia*, 1599

which, together with Via della Topaia as far as the junction with Via di Carmignanello, mark the network of lower roads running along the foot of the hillside. Roads branching off on the first level include, from east to west, Gore, Quarto, Petraia, Brache, T. Gaddi, Mula and Strozzi roads; Via di Palastreto, del Bronzino, della Fonte, dell'Alberaccio and di Malafrasca in the second strip. The area contained in the first two strips is more heavily built-up, principally along the main roads, while in the third strip the preponderance of woodland over arable land (due to the morphology of the rougher ground) led, not only to the building of fewer roads, but also to a reduced number of habitations.

Clusters of buildings developed along Via di Castello, and these included the stately villas of estates with agricultural land on the plain, today mostly converted or demolished. The first road along the foot of the hillside, at an altitude of between 70 and 90 metres, forms the main axis for the grand villas which were built at fairly regular intervals on sites leading off one side of Via Maestra. Starting from the Terzolle border, Villa La Quiete had an approach road about 500 metres from the originally tree-lined avenue which led from Via Maestra to Villa il Chiuso. Via della Petraia is at almost the same distance, followed by the avenue leading to Villa di Castello, the Via di Bellagio connecting the villa of the same name to Via Taddeo Gaddi, in line with the entrance to Villa Baldini. Via della Mula, which leads to the Torrigiani and Strozzino villas as well as Villa della Mula is at similar distance. The Pozzino, Gondo, Terrio, Poggiochiaro and Fontenuova villas are reached from Via Giovanni da San Giovanni, which joins Via di Castello on a level with Villa Fontenuova. At between 150 and 200 metres are other villas which have no direct access to the valley road but are connected to the system of transverse roads on the upper level. Via della Topaia provides the link for the Malafrasca, Belvedere, Topaia, Casale, Torre, Covacchia, Servadio, Palastreto and Moreni villas, the latter being at the crossroads of Via F.lli Roselli and Via della Castellina.

This was the setting for various kinds of building and varying types of relationship with the countryside, depending on the different historical origins. In the case of the more complex organization of pre-19th-century establishments, a landowner's villa and estate, the residence's mixed use was emphasized in terms of both form and structure by the inclusion of particular features such as gardens, parks, tree-lined avenues in an increased spatial network. This occurs similarly, in terms of the landscape, in pre-19th-century establishments with a simpler working arrangement

(owner's villa and farm), which have a different typological and situational layout for the owner's house and the farmhouse. In buildings constructed during the late 19th-century, there was a repetition of earlier established models with the addition, to the existing farm buildings, of an owner's residence, sometimes attached to the farmhouse.

The historical continuity of the countryside's occupation and the particular political, economic and cultural conditions which gave rise to this continuity produced a pattern of land development which was in many ways unique, an organized architectural design, as complex and articulated as that in the city.

The flow of city capital into the outlying districts, was related to the consolidation of the share-cropping system and the subsequent division of land into small farms, which formed the basis of this full integration of town and country. The farm, the *podere*, was the most rational means of organizing agricultural production. The continuation of its essential components (farmhouse, arable land planted with olives and vines, often accompanied by some pasture and woodland) is attested to by the vast number of archival documents which confirm the prevalence of share-cropping as the system for running farms. Apart from physical descriptions of the properties, the documents also carry the names of share-cropping families. Landowners' villas serving as organizational centres of an agricultural estate occur most frequently on the land near the city, providing a "second house" which could even be visited on a daily basis, and in the 15th century this was one of the principal investments for the capital of the aspiring merchant class.

Greater stress is laid on the formal aspects of the complex of the Medici villas of Petraia and of Castello, which is in the middle band of the area we have described. This large complex, when examined from the viewpoint of how its presence and evolution affected the area's structure, as a reflection of the changes in farming life, exemplifies the well-considered rational order which, albeit with a number of variations, was to remain a recurring characteristic of Renaissance operations of urbanization in the Florence area. Furthermore, the Castello estate also encouraged other more modest ventures, ones which gave this countryside its particular and highly personal character.

The Medici property of Castello constitutes, in its entirety, a remarkable example of rural organization, with an overall plan which concerned the scale of the buildings and the aspect of the land. The structure of the highly elaborate

121

agricultural landscape forms the background for the monumental complex of the stately villa. Villas, gardens, park areas, farmlands, precise plans of cultivation, roads, choice of crops and the situation of farmhouses were all the result of a combined process developed over the course of centuries, never substantially swerving from its Renaissance beginnings. Today, despite the scars produced by the invasion of recent large-scale building developments, it is still possible to decipher the rural framework which was established back in the 15th century.

Aerial view of the Villa Medici and its garden at Castello

CHAPTER SEVEN

The History of the Area

The Medici family's operations in the countryside around Florence followed, albeit on a considerable larger scale, a similar course to that of the bourgeoisie which we have described, if it is true, as it states in the 1427 land register, that the goods and possessions of Giovanni, Cosimo the Elder's father, were valued at 180,000 florins, making him the richest man in Florence after Palla Strozzi.

In 1477, when work began on the Castello estate, the Medici acquired the most important of its country properties in the immediate vicinity of the city, and this led to a change in the character of the area itself, both from a socio-economic point of view and a physical one. This was the time of a new shift in social classes, with the ousting of the bourgeois-merchant classes, the leaders of the first colonizing movement, in favour of the families of those forming part, later on, of the Grand Duke's bureaucracy.

The area around Castello was directly caught up in the desire of those moving up the social scale to invest in agricultural property and extra-urban villas, since owning a villa in the same area as the prince conferred a further rise in status. We should look here at the property transfers of some villas to the Grand Duke's secretaries: the Casale villa to Lorenzo Pagni, the Covacchia villa to Ippolito Bassetti; Querciola to Antonio Tarchiani, Cosimo III's secretary, and to Bartolomeo Corsini, the court poet. The same occurred with the court physicians: the Quarto villa to the Pasquali family; Gondo to Francesco Redi. A whole series of courtiers, writers and artists gravitated to the surrounding houses. Giuliano Ricci lived in what in the 19th century was to become Villa Amalia, Benedetto Varchi and Scipione Ammirato, Pier Francesco Giambullari and Giovanni Bilivert made the lodges of the Grand Ducal villas their more or less fixed abodes (Topaia, in the first instance, and Poggio Secco in the second).

It is interesting to follow, with the aid of archival documents, the course of the development of the Grand Duke's estate and the changes which occurred both in terms of size (purchases, transfers, divisions, etc.) and of physical aspect (changes in crops, new roads, elimination of farmland to create gardens and parks).

Castello was first owned by Pier Francesco de' Medici's sons, Lorenzo and Giovanni, who bought it from the prominent Della Stufa family.[1] An examination of the declarations for the land register, in chronological order, allows us to follow how the original nucleus was changed through a series of acquisitions. The 1498 land registry declaration states: *"A gentleman's residence at Castello with a fish-breeding pool, at a place called Vivaio with a farm belonging to the house, bordered by road and track, worked by Simone di Mariotto. A farm in the same borough as the above, abutting on road, path and on the others, worked by Jacopo di Mateo di Nanni. A farm at the said house, abutting on the road and Mariotto Carnesecchi, and on the others. A worker's house with a dovecote and 40 stiora of arable land, abutting on the road and Mariotto Steccuti; worked by Jacopo di Matteo di Nanni"*.[2] A later declaration of Cosimo's property made in 1534 by Giovanni de' Medici, apart from the properties already listed, shows an increase in the property around the villa. Indeed, this declaration tells us that Cosimo, having inherited the property from his father, carried out a series of purchases to augment the agricultural land around the villa, which was given his close attention in subsequent years. These new acquisitions concerned a farm *"a place called Pozzino"*, which does not reappear on subsequent documents; a farm with a house for owner and worker *"a place called Topaia"*; an inn on Via Maestra and two pieces of land to the south.[3]

Changes which took place between 1498 and 1534 would suggest that the aim was to enlarge and consolidate the estate around the Castello villa. This was related to the consolidation of the institutional role of its proprietor at this period, which led, after the fall of the Florentine Republic and exile, to Cosimo's assumption of State power.

In 1538 Cosimo embarked on major restructuring works which affected not only the building but also the whole aspect of the surrounding land. The architect Tribolo soon replaced Piero da San Casciano as master of operations and, in his *Life of Tribolo*, Vasari includes a detailed description of the original project for the design of the villa and garden. If Tribolo's grandiose project had been fully realized it would have been one of the most magnificent examples of mannerist remodelling in Tuscany. Alongside operations aimed at beautifying and perfecting Cosimo's favourite country residence (particularly the garden which, on Benedetto Varchi's suggestion, focused on repeated references to the glories of the House of Medici), all the agricultural land underwent major reorganization, being planted with orchards and vineyards; they covered the land beyond the actual garden,

[1] In 1470 Andrea di Lotteringo della Stufa declared *"a farm with a gentleman's palazzo at Castello, a place called Al Vivaio"*. A.S.F. Archivio delle Decime, Campione del Catasto di San Giovannni, Leon d'Oro of 1470, map 161.

[2] A.S.F. Archivio delle Decime, Campione dei Secolari, divided into *popoli* (similar to English parishes or boroughs), Quarter of Santa Maria Novella, 1498 I, map 81, see C. O. Tosi, *Castello nel Comune di San Fiorentino*, op. cit., p. 2.

[3] A.S.F. Campione dei Secolari, Quarter of Santa Maria Novella, in G. Gobbi, *Documenti per una storia del territorio: interventi granducali nell'area fiorentina*, in "Bollettino degli Ingegneri", 7, Florence 1978, pp. 7–13.

[4] Planting these vineyards (which were to produce a muscatel praised in verse by Francesco Redi in his *Bacco in Toscana*: *"Ma lodato, celebrato, coronato / sia l'eroe che nelle vigne / di Petraia e di Castello / piantò primo il moscatello"*) involved importing cuttings from Spain, the Canaries and France, see C. O. Tosi, op. cit., p. 8.

[5] C. Acidini Luchinat, G. Galletti, op. cit., p. 9.

[6] A letter of 9 October 1544 from Lorenzo Pagni, administrator of the Castello buildings, to Pierfrancesco Riccio, the Grand Duke's secretary, states: *"We have ordered four pounds of tallow candles to illuminate my tower at Petraia"*. D. R. Wright, *The Medici Villa at Olmo a Castello: Its History and Iconography*, Princeton 1976.

Right: Plan of the vineyards at Castello (A.S.F. Piante Scrittoio RR Possessioni, Vol. II, c. 5); project for creating two poderi (A.S.F. Piante Scrittoio RR Possessioni n. 551); the church of Boldrone Monastery and the corridor connecting it with La Quiete from the sketchbook of Diacinto Marmi 1632 (G.D.S.U. 5049A); plan of the podere della Querciola and the Osteria di Castello (ibid., 5048A); plan and elevation of the Osteria di Castello (A.S.F. Piante Scrittoio RR Possessioni, Vol. II, c. 14).

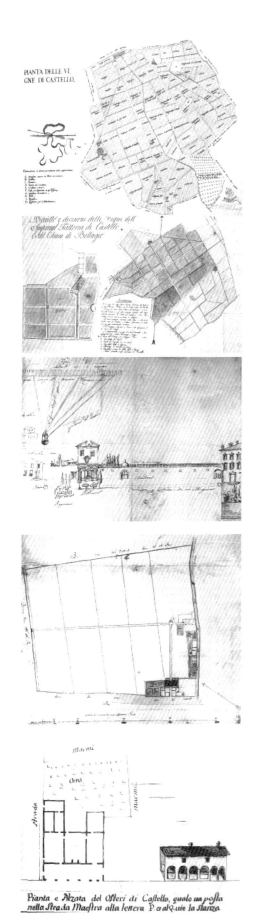

PIANTA DELLE VI
GNE DI CASTELLO.

Veduti e dicumeni delle Vigni dell
Imperial Fattoria di Castello
All Chiuso di Bellagio

mermi

Pianta e Alzata del Osteri di Castello, quale un posta
nella Strada Maestra alla lettera P. er al Q. uie la Stanza

the so-called *Chiuso di Bellagio*, in the area lying between the San Michele church, Villa della Petraia and the present Via della Topaia, as far as the estate's northern boundary.[4]

A document that is of fundamental importance to a knowledge of the structure and organization of the estate, and of its composition, in the mid-16th century is the *Campione di Beni di Cosimo I* (Inventory of the Goods and Properties of Cosimo I), in the 1566 and 1568 versions in the Florence State Archives. In the 1566 version the Petraia villa appears among the properties belonging to the Castello estate. There are contrasting views on the arrival of the Petraia villa among the Medici properties.[5] However, there is no doubt that the former ancient property of Palla di Noferi di Palla Strozzi, declared in the land register in 1427 as *"a property called Petraia in the parish of San Michele at Castello which is a ruined noble residence with workers' houses and olive presses with CXL stiora of land, part vineyard and part arable and planted with olives"*, in 1544 belonged to Cosimo I.[6]

The 1566 *Campione di Beni* of Cosimo I declared ownership of a *"farm in the place called Petraia with house for Signore and worker"*. The villa is registered as the house for Signore, accompanied by a farm (corresponding to the land to the north and east of the villa, later turned into vineyard). The 1568 inventory relating to the Castello property, is divided into *Nota di beni sottoposti alla fattoria di Castello*, which includes the farms of Querciola, Viottola, Vivaio, Steccuto or Arco, and Bellagio, as well as numerous houses assigned to farm workers, and a *Nota di beni sotto la Petraia* which includes three farms and some pieces of scattered land, houses for farm workers and a forge.

This separation in the 1568 document is probably due to the fact this was the year Cosimo divided the property between his two sons, Francesco I, the future Grand Duke, who received the villa and its appurtenances, and Cardinal Ferdinando, who came into the Petraia property. Both expanded the properties by buying extra land but particularly Ferdinando, who inherited the Castello property after his brother's death (19 October 1587), reuniting it with his property, and further enlarged it by buying the Colatoio farm, north of the church of San Michele, and, in 1576, land bought from the Sisters of San Piero to the west of Petraia, turned into a bird-netting area.

Following in the family footsteps, Ferdinando I further extended his already rich network of extra-urban villas in a series of operations which taken together suggest a specific general plan. He was responsible for the transformation of the Petraia villa, carried out between 1587 and 1589 by Raffaello di Zanobi di Pagno. But the cardinal had already shown his interest in the property earlier, as shown by documents recording the use of slave labour between 1573 and 1574 to produce the terraced banks in the garden.[7]

On the death of Ferdinando, Petraia with its annexes and farms passed to a younger son, Don Lorenzo, who bought another adjacent farm and introduced changes to the house and garden, work being directed by Parigi. This is when the great banked avenue was built linking the villa with the road below, and when the cypress wood to the north of the villa was enlarged. On Don Lorenzo's death, the Petraia returned

[7] S. Butters, *Le Cardinal Ferdinand de Médicis*, in *La Villa Médicis*, ed. A. Chastel and P. Morel, Rome 1991.

[8] A.S.F. Regie Possessioni, n. 725, Contratti, Vol. IX, cc. 43–45.

Left: A view of the city of Florence from the garden of Villa Petraia at the beginning of the 20th century.
Below: A projet by Leopoldo Veneziani to transform the casa di Fattoria at Castello 1818. (A.S.F. Piante Scrittoio RR Possessioni, n. 559).

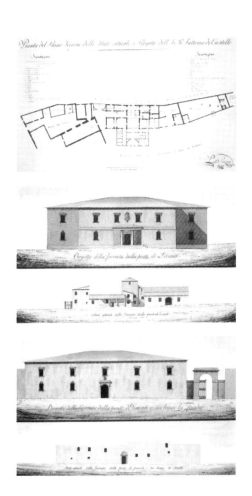

to the management of the Castello estate, and so it remained until the property was finally broken up. In 1618 the property was expanded by the addition of the nearby Rinieri villa, bought by Cosimo II for 4400 *scudi* to increase the annexes of his residence. The building and the agricultural property remained in the possession of the Medici family for a brief period only. On Cosimo's death in 1620 part of the farm was ceded to Cardinal Giovan Carlo, while the villa was ceded to Robert Dudley, Duke of Northumberland, who rebuilt the port of Livorno, a task which occupied him until his death in 1649. The following year Ferdinando II sold the villa and two farms to Pietro Cervieri, as shown by the following contract drawn up on 18 October 1650: "*Pietro Cervieri most respectfully entreats V.A.S. to graciously allow him to buy the Rinieri villa, with the seventy-seven stiora of land annexed to it including arable, vineyard, orchards, with bird-netting areas, fountains, meadows, gardens and such matters: and other possessions and particularly asks Your Highness to be so gracious as to reserve the water of the spring solely for use in the said villa, the villa and lands situated in the parish of San Michele at Castello and within its boundaries for the sum of two thousand two hundred and fifty ducats and seven lire per scudo and all taxes and expenses of Your Highness the said price to be paid when the contract is executed with those provisions and conditions to satisfy the contractor which Your Highness has been pleased to concede on similar occasions.*"[8]

The property holdings at the time of Grand Duke Cosimo III, towards the close of the 17th century, are recorded not only by an inventory of goods and properties but also by a precious series of illustrated records in the State Archives in Florence entitled: *Descrizione geografica di tutti I beni che nel presente stato gode e possiede il S.mo Granduca nostro S.re nella sua Fattoria di Castello, fatta l'anno 1697*. Apart from a general map of the whole complex of villas, gardens, vineyards and farms it includes illustrations of the layouts of the individual farms, identifies the crops in the various sections, presents a plan of the buildings of the farm concerned, and a perspective view at the foot of each sheet.

Indeed, the importance of these documents, whose fineness of detail reflects the precise work of contemporary cartographers, lies in the value of the evidence they supply concerning agricultural structure: details of the farming system, with illustration of the cultivated plots showing their various sizes and outlines, and of the buildings involved in agricultural production. This documentation shows that while Cosimo III was Grand Duke the *Fattoria di Castello* was composed of:

PODERE DEL VIVAIO

This is shown extending south of the Villa di Castello, cut in two by the tree-lined avenue which leads to the villa from Via Maestra. A farm road, crossing the avenue, leads to the modestly sized one-storey farmhouse, with a front portico, continuing as far as Via Quintigiana, which marks the confines of the farm and of the property. On the opposite side a barrier of trees marks the boundary with the Querciola farm, the property of Sig. Diacinto Marmi. The Querciola farm was part of the property of Cosimo I, as is shown by the *Nota di Beni sottoposti alla Fattoria di Castello*, and was ceded to Marmi in 1669, together with the adjacent Ragnaia and eight plots of land south of Via Maestra, in exchange for a farm which Marmi owned, included in the Calappiano estate (cf. A.S.F., Vol. 37, n. 68; see illustration). On the same sheet is a drawing of the "Osteria di Castello", an inn on the other side of Via Maestra which formed part of the estate, along with other small lodgings for farm-workers. The farm took its name from the great fish-breeding pools in the villa's forecourt.[9]

PODERE DELLO STECCUTO E DELL'ARCO

In the inventory of Cosimo I's properties this is described as *"a farm with house for gentleman and worker at the place called Stechuto all'Arco"*, while the 17th-century map shows two quite separate farms, although they appear on one sheet. Later the name *"all'Arco"* disappeared and the two farms became merged into a single unit called Steccuto. The gentlemanly residence is not shown on the map and was probably one of the two turned into *"house for worker"*. The Arco farmhouse has a rather unusual plan with two separate blocks joined by a central portico, and a dovecote tower at the west end of the building. The Steccuto house sides the approach to the courtyard which leads to a transverse tree-lined path, and there is an enormous fish-breeding pool in front of the building. On the same sheet is a drawing of land belonging to the farms, called *"le Terre del piano"* (lands on the plain). In fact, hillside farms in this region often had some fields elsewhere, usually south of Via Maestra. There is also a perspective view of the *"Case del Poggio"*, on the northern boundary of Steccuto, occupied by farm workers, corresponding with what is today the centre of Poggio Secco.

[9] These were later filled in on the orders of Pietro Leopoldo of Lorraine. In *Protocollo dello Scrittoio delle Reali Fabbriche del dì 19 Agosto 1773*, in reference to works of renovation considered necessary for the visits of the Prince and the Grand Dukes to the Petraia and Castello villas, we read: *"Once it has been decided . . . there remains the work on the conduits at Castello, and the two fish-ponds on the lawn of this villa which, quite apart from being in no way beautiful, spoil the air of the place, which would otherwise be excellent"* (A.S.F. Scrittoio delle Reali Fabbriche 526). As Tosi tells us, operations in 1904 to erect a monument to Umberto I uncovered walls *"which still had the iron rings used to secure the boats kept for fishing. On the same occasion a fully vaulted conduit full of pure fresh water was discovered, forty centimetres in diameter, running from west to east parallel with the villa,"* C. O. Tosi, op. cit., p. 6.

Right: Podere del Vivaio (A.S.F. Piante Scrittoio RR Possessioni, Vol. II, c. 14); *Poderi dello Stechuto e dell'Arco* (ibid., c. 11).

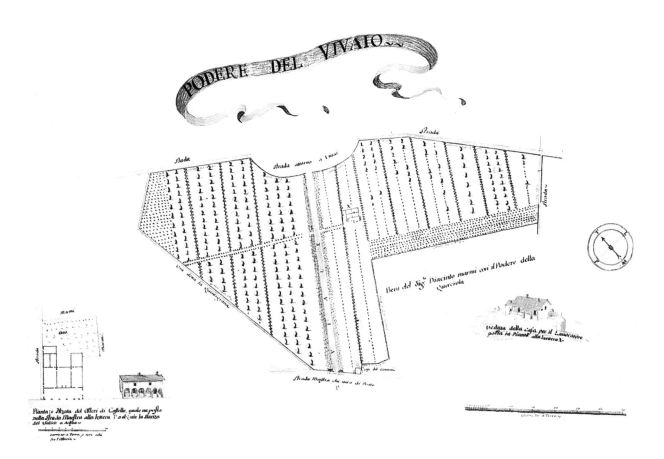

PODERE DEL VIVAIO

PODERI DELLO STECHVTO E DEL ARCO

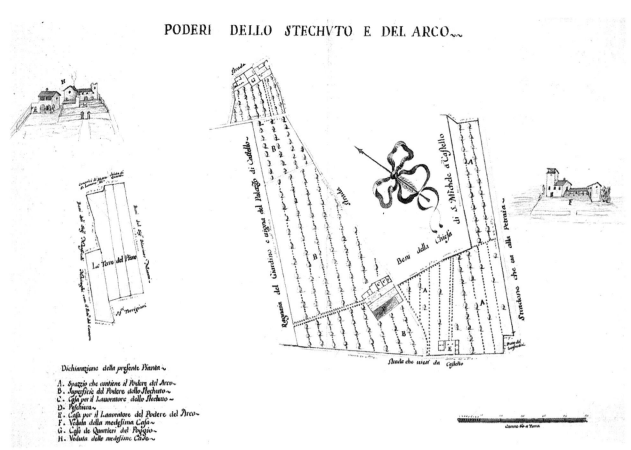

Dichiarazione della presente Pianta

A. Spazio che contiene il Podere del Arco
B. Superficie del Podere dello Stechuto
C. Casa per il Lavoratore dello Stechuto
D. Peschiera
E. Casa per il Lavoratore del Podere del Arco
F. Veduta della medesima Casa
G. Case de Quartieri del Poggio
H. Veduta delle medesime Case

PODERE DELLA RAGNAIA

This farm is shown adjoining the garden of Villa della Petraia and is divided lengthwise by a *ragnaia* (a densely planted area used for snaring birds). The farmhouse stands on the southern boundary of the land and has an L-shaped plan with a loggia on two sides. Two-thirds of the farmland was later transformed into a park by Grand Duke Leopoldo of Lorraine.

PODERE DELLA TOPAIA

The farm consists of two detached and modest plots of land (one is identifiable on the general planimetric map of the Covacchia lands and is marked with the letter R), a house for a worker and for "*the guard*". There is an interesting view of the villa which Cosimo III transformed into his "house of delights" and provided, in accordance with his interest in botany and fruit-growing, with a garden planted as an orchard with dwarf fruit trees.

PODERE DELLA COVACCHIA

This complex consists of a gentleman's residence and a worker's house and farm. It appears for the first time in the 1697 *Descrizione* of Medici properties. During the rule of Cosimo III it was used by his secretary Ippolito Bassetti. The layout of the land is well-organized, with a tree-lined avenue running between the villa and the chapel, which stands in a grove of trees bordering the woodland to the west. The bird-netting areas border two small courses of water which divide the various areas under cultivation and the woodland. The interesting design of the villa is probably the result of additions made to an original nucleus with a dovecote tower.

Above: The house of the *Podere della Ragnaia*, detail from map (A.S.F. Piante Scrittoio RR Possessioni, Vol. II, c. 9)
Below: The house of the *Podere della Covachia*, detail from map (A.S.F. Piante Scrittoio RR Possessioni, Vol. II, c. 13).
Next page: *Podere della Ragnaia*; details of *Podere della Topaia* and *Podere della Covachia*.

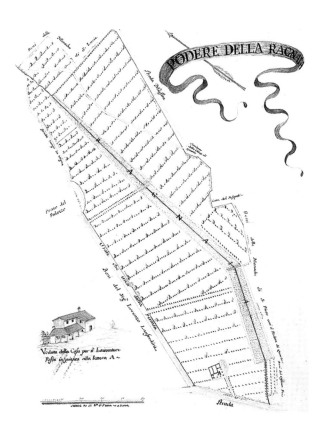

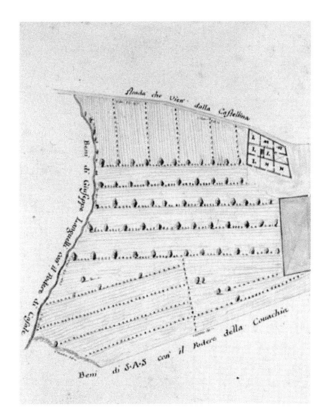

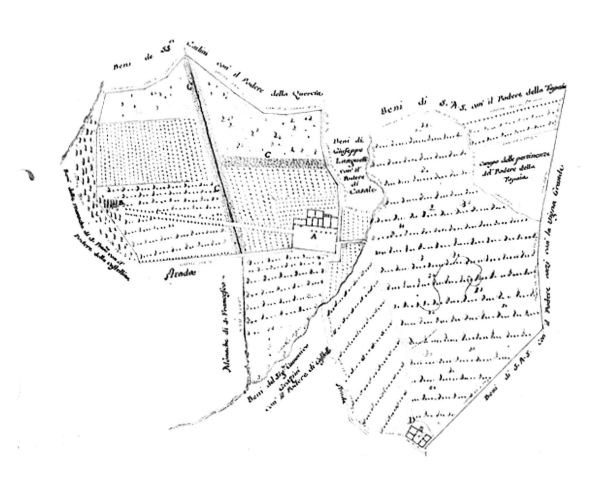

131

PODERE DEL TERRIO

This property consists of a master's and a worker's house, and plots of land bordering the road to Castellina and the property of the Sisters of San Francesco. We have no record of the date that it became part of the Medici estate, and it does not appear on the general planimetric map of the property. The remaining land of this estate, with the exception of the farms above, was occupied by vineyards, a particular feature of this property.

With the extinction of the Medici line and the establishment of the House of Lorraine, most of the landed properties passed to their successors and it was almost certainly this shift in ownership which gave rise to the surveys and technically accomplished maps which provide a more accurate image of the properties that were accumulated over the centuries. Among the estate maps in the State Archives in Florence, we should mention in particular the *Pianta dei poderi vigne e fabbriche della Fattoria di Castello di S.M.I.* drawn up by Bernardo Sgrilli in 1747, in which the map's precision is further enhanced by skilful draftsmanship and clear presentation. A comparison of this map and the one made in 1697 allows us to see that the property remained more or less unchanged over this period except for the acquisition of Petraia, which on the 1697 map appears as the property of Lorenzo Lanfredini (at this time the owner of the adjacent I Rinieri villa, later bought by Cosimo), while on Sgrillo's map it is encapsulated in the estate.[10]

During the last years of Medici rule, the stagnation of the State economy extended to management of the family's properties, passively exploited by the concession of countless privileges. During the years immediately following the end of the Medici dynasty, the Castello-Petraia estate was incorporated in the administration of the nearby Careggi property. The fullness of the description in *Nota dei poderi, orti, vigne Palazzi case ed altro esistenti e di attinenza a detta Fattoria di Castello Petraja e Careggi*, drawn up at the wishes of Francesco Ricoveri when he rented the estate in 1740, makes it a noteworthy record.

The reorganization introduced by Pietro Leopoldo of Lorraine,[11] with measures aimed at encouraging capital investment in agriculture, involved State property too and this was tackled through a programme of general readjustment which provided for only four estates to be left under direct administration: Poggio a Caiano and its ten farms; Castello

[10] Villa I Rinieri passed from Pietro Cervieri to the Jesuit Fathers of San Giovannino, his universal heirs on his death in 1665. The villa was bought from the Fathers by Ottavia di Gismondo della Stufa for 5400 *scudi*, to form a dowry on her marriage to Lorenzo di Girolamo Lanfredini. Her son Lorenzo inherited it on her death in 1687. The Corsini were already interested in acquiring the property at this period, for reasons of investment as well as prestige, as we read Marquese Filippo Corsini's letter to the estate manager Luigi Arrigucci, dated 19 July 1687: "*I would like to know if you hear that Lorenzo Lanfredini is selling his Castello villa*" (cf. "*Il giardino di Villa Corsini a Castello*", doctoral thesis of Patrizia Santangelo, Department of Architecture of Florence University, 1995–1996).

[11] A. Salvestrini, *Pietro Leopoldo. Relazioni sul Governo della Toscana,* Florence 1968, p. 352. See also G. Gobbi, *Documenti per una storia del territorio*, op. cit., p. 11.

Right: *Podere del Terrio* (A.S.F. Piante Scrittoio RR Possessioni, Vol. II, c.12).
Next page: A projet to transform the Casa del Colatoio by Giuseppe Del Rosso. Plan of the vineyard of Castello (A.S.F. Piante Scrittoio RR Possessioni, 475/3, 475/2, 475/1).

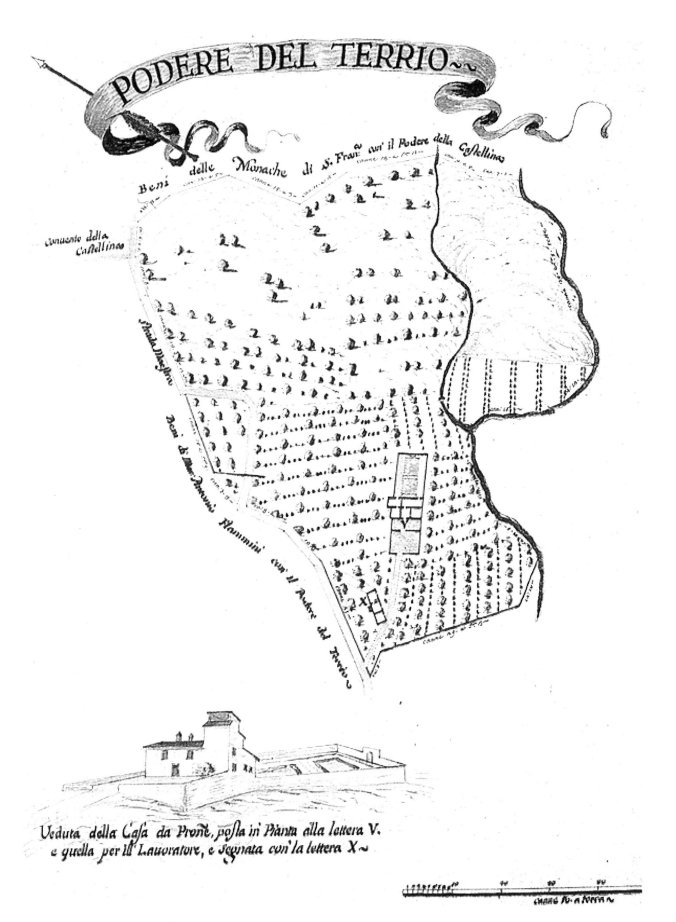

PODERE DEL TERRIO~

Beni delle Monache di S. Franc. con' il Podere della Castellina

Conuento della Castellina

Veduta della Casa da Pront. posta in Pianta alla lettera V.
e quella per lli Lauoratore, e segnata con la lettera X~

with its vineyards and four farms; Cascine del'Isola with eleven farms and Poggio Imperiale with twelve.

After this period we find a notable increase in the number of documents concerning the estate: administration books, inventories, estimates of maintenance works to be carried out on the buildings, drawings of a building for drying grapes, and a plan of the 1792 vineyard, which it is interesting to compare with its successor, the first project to transform the vineyards of Castello and of Chiuso di Bellagio.

The map of the lands making up the Imperiale Fattoria di Castello, drawn up during French rule in 1810 by De Carcopino, allows us to compare the situation of the property at this date with the position shown on Sgrilli's 1747 map. A comparison shows that the Covacchia villa and farm no longer form part of the estate, while the Gondo villa and farm above the Castello garden have been added. It was beside this building that Grand Duke Leopoldo II installed modern equipment for producing olive oil, including a hydraulic press which was to serve as a model for the improved production of oil. We should note plans for other projects which, in keeping with the prevailing rules of neo-classicism, even include ornamentation of the farm buildings. Among these are Leopoldo Veneziani's plans for converting the house of the Castello estate and for alterations to some farmhouses belonging to Chiuso, owned by Del Mazza, which had just been purchased and joined to the Castello estate. Although these projects remained on paper they reveal a re-awakened interest in caring for the land and, more generally, a new drive to improve agriculture development.

As regards the outward order and aspect of the land, a major change was made in 1836 at the wishes of Leopoldo II. This consisted in turning the land of the Ragnaia farm (between the Quarto villa and the villa Petraia) and part of the vineyard to the north into a romantic park, and building a curving avenue with double rows of trees to link the parks of the Petraia and Castello villas, designed by the Bohemian engineer Fritsch. The public road to the west was closed to prevent transit through the park (the old road from Boldrone being already encapsulated in the park) and the new Via di San Michele was opened.

This reorganization introduced drastic changes to the land, interrupting the traditional established pattern of farmland with large stretches of open green spaces. Moreover, the creation of these parks brought other changes to the surrounding area, and the "up-dating" of villas and gardens to accord with the current fashion. The Quarto, Torrigiani

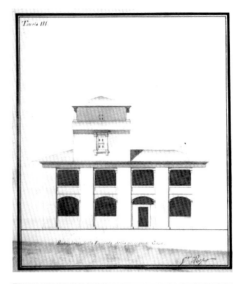

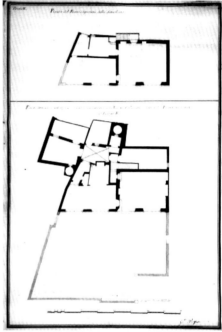

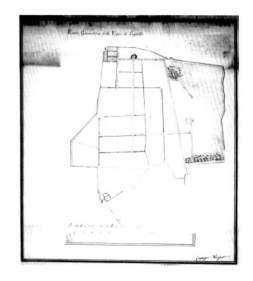

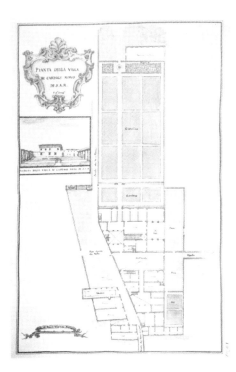

Above: Plan of the Villa di Careggi Novo 1736.
Below: *Pianta del Palazzo e Giardino della Petraia* (A.S.F., Piante Scrittoio R.R. Possessioni, Vol. II, c. 7/1).

and Borghese villas are telling examples of this fashion for turning green areas into romantic parks in the English style, almost, but not quite, the last evidence of the villa's impact on the countryside. These changes soon formed a pattern of organized green spaces which occurred repeatedly between the districts of Quarto and Quinto in a series of ornamented parks. This pattern was developed across a network of small farms and represents the first decisive change in the relationship of villa and agriculture in its traditional sense. A change of such magnitude had not occurred in the previous centuries, even when the Medici residences were turned into palaces of pleasure, because while alterations were indeed made to enhance the recreational facilities of the stately villas attention was still paid to aspects involved in exploiting an estate's agricultural production. Other instances where villas were provided with romantic parks all involved eradicating farmland, proof of this being shown by the shift from "villa-agricultural production" to "villa-place of recreation". However, the final outcome of this change in a traditional rural structure, still based on economic conditions established in the Florentine area over four centuries earlier, did not yet cause a break in the continuity of the pattern of settlement and of land being

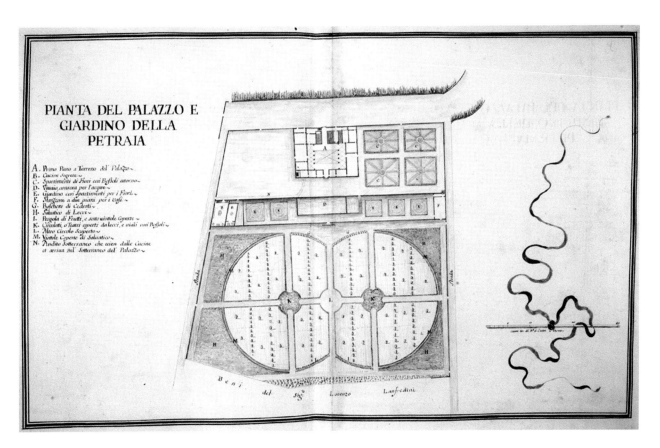

organized around a villa, although this began to have a different significance.

The Castello estate began to be broken up in 1848 when plots of land on the plain were sold for building the new tarmacked road. Chiuso, the property of the Del Mazza family, bought in 1817 from the Scrittoio delle Reali Possessioni, was sold in 1849 to Gaspero Viti. In 1869, Law n. 4547 of 26 August 1868 on crown properties permitted the farms of Vivaio and Steccuto to be bartered, although in the pre-sale agreement the property agent had remarked: "*I cannot fail to point out that the lands making up the Vivaio farm surround the great avenue and parterre in front of the Royal Villa of Castello, which leads me to consider that over the course of time the alienation of this property might occasion such inconvenience as to far outweigh the value that this farm has today . . .*"[12]

The traditional appearance of the countryside, crystallized into an organized pattern, one which gave the landscape a place in the cycle of historical events, was brusquely interrupted in the decades following the breakdown in the traditional farming system. Various developments altered the established order in the countryside without giving evidence of any new structure, while, in the absence of any organizational alternatives for land which had been settled and cultivated for centuries, the agricultural crisis became a crisis for the rural world as a whole.

Instances of transformation which have taken place, and continue to do so, chiefly consist in superimposing the constructions typical of fringe development on the crumbling agricultural structures. A major role in this has been played by the growing demand for building land and the total disregard for the countryside shown by private enterprise.

When examining the changing pattern of the rural structure in the Florentine area it should be remembered that this process was sparked off by the breaking up of the large estates. The collapse of traditional structures of farming and habitation, with farms being abandoned by share-croppers, had a dramatic effect on a system which was already fragile and, given the area's particular location, subject to increasing pressure from the city. A further result was that some estates became completely fragmented, with the ensuing uncontrolled and unplanned use of the hillsides by private enterprise for building sought-after residences, frequently involving property speculation. This led to farmland in the area being split up into building lots, particularly in the stretch between Via Sestese and the first road in the foothills, Via di Castello, and to the changed use of the old farmhouses.

[12] Despite this opinion the farms were separated and the land of Ottavio Gigli were bartered for. In the opinion accompanying the agreement in September 1868 the value was estimated at: "*L. 27, 378.80 for the Vivaio farm and for the Steccuto farm L. 31,967.28 more for the addition of the villa*". The Steccuto farm included two houses, one of which was to become Villa Il Riposo, or Belriposo, while the other became Villa Pallestrini, and later Cini. In 1860 the Querciola farm returned to the Castello estate before being sold in 1872, when the farmhouse became Villa Ricceri.

Fattoria di Castello: the formation:
1 the land property in 1498;
2 the enlargment between 1498 and 1534;
3 the situation from Cosimo's I Campione di Beni 1566, the villa Petraia is included in the land property;
4 lands acquired until 1585;
5 the Rinieri villa with poderi bought in 1618 and sold in 1650;
6 land bought until 1697;
7 after the passage of the Grand Duchy to the Lorraine dynasty;
8 Chiuso dei Mazza, bought in 1817, sold in 1849.

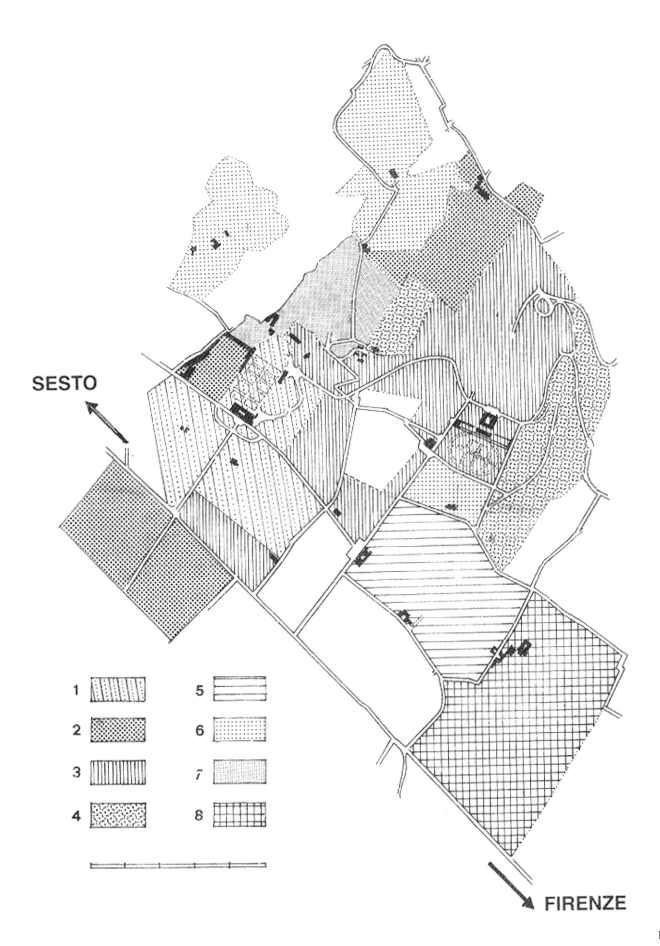

SESTO

FIRENZE

1 [▨] 5 [▤]
2 [▦] 6 [⋯]
3 [▥] 7 [▒]
4 [░] 8 [▦]

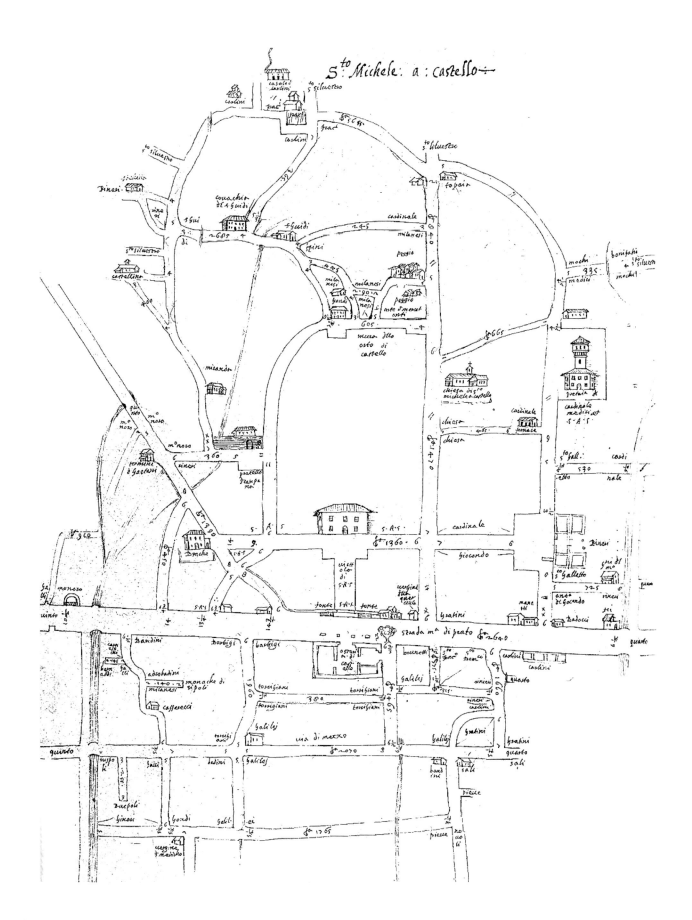

CHAPTER EIGHT
Mapping the Area

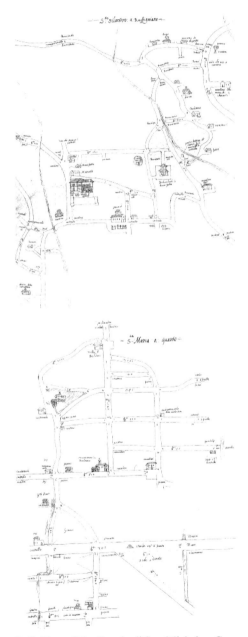

Left: Plan of the Popolo di San Michele a Castello (A.S.F. Piante dei Capitani di Parte Guelfa, Popoli e Strade, Vol. 121).
Above: Plan of the Popolo di San Silvestro a Ruffignano; plan of the Popolo di Santa Maria a Quarto.

THE MAPS OF THE *POPOLI DEI CAPITANI DI PARTE*
The Magistratura dei Capitani di Parte Guelfa came into being during the struggle between the Guelph and Ghibelline factions and, after merging with the Ufficiali della Torre, it became the body in charge of public building and water and road works, leaving us a highly important series of illustrated documents drawn up during the last decades of the 16th century. These maps were produced by official draftsmen, including famous figures such as Buontalenti (who, apart from other work, has left us surveys and proposals for regulating the course of the River Arno), and they provide us with an extremely valuable picture of the area. The maps apply to the *Popoli*, that is, the various districts around Florence which came under the authority of the higher offices of the *Podesterie*, in turn answerable to the *Vicariati*. This territorial organization was introduced by the *Signoria* in 1423 and remained in force until the reforms embarked on by Pietro Leopoldo in 1772. The particular area under study came under the Podesterie of Sesto and of Fiesole, both under the authority of the Vicariato of Scarperia. The Podesteria of Sesto was responsible for the *popoli* of Santa Maria a Quarto, San Michele a Castello, San Silvestro a Ruffignano and Santa Maria a Quinto, while the parish of Santo Stefano in Pane came under the Podesteria of Fiesole. The map survey, in two versions which are almost identical and practically contemporary, is accompanied by a document carrying information about the layout, boundaries and properties in the outlying areas.
The map is of the planimetric type, drawn by eye, and measurements are included expressed in Florentine *braccia* (equivalent to a yard), to indicate the width of roads, besides every kind of landmark, such as shrines, springs, enclosing walls, the boundaries of every land division with the names of the proprietors and elevations of the principal buildings which help to identify the paths.
Nevertheless, under close scrutiny some differences emerge, probably due to a more hastily produced drawing and less attention to detail. For instance, if we compare the two

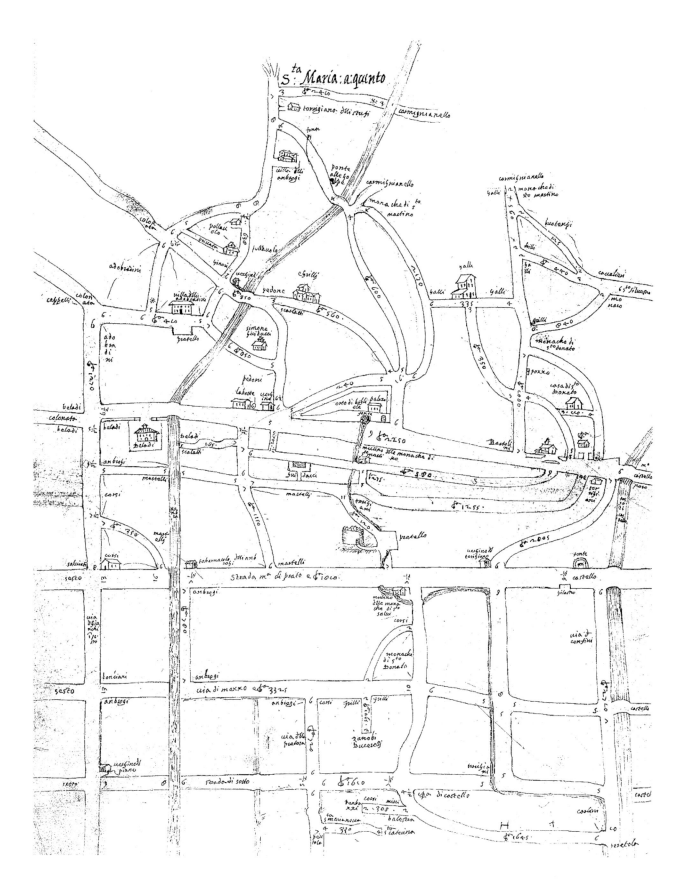

Above: Plan of the Popolo of Santa Maria a Quinto.
Right: Maps of the Istituto Geografico Militare I.G.M (1896, 1923, 1936).

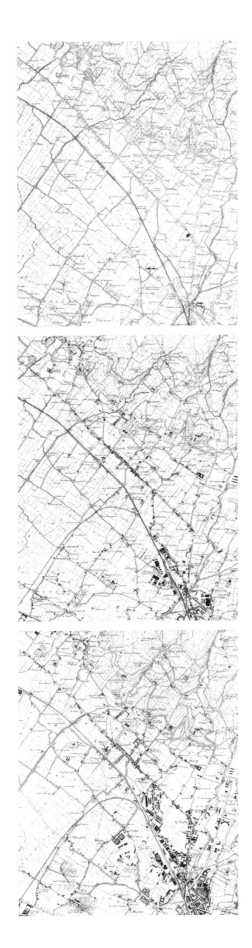

versions of the parish of San Michele a Castello (Vol. 120 c. 285 and Vol. 121 c. 375): on map 375 the open space in front of the villa is marked, with the words "*viottolo di S.A.S.*"; on the other side of Via Maestra appears the layout of the "*Osteria di Castello*" while in the other (map 285) only the name is shown. The façade of Petraia is accurately depicted (more sketchily in the Vol. 120 version) above the words "*Cardinale Medici et S.A.S.*". On the same map, we can see the different way that villa "*I Rineri*", later Villa Corsini, is depicted, by a sketchy elevation in one instance, and in the other by a plan showing a loggia at the back, on the garden side. The Brache villa is not illustrated on the sketchier map (c. 285), being marked simply with the name, while it is depicted in detail on the other (c. 375).

Despite the fact that the maps are based on a visual survey and are not in scale the accuracy of the skilled draftsmen provides a clear picture of the area, one that is convincing and realistic, enabling us to make an exact reconstruction of the layout of these outlying areas at the close of the 16th century (1580) and to compare it with the present situation, in many instances little changed.

A MODERN MAP

Research has led to extremely detailed analyses of the settling of this extra-urban area (analyses of the typological components: villa, farmhouse, landscaped green spaces, crops, roads, etc.). These analyses were realized through cataloguing important buildings and constructions and, at the same time, creating a map to serve not only as a record of the purely functional aspects but also to provide a consistent central reference point for an informed study of the area itself.

A first outline of this work appeared in the journal "Controspazio", 2 (1977), edited by G. Gobbi and T. Gobbò, with L. Capaccioli and L. Lazzareschi, entitled *Interpretazione grafiche del sistema collinare fiorentino: studi e ricerche per la formazione di un sistema di parchi territoriali*. The aim of the study was to produce an experimental map of the area, in appropriate scale, and one compatible with the architectural representations. The intention was to reintroduce drawing to create a map that would make it possible to analyse and interpret the features of this area. When the work was carried out (in the early 1970s) as part of the studies conducted in the Architectural Department of Florence University, this objective was largely abandoned in favour of an inter-departmental approach, drawing on disciplines such as sociology, which clearly had little to do with the theme of visual representation. The specific goal was to succeed in showing the value of an intensely cultivated and elaborately developed area like the Florentine countryside, where every feature is united in an apparently unstudied overall design, in reality the result of well-considered and long-established practical use. Apart from studying the most appropriate drawing methods for recreating the wealth of objects to be included (without resorting to using symbols or imitating the graphic realism of the early maps), the problem lay in the scale of the representation necessary to give a precise and well-defined visual image of the subject. When a map introduces symbols to replace realistic drawing a key is required to decipher it; the key must respond to the particular purpose and objective of the map. Moreover, a precise relationship is established between the abstract and the real, between illustration and established symbol, between the scale of the symbol and the scale of the map. In other words, if the realistic figure-symbol has been abandoned as sign-unit in modern cartography, a different illustrative code is needed to provide an overall image which is more truly realistic. Thus, drawing up a map meant establishing a specific relationship between the size of the images and the scale of the map which, while not reaching the paradox of realism of the imperial Chinese cartographers described by Borges, was nevertheless in keeping with the features represented and therefore, also, with the scale of the buildings.

This operation was designed to produce a life-like interpretive illustration that was self-explanatory and it was necessary to discover a form which would, with comprehensive and concise imagery, restore the area's character as a physical framework, one which reveals the signs of the various stages of the advance of civilization. This form of representation cannot, therefore, be reduced to a mere code, but must employ a range of images which contribute to the character and form of the reconstruction. The choice of scale was no longer simply an automatic process, but intrinsically related to the object represented and therefore relevant to its particular size and nature.

Indeed, one particular purpose of this information, in its different scales, is the support it can provide in view of any environmental changes which might be introduced through operations carried out on natural and historical formal structures in which there is frequently a succession of environmental and social events and processes. The map's "realistic" style (albeit a selective and functional realism) weaves a network of pre-established patterns and objects which offer quite different possibilities from, for example, an aerial photograph. A photograph offers a full, but basically neutral view, full as it may be of information, while a map

PLANNED TRANSFORMATIONS

Villa and annexes

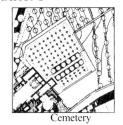
Cemetery

Italian garden

Park

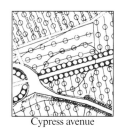
Cypress avenue

CONNECTIONS BETWEEN CULTIVATIONS AND SPATIAL ELEMENTS OF PODERE

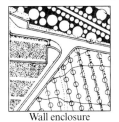
Wall enclosure

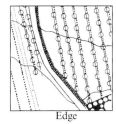
Edge

Row of olives

Row of vines

Mixed row olive-vine

CULTIVATIONS AND STRUCTURAL ELEMENTS OF PODERE

Farmhouse

Path

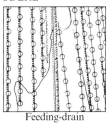
Feeding-drain

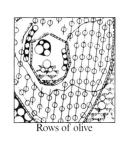
Rows of olive

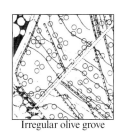
Irregular olive grove

Olive grove on edge

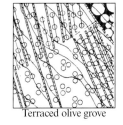
Terraced olive grove

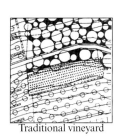
Traditional vineyard

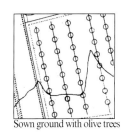
Sown ground with olive trees

Sown ground with vineyard

EXTRA-AGRICULTURAL VEGETATION · EXTRA-AGRARIAN BUILDINGS

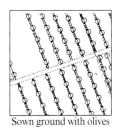
Sown ground with olives
and vines

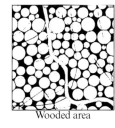
Wooded area

Green along water-
course

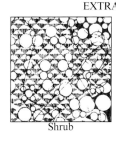
Shrub

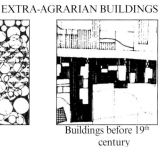
Buildings before 19th
century

Before 19th century
of architectural value

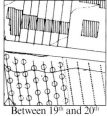
Between 19th and 20th
century

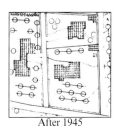
After 1945

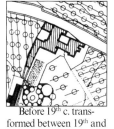
Before 19th c. trans-
formed between 19th and
20th c.

Before 19th century
transformed after 1945

143

offers an ordered sequence of carefully chosen images to reproduce the pattern of the major features which contribute to the character of the area and, in this way, the map also helps to re-establish the importance of this territory.

The map is on a 1:2000 scale and is not limited to showing major buildings and constructions (the outcome of a survey) and recommending their preservation, but is also intended to illustrate the enduring organizational power that these structures exercise, and stress the underlying network of relationships linking the various aspects of the landscape. The map provides a reference point that can be used to safeguard buildings and countryside in this area, besides offering a guide for any future operations of conservation and for controlling conversions and rebuilding operations, serving as matrix and framework. This kind of graphic representation can therefore serve as a thematic map to provide established guidelines for any form of planning activity. Several different graphic techniques were studied to identify the one best suited to illustrate both the layout of the buildings and the different texture and quality of different surfaces (olive groves, vineyards, etc.), as well as the rural patchwork created by the division of land into farms, by farm tracks and by water courses, as well as by the different character of thickly, or sparsely, planted woodland. The type of representation chosen therefore not only goes further but also integrates the material, compared with studies based on a subjective view of the elements in the landscape (preferential views, openings, barriers, etc.) since the aim was to restore the components of the landscape. It should be said that in traditional methods of cartography the land was treated as a *pure extension*, a geometric surface reduced to a mere material resource, open to any sort of abuse. Moreover, these examples of standardized maps are perfectly in keeping with the *laissez-faire* attitude which prevailed at an operational level. Whereas an attempt to restore and map the true quality and character of this area, imprinted over the centuries, obviously implies respect for the integrity of cultural values as a fundamental parameter and condition for carrying out the work.

The villas and gardens in the area are also shown on a larger and more detailed scale (1:400), in accomplished drawings in which intensive graphic research has been aimed at illustrating the particular characteristics of the component elements, in relationship to each other and in structural and visual form. It should be said that this research, and the production of the maps, was conducted in the early 1970s and that changes have taken place in the intervening years, largely to the further detriment of the quality of the landscape and the environment.

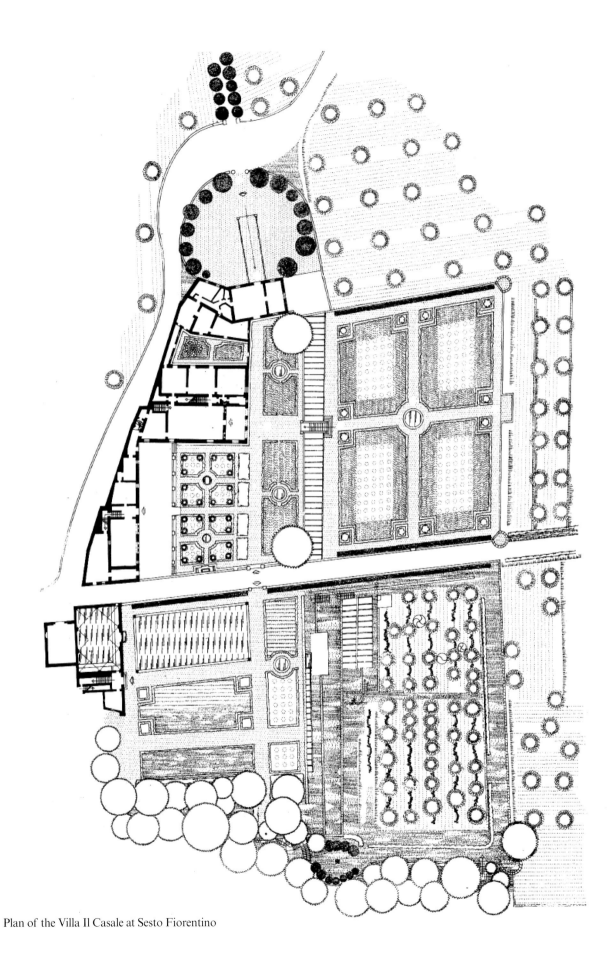

Plan of the Villa Il Casale at Sesto Fiorentino

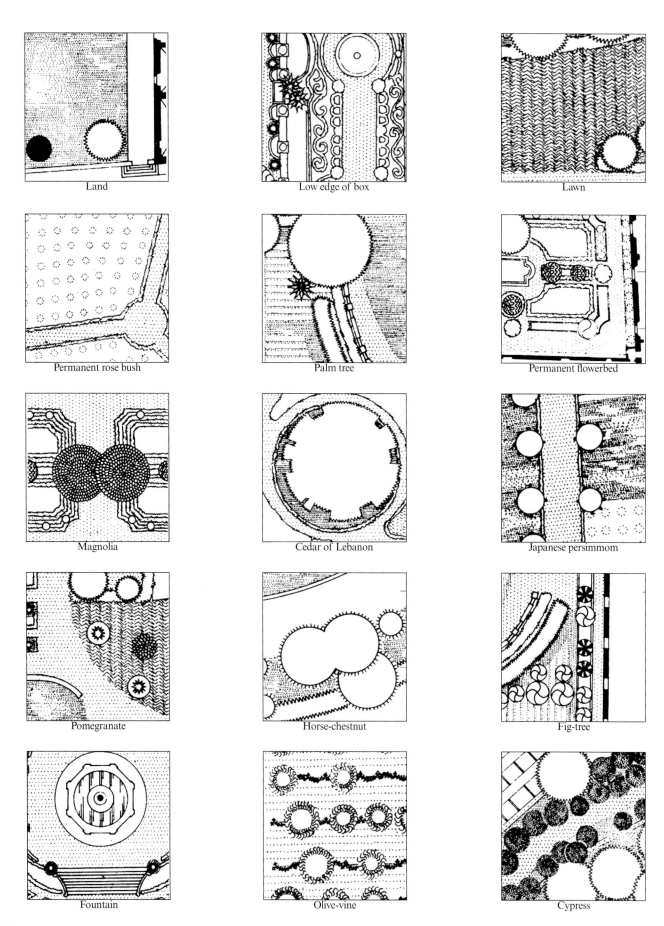

Land

Low edge of box

Lawn

Permanent rose bush

Palm tree

Permanent flowerbed

Magnolia

Cedar of Lebanon

Japanese persimmom

Pomegranate

Horse-chestnut

Fig-tree

Fountain

Olive-vine

Cypress

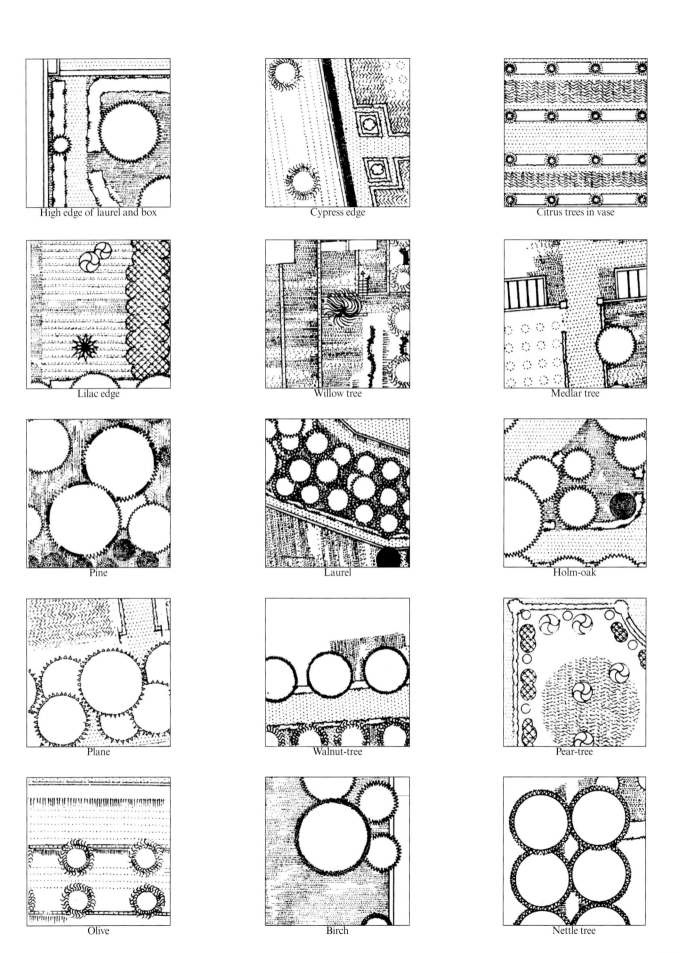

High edge of laurel and box

Cypress edge

Citrus trees in vase

Lilac edge

Willow tree

Medlar tree

Pine

Laurel

Holm-oak

Plane

Walnut-tree

Pear-tree

Olive

Birch

Nettle tree

147

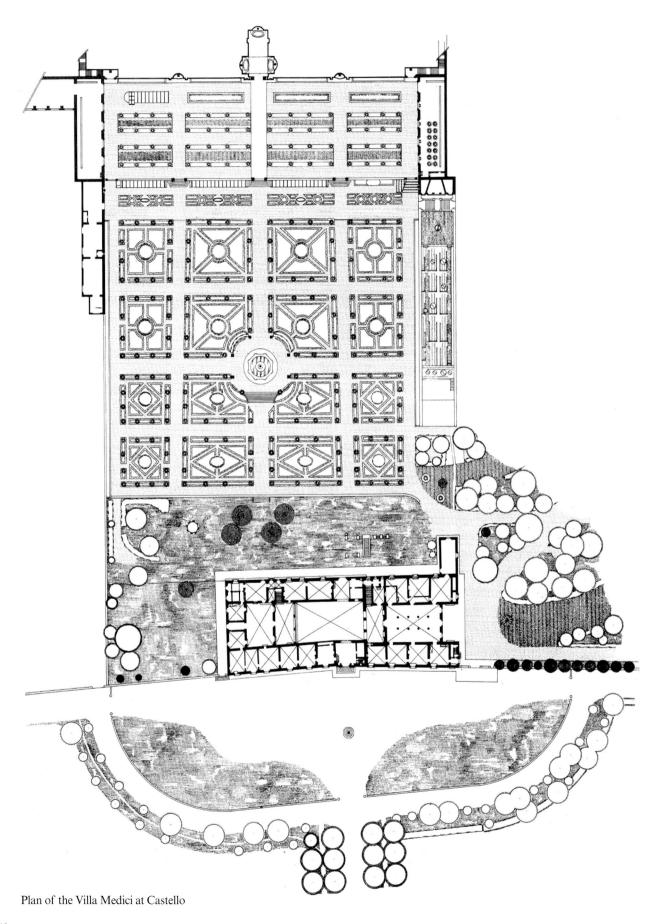

Plan of the Villa Medici at Castello

PART THREE

VILLAS IN THE CASTELLO-SESTO FIORENTINO AREA
LE PANCHE, VILLA DELLE FILIPPINE
LE GORE, VILLA CARAMELLI
LA CORTE, formerly VILLA BALDINI
VILLA BELLINI
LOGGIA DEI BIANCHI
IL GIOIELLO
VILLA EMILIA
VILLA CORNELISEN
BELLARIVA, VILLA MORIANI
CASTELQUARTO
VILLA LA LIMONAIA
VILLA GUASCONI
LA QUIETE
VILLA CASINI
VILLA AMALIA
IL CHIUSO, VILLA ORSINI
VILLA CORSINI
VILLA MAFFEI
VILLA BELGIOIELLO
VILLA MALAFRASCA
VILLA BELVEDERE
IL RIPOSO or BELRIPOSO
VILLA LAWLEY
VILLA DI QUARTO
VILLA PETRAIA
IL QUADRIVIO
VILLA RICCERI
VILLA DEL PANTA, BELVEDERE
POGGIO SECCO
VILLA DI CASTELLO
IL GONDO
VILLA IL POZZINO
BELLAGIO, VILLA LE BRACHE
TERRIO, VILLA GIRALDI
POGGIO ALLEGRO, POGGIOCHIARO
VILLA FONTENUOVA
VILLA COVACCHIA
VILLA IL CASALE
VILLA LA TORRE
VILLA DELLA CASTELLINA
VILLA PALASTRETO
VILLA TOPAIA
IL CANTONE, VILLA BILLI
VILLA VILLORESI
LA FONTE
VILLA BALDINI-BORGHESE
VILLA LA MULA
VILLA EUGENIA-NENCETTI
VILLA LAPI-WINTELER
BOGLIOLO, VILLA MORENI
VILLA TORRIGIANI
LA ZAMBRA
IL POZZACCIO, VILLA PARENTINI
LO STROZZINO, VILLA MANFREDI

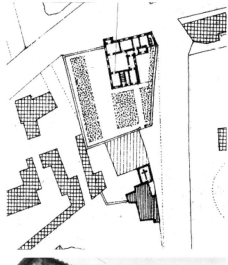

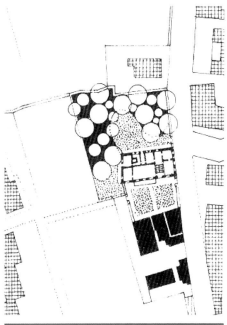

LE PANCHE, VILLA DELLE FILIPPINE

This ancient building appears as "Villa delle Filippine" on the 1896 and 1923 I.G.M. maps. On the 1936 map it is called "Podere delle Panche". Carocci tells us that during the 15th century the villa was owned by the Brunelleschi family. A 1498 declaration to the Decima announces the division of the property, one half being given to a daughter, Agnoletta. In the early 16th century the building was sold to the Orlandini, from whom it passed to the Marchionni family who turned it into an inn. In 1681, after further changes in ownership, it was bought by the Vettori who returned it to its original residential use. The Vettori remained the proprietors into the last century and their coat of arms appears above the entrance. The sadly dilapidated villa has been divided into separate apartments. The plan is L-shaped and the wall of the east wing shows fragments of door posts and the frame of a window, later walled up; the corners are built with blocks of limestone. The rear part of the villa, slightly smaller in scale, has an 18th-century look. *"The windows are large and rectangular with stone frames carved to simulate rustications, separated by parallel lines of bands and grooves. On the ground floor they have projecting architraves and bars, with sills supported on corbels. On the west face is a rusticated door with a round intrados and ogival extrados surmounted by an 18th-century-style coat of arms flanked with volutes and indecipherable arms. On a projecting body on the north face is a small door with an architrave and round-arched lunette. A convex stone cornice runs below the roof timbers. The low enclosing wall formed part of the early road walling. On the side of Via Niccolò da Tolentino, corbels and the arched line of a lintel reveal the position of the 18th-century entrance, now closed"* (R. Bartoli, L. Venturini). The new roads which have replaced the old farm roads and the buildings lots which have invaded the landscape with inappropriately large buildings, by comparison with the original scale in this outlying district, have deprived the building of its original setting, placing it at the junction of two roads, the old Via delle Gore and the new Via N. da Tolentino which retraces the course of an old farm track.

Bibliography:
Carocci, 1906, p. 260.
Lensi Orlandi, 1965, p. 13.
Castello campagna medicea periferia urbana, 1984, p. 85.

LE GORE, VILLA CARAMELLI

This building, looking onto Via delle Gore, almost opposite Villa La Corte, has been much reworked and turned into an infant school. Today it is of little interest except for its handsome 17th-century windows on the side facing the road, and a few 15th-century features in the interior. It was the property of the Martelli family who owned it for five centuries, part of their Commenda di Santo Stefano. In the 19th century it belonged to the Capei and then the Caramelli families, as recorded on the 1936 I.G.M. map (on the earlier 1823 and 1896 versions it has no name). Its agricultural setting has been totally lost and the land almost entirely divided into building lots, with the exception of one remaining narrow strip.

Bibliography:
Carocci, 1906, p. 261.
Lensi Orlandi, 1965, p. 13.

LA CORTE, formerly VILLA BALDINI

The 1896 and 1923 I.G.M. maps record the name "Villa Baldini", the 1936 version "Villa Campa". The earlier names used by Carocci ("La Corte" and "Le Gore") are derived, in turn, from the planimetric layout of the complex, and from its location. The property recently passed to the Masini and this ancient building, owned by the Rondinelli family in the 13th century, is being faithfully restored. In 1429 we find it was sold to Niccolò Cambini, then inherited by Giuntini before being bought in 1533 by Giovanni di Francesco da Magnale and, in 1699, a century and a half later, the Ufficiali dei Pupilli sold it to Giovanni di Francesco Giudici. During the 19th century it was owned by the Baldini family. The complex stood on land which, until the 1950s, stretched from the Terzolle stream to Via delle Gore. The major changes introduced by the now heavily populated area have changed the villa's relationship with its agricultural land. A walled garden, run wild with vegetation, separates the old building from the encircling building lots. The façade with the main entrance is approached by a tree-lined avenue and has two side-wings, a fairly common feature in this area (also to be found at Villa del Gondo), providing the building with a courtyard closed on three sides. The octagonal pilasters in the courtyard are the remains of 12th-century columns (now visible on the right wing where an open loggia has been closed), and the Rondinelli arms on the tower above the façade show its noble origins. The interior has handsome rooms with vaulted ceilings supported on *pietra serena* corbels.

Bibliography:
Carocci, 1906, p. 261.
Lensi Orlandi, 1965, p. 13.

VILLA BELLINI

The name recorded on the 1896 and 1923 I.G.M. maps is "Villa Bellini", on the 1936 map "Villa La Quiete". The villa stands in a set-back position on Via delle Quiete, the façade looking over a porticoed courtyard. The building was originally connected to Villa delle Montalve and the surrounding farm buildings, property of the convent, and has been much remodelled and altered.

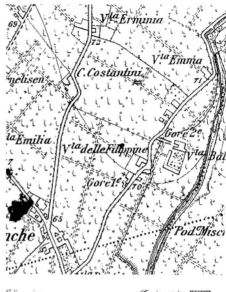

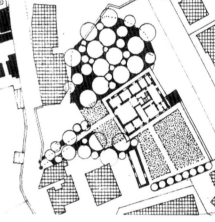

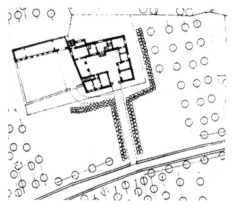

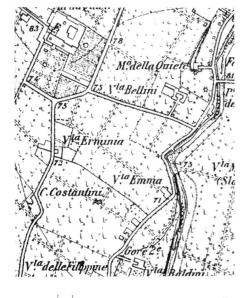

LOGGIA DEI BIANCHI

According to a 19th-century scholar this interesting complex may have derived its name from a company of white-robed Penitents from northern Europe which sought refuge here from the city during the 14th century, for fear of the plague. The monks are said to have sought refuge under a loggia by the Terzolle stream, in the *popolo* of Santa Maria di Quarto (*popolo* = parish or borough). However, although this is an interesting idea it does not appear to be attested to by firm evidence. Nevertheless, it seems very likely that a company of monks did travel to Rome along the banks of the Terzolle, as depicted in the oratory of Santo Stefano in Pane. The church is dedicated to the Company and has a fresco showing two white-robed, hooded figures worshipping at the Cross. There is no doubt that the name "a' Bianchi" recorded in the 1427 Florentine land register refers to this complex: "*a farm with a house for master and worker, dovecote, mill and forge*", the property of the Mazzuoli family. In 1453 it passed from the latter family to the Rinieri, remaining in their possession until 1557 when it was sold to Giovanni di Matteo Concini. Bought in 1568 from Benedetto Pandolfi it came again into the hands of the Rinieri family who sold it in 1598 to Bernardo di Giovanni Corona Da Ponte, a merchant from Bergamo who lived in Florence and founded the nearby oratory. The map of the Capitani di Parte of the parish of Santa Maria a Quarto has a sketch of a simple building, and written below: "*Loggia dei Bianchi*". The property moved from Da Ponte to the Alborghetti family, also merchants from Bergamo, and in 1774 they ceded it in perpetuity to the congregation of the Sisters of Minims, the Order at the nearby convent.

The building has been recently restored and divided into apartments and is now a handsome villa composed of three bodies forming a U, the result of different building operations at different periods. The façade on Via della Loggia dei Bianchi has a markedly 16th-century look: in the centre is a large rusticated entrance, with a slightly projecting keystone; the ground-floor windows have convex, or "kneeling", bars, while those on the first floor are smaller with simple *pietra serena* surrounds. The dovecote and supporting buttress probably represents the original core of the complex which expanded around the Renaissance structure. The inner side, giving onto the garden, has a loggia on two sides supported by fluted columns and capitals of a type much used in Florence during the late 15th century. The loggia, if we accept the tardy arrival of ornamentation in outlying areas, is datable to the late 15th or early 16th century. Other periods appear in some features, including the doors leading to the loggia. The keystone above the entrance on Via delle Gore bears the date 1790.

Outside the walled enclosure, but still part of the complex, at the corner of Via Delle Gore and Via della Loggia dei Bianchi, is a 15th-century oratory with a small covered portico supported by slim stone columns topped with wooden roof trusses. The building, which bears the Da Ponte arms, consists of two quadrangular spaces, one of which is covered by a small hemispherical cupola and drum covered with "fish-scale" terracotta tiles. The façade on Via delle Gore has two simple windows bordered with stone and crumbling traces of extremely interesting coloured graffito work and *trompe l'oeil* decorations in the late-mannerist style. The portico is also frescoed with grotesque decorations, now in very poor condition. The building is entered through a classical stone doorway crowned with a broken pediment.

Bibliography:
Castello campagna medicea periferia urbana, 1984 p. 86.
Antico e futureo nel territorio mediceo di Castello I giardini della chimera, 1989, p. 64.

IL GIOIELLO
The name "Il Gioiello" in the 1896 and 1923 versions of the I.G.M. maps, appears as "Villa Il Gioiello" in the 1936 publication. The name captures the spirit of this building, almost hidden behind a high wall flanking the road (of the same name) bordering the park of Villa di Quarto and the Quarto cemetery. The house has an open courtyard and adjoining farmhouse. The complex formerly belonged to the art historians Ludovico Ragghianti and Licia Collobi and is still occupied by their descendants.

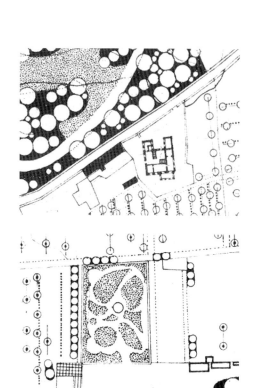

VILLA EMILIA
The 19th-century name "Villa Emilia" appears on the I.G.M. maps. This was once the property of the Deti family of the parish of Santa Felicita; later owned by Filippi and Del Turco before returning, at the beginning of the 17th century, to its earlier owners, the Deti family. After changing hands several times it was bought at the beginning of the 20th century by the famous singer Enrico Caruso. In order to modernize it to suit current tastes he carried out drastic alterations, almost totally effacing its original character. Some details of the conversion reflect a wide range of styles, including the Moorish air of the street entrance. Particular features include an annex in *art nouveau* style, a glass and iron conservatory in the garden and handsome wrought iron brackets supporting the overhang of the roof. It is now a clinic, "Villa Gisella", and the roadside frontage retains some features of the earlier building.

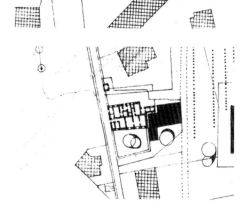

Bibliography:
Carocci, 1906, p. 262.

VILLA CORNELISEN
The building, 19th-century in appearance, stands on the road linking Villa della Quiete and the old Via Maestra and on the 1896 and 1923 maps it is recorded as "Villa Cornelisen". This is almost certainly one of those late-19th-century suburban houses with architectural features of only minor interest which are the result of the transformation of pre-existing rural buildings. In this instance, the villa stands where there were once two small houses, belonging to a farm. In the 1427 land register the property belonged to the Guasconi family, the owners of the villa on Via Maestra. At the end of the 15th century it was bought by Mariano di Tommaso Deti and became an annex to Villa dei Pini (later Villa Emilia, the property of the tenor Caruso in the early 20th century). As Carocci reports, the property underwent various changes in ownership during the course of the 17th and 18th centuries. In 1828 it was bought by Margherita Corsi, Baldi's widow, and this probably marked the start of operations to convert the early rural buildings into a holiday villa.

Bibliography:
Carocci, 1906, p. 264.

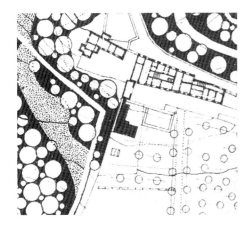

BELLARIVA, VILLA MORIANI

A 19th-century conversion has almost totally obliterated any trace of the original Silvestri villa, given in 1565, together with the adjoining farm, to the sisters of San Pietro Maggiore, after the end of the suppression of the monasteries. On the 1896 I.G.M. map it is called "Villa Moriani", and "Bellariva, Villa Chirici" on the map of 1936. It belongs to the descendants of the painter Giovanni Colacicchi, who lived here. The surrounding area has particular charm with the ancient park of Villa di Quarto to the north and an olive-growing farm to the south.

Bibliography:
Carocci, 1906, p. 268.
Lensi Orlandi, 1965, p. 15.

CASTELQUARTO

This was originally called "Le Panche", like other complexes in the area. On the 1896 and 1923 I.G.M. maps it is called "Villa Erminia" and on that of 1936 "Castelquarto". Its origins are 13th century, when it was the property of the powerful Adimari faction, later passing to the family of one of its members – the Della Trita family – and in the mid-15th century to the Cambini of Via Larga. In 1660 it became the property of the Albizi family, who continued to own it for some time. This is the period of the architectural style of the building, which reveals no trace of its original medieval structure but has all the elements of a luxurious 17th-century country house. The façade on the old Via di Quarto has a window with outward curving bars (the famous *inginocchiata* window, literally, "kneeling") and an 18th-century cuspidate doorway leading to the courtyard, surrounded on three sides by the building. The interior façade also shows traces of two *inginocchiate* windows and others with *pietra serena* surrounds decorated with 18th-century motifs, such as the guttae in the upper corners and an entrance-door with a simple frame crowned by a modern-day coat of arms displaying a double-bowled fountain and the word FONS. The unitary character of the whole complex is also clear from the two walls facing the courtyard, where the architectural and decorative features are regularly repeated. At right angles to one of these is a small loggia with slender Tuscan columns and wooden corbels, now glassed in. In the interior is a central two-storey drawing-room with galleries which lead to the rooms on the upper floor. Some rooms are decorated with 18th-century landscape murals, and there is a study painted with architectural scenes. At the beginning of the 20th century it was owned by the Otto family, who made changes to the garden and to the façade looking towards Monte Morello, disturbing its 17th-century character by adding a heavy balcony. This side of the villa overlooks a walled garden which has remained unchanged in size. The villa now houses a religious institution. Some of the adjacent farmland has been turned into building lots.

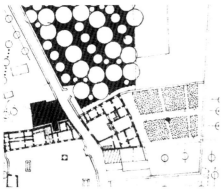

Bibliography:
Carocci, 1906, p. 262.
Lensi Orlandi, 1969, p. 15.
Castello campagna medicea periferia urbana, 1984 p.84.

VILLA LA LIMONAIA

This interconnected series of buildings was divided into a farmhouse and landlord's residence and is the result of the major changes which took place when the differently sized buildings were joined together. This was in all likelihood the lemon-house of the nearby Villa di Castelquarto and four columns from the original building still survive, possibly part of a loggia, now preserved as decorative features for the garden. The farmhouse has the usual features of 19th-century rural architecture.

Bibliography:
Lensi Orlandi, 1965, p. 15.
Castello campagna medicea periferia urbana, 1984 p.84.

VILLA GUASCONI

The Villa Guasconi complex stretches along what was once Via Maestra, just after the hamlet of Le Panche (the name of which, according to Carocci, is derived from the barriers placed to ward off the waters of the Terzolle). In the 15th century it was the country house of the Giugni family, passing in 1652 to the Salviati and, in 1688, to the Marchese Guasconi, the proprietor of numerous farms in the area. Today it is in very poor condition but some traces of what was once a handsome and well-designed house can still be seen in the roadside façade and in the colonnaded courtyard. Building lots have completely removed its original agricultural setting, still clearly marked on the 1936 I.G.M. map.

Bibliography:
Carocci, 1906, p. 263.

LA QUIETE

The buildings making up Villa La Quiete (formerly Palagio di Quarto and later Conservatorio delle Montalve) have some features which have been preserved in virtue of its continuous occupation and use from the 17th century to the present day. The building has a long history and its composite style is the result of successive stages of development. The earliest records are 15th century. Owned by the Orlandini family, in 1438 it passed to Niccolò da Tolentino and in 1453 to Pier Francesco de' Medici. In the following century it was confiscated by Cosimo I who ceded it to the Commenda dell'Ordine di Santo Stefano. At this time, the building and the surrounding land, abutting on Via di Boldrone and other roads which have now disappeared, were recorded on the map of the Capitani di Parte of the parish of Santa Maria a Quarto as being the "property of Cavalieri". The building, even in the summary view offered by the maps, has no particular architectural features and corresponds with its appearance before the 17th-century alterations. Grand Duchess Christina of Lorraine bought the property from Cavalieri in 1627. This was the time of the villa's greatest splendour, when it was decorated by Giovanni da San Giovanni with frescoes which included *Quiet calming the winds*, painted in 1633 and commissioned by Cristina, as is shown by her name painted on the ceiling of the gallery. On the duchess's death in 1636 her son Ferdinando II gave the villa to the aristocratic Eleonora Ramirez di Montalvo who, in 1650, converted it into a school for well-born girls. After the founder's death the school came under the protection of Vittoria della Rovere and in 1686 work began on building the church, completed by Gherardo Silvani. The façade by the entrance to the villa has a portico with three arches, with the della Rovere arms emblazoned in the centre.

Inside lies Vittoria's marble tomb which was produced in 1698, probably by Giovan Battista Foggini.

In 1724 the villa became the home of Anna Maria Luisa de' Medici, Palatine Electress, the last descendant of the House of Medici. She had the villa ornamented with sculptural works, still *in situ*, by the finest artists of the day, such as Soldani, Foggini, Piamontini and Montauti. During the following century major changes were made to the complex with two wings being added to the second courtyard, one of which, on the garden side, has a covered roof-terrace echoing the one in the original body of the building. The villa has a spacious garden which was begun by the Electress Palatine when she purchased some land, had water brought in a long pipe from the Lepricine fountain, and built a large lemon-house. This is a rare example of a surviving 18th-century garden, still complete with its ornamental and some of its botanical features. As G. Galletti says in his entry on the garden: "*Setting aside the compound styles of the fountains, the baroque stairs and the terracotta and rough stone rococo additions, the morphology of the garden is still in the Renaissance tradition. Rational criteria of layout and simplicity of forms arranged in a walled garden and subdivided on two levels. The upper level is divided into rectangular parterres with a quarter of a circle removed from the corners to accommodate the bases for the pots of citrus trees. The main sides are bordered by a double row of box, broken at intervals to hold further bases for pots and rows of what were probably plants grown from bulbs. The four-sided area of the lower level, between two paths leading to a fountain in the centre, is divided into five large parterres on each side, bordered by box hedges about a metre thick. The parterres were once undoubtedly used for growing fruit, as was the trellis along the west wall. Immediately below the upper level, in front of the main rooms and the small grotto, framed by the double-ramped staircase between the levels, are two beds formerly used for groves of bitter orange trees. . . . The netting-grove on the east side of the lower garden, marked as 'wild' in the preparatory drawings, is one of the few in the Florentine area not to have fallen into ruin and to have retained its original form, thanks to the espalier pruning. . . . The ten rectangular compartments that it contains faithfully echo, in their unitary composition, the perspectived arrangement of the garden, vistas ending with the more dramatic architectural features, such as the imposing baroque shrine at the end of the third transverse path, or the entrances to the wine-cellar or the lemon-house. Each section, or compartment, has a framework composed of rows of evergreen oaks, planted in regular fashion along the perimeter and forming the upper part of the espalier hedge bordering the path. The lower part is a box hedge which reaches the remarkable height of four to five metres. This pattern of double-layered tall hedges reveals what, before 19th-century alterations and repeated pollarding, must have been the layout of the bird-netting areas in the Boboli Gardens. In one part of the netting area, two compartments hold two rooms, real garden-rooms, open to the sky . . . To the still fully Renaissance atmosphere of thoughtful reflection and delight is added the unusual one, for a garden, of a religious collection. The grotto of the* Good Samaritan, *and especially the* Noli mi tangere *shrine were conceived as places of prayer. The small chapel, never completed but designed almost like a nymphaeum, would have further emphasized the use of purely profane models in a Christian context.*"

Bibliography:
Castello campagna medicea periferia urbana, 1984, p. 81.
Antico e futuro nel terriorio mediceo di Castello I giardini della chimera, 1989, pp. 37–39.
De Benedictis, 1997.

VILLA CASINI

Referred to as "Villa Casini" in the 1896 and 1923 editions of the I.G.M. maps, and "Podere Il Frantoio" in the 1936 one, it was later called "Villa Italia". Its appearance today is that of a late 19th-century residence. Traces of the earlier building can be seen in the walled-up entrance on the road and the three windows with corbels, but it was much affected by a recent restoration which left its mark on the whole building.

Bibliography:
Lensi Orlandi, 1965, p. 15.
Castello campagna medicea periferia urbana, 1984, p. 113.

VILLA AMALIA

The I.G.M. maps record the building as "Villa Amalia" in their 1896 and 1923 versions, and "Il Cedro, Villa Lavaggi" in 1936. "*It stands almost in front of the Petraia, with its façade on Via di Mezzo which joins the provincial road by means of a farm track.*" This is how Tosi described it early in the last century. Today its original setting has been totally ruined by the construction of the Saivo factory on the old farmland, the surroundings being now reduced to a strip of garden separating the villa from the adjacent factory buildings. It now stands on Via Giuliano Ricci (formerly Via di Mezzo), heavily altered and converted and is surrounded by an exposed stone wall, a continuation of the one bordering the old road. There are two entrances, the first on Via Ricci, with a keystone carved with a coat of arms displaying three tortoises on a diagonal band. Modern iron gates to the right of the villa lead into the garden. On this side is the second entrance, a 19th-century rusticated stone doorway. At the end of the 15th century the house belonged to Salvi Panuzzi; transferred in 1508 to the sons of Niccolò del Maestro Luca of the parish of Santa Trinita, and from them to the Del Zaccaria family; on 12 February 1591 it was bought by Giuliano Ricci, a man of letters and a member of the Accademia della Crusca, a grandson of Machiavelli. Ricci lived in the villa, which he called "I Cancelli", until his death in 1606. In 1613 his sons sold the property to Alessandro di Antonio di Matteo Latini. It was later owned by the Casini (1622), Baldanzi (1631) and lieutenant Annibale Cecchi (1651). During the 19th century the villa and adjoining farm became the property of the Marchionni family and then of the singer Carlotta Zucchi who, in 1891, transferred the property to Pallotti, an antiquarian, from who it was purchased by the Gozzini.

Bibliography:
Tosi, 1905, p. 43.
Carocci, 1906, p. 281.
Castello campagna medicea periferia urbana, 1984, p. 79.

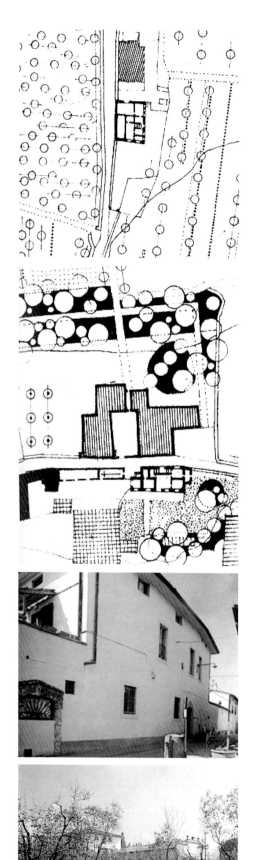

IL CHIUSO, VILLA ORSINI

This villa stands on a plain and has had various names, "Le due colombaie", "Il Sodo" and "Il chiuso dei Mazza", the latter referring not to the name of the proprietors but to the layout of the farmland around the villa. The estate included four farms and four farmhouses (Sodo, Panche, Via Erbosa and the Villa) bordered by the surrounding roads: Via delle Panche, Via del'Osservatorio, Via di Boldrone and Via della Quiete. The principal building is a 17th-century remodelling of a pre-existing structure. The present layout is of the typology with a courtyard closed on all four sides and it has two symmetrical placed dovecotes (hence the name "Le due colombaie") at the ends of the façade on the garden side. In the centre is a loggia and handsome barred (*inginocchiate*) windows on simple corbels which grow denser towards the centre, emphasizing the entrance, set in alignment with the main garden pathway and with the cypress-lined avenue which once reached as far as Via delle Panche. Alas, the trees in the avenue were largely cut down during the late 1960s to make it easier to divide the farmland along the road into building lots. The enclosed courtyard at the centre of the building is reached from the walled garden and from the entrance on Via del Boldrone (originally the main one), through a grandiose 18th-century rectangular doorway. One side of the courtyard has a loggia with composite columns and capitals, while the side facing the Observatory has a *pietra serena* doorway from the mid-15th century. The first-floor rooms are decorated with 17th-century frescoes.

According to Carocci, in the 1427 land register the property belonged to Antonio di Taddeo Tommasi, of the Lion Bianco gonfalon. In the second half of the century it passed to the Del Barbigia, or Barbigi, wealthy merchants who lived in Piazza Santa Croce, and in 1599 it was brought as dowry by Francesca di Francesco Barbigi on her marriage to Lorenzo di Francesco Palmezzini, being ceded the same year to Alberto di Cristofano Lambardi of Venice.

Sold in 1661 to Lorenzo Gamucci and in 1686 to the Consolini family, it then passed to the Gori and the Del Mazza, from whom it was purchased, in 1817, by the office of "Regie Possessioni", becoming part of the Castello estate until 1849 when it was alienated as part of the programme to reorganize grand ducal property. Tosi tells us that it was owned by the famous military commander, Niccolò da Tolentino; his offspring would have transferred it in 1453 to Giovanni di Bicci dei Medici, who passed it in 1495 to Piero d'Andrea Taddei. With the collapse of the Florentine Republic, when his son Filippo Taddei was declared a rebel, the estate would have been confiscated and passed into the possession of Cosimo I and the villa, according to this account, continued to belong to the Castello estate for a considerable period.

In 1882, the villa and its agricultural holdings were sold to Contessa Ludovica Bourbon di Sorbello, the widow of Count Orsini, and was later inherited by its present owners, the De Pazzi Morelli family.

Bibliography:
Tosi, *Santa Maria a Quarto*, 1892, p. 16.
Carocci, 1906, p. 207.
Gobbi, 1978, p. 12.
Castello campagna medicea periferia urbana, 1984, pp. 79–80.

VILLA CORSINI

"*The most beautiful example of an extra-urban baroque residence near Florence*", is how Edith Wharton described this villa in her book *Italian Villas and their Gardens*, published in New York in 1904. From documentary evidence the Villa Corsini can be traced to the 15th century. In the 1427 land register the villa was owned by the influential Strozzi family whose leading member, Palla Strozzi, had such power in the city that he was exiled on the wishes of Cosimo the Elder, fearful that his fame would make him a rival in his rise to political power. The widow of Palla's son, Alessandra de' Bardi, sold the villa, up to this time called "Palagetto", to Bernardo di Stoldo Rinieri. In the contract of sale, drawn up on 19 December 1460, the property is described as follows: "*a farm with a house for owner and worker with garden and arable land, vineyard, orchard, olive groves and untilled ground, situated in the parish of San Michele at Castello, known as the Piazza or Palazzetto, sixty* 'staia' *in all. Another farm with a worker's house and fifty* staia *of land, known as Chiasso, all for one thousand gold florins.*"

This was the first core of the future Villa Corsini which, at this period, had all the usual features of extra-urban "manor" houses in the area. When the villa passed to the Rinieri family, prominent merchants, it took on a new name, "Il lepre dei Rinieri" or "I Rinieri". Apart from the villa in question the family also owned other property in the area, having bought a villa and part of a farm and a mill at the Loggia dei Bianchi, a farm called Le Brache in the parish of Santa Maria at Quarto, and another near the village of Le Panche. As we see from the maps of the Capitani di Parte, the Rinieri also owned land in the parish of Santa Maria at Quinto, near Villa Covacchia. The property remained in the possession of the Rinieri family until 1571. In this period were commissioned by Christofano Rinieri to Tribolo the first works to transform the villa and gardens. It subsequently belonged to the Sangalletti. The first version of the Capitani di Parte maps carries an elevation of a simple building, the property of the Rinieri, while the following version gives a truer planimetric image, with the name "Galetto" appearing beside it as well as the Rinieri name. The property was confiscated from the Sangalletti by the grand ducal authorities and resold in 1597 to Pagolo Donati. After this it changed hands on several occasions before being bought in 1604 by Dianora Malaspina, and sold again in 1618 to Grand Duke Cosimo II for 4400 *scudi*, enlarging the already sizeable Medici holdings in the area. A guest at the villa during this period was Robert Dudley, Duke of Northumberland, who rebuilt the port of Livorno.

But the villa did not remain a grand ducal possession for long. In 1650 Cosimo Sassetti, minister general of the property office, sold it to Piero di Bernardo Cervieri, who bequeathed it in his will to the Jesuit Fathers of San Giovanni in Florence. In 1678 the villa and its possessions were bought by Ottavia di Gismondo della Stufa, as the basis of the dowry for her marriage to Lorenzo di Girolamo Lanfredini. In 1697 financial difficulties caused the son, also Lorenzo, to begin to sell the property. He first sold the "Ragnaia" farm to Cosimo III and, in the same year, he sold the villa for 6880 *scudi* to Lucrezia Rinuccini, wife of the Marchese Filippo Corsini. The villa remained in the family's possession until the Second World War and after various events had reduced it to a ruinous condition it was bought by the official Soprintendenza ai Monumenti. Interesting correspondence in the library of the Accademia Nazionale dei Lincei e Corsiniana in Rome, published by Luigi Zangheri, gives us a detailed account of the history of the villa and the changes introduced by the Corsini.

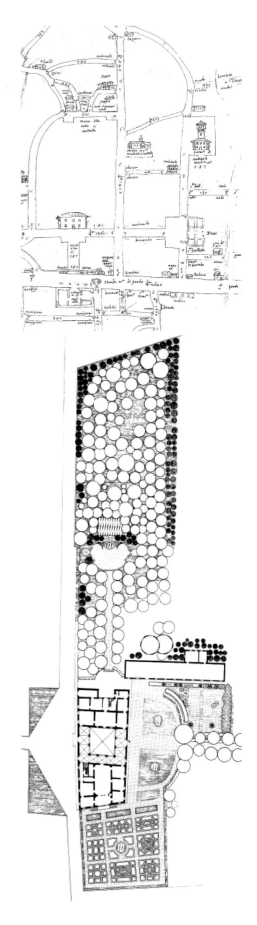

"The villa might suit you very well", writes the Marchese Filippo to his brother Lorenzo (later Pope Clement XII), *"there is a nearby farm with easy access, and another not far away, which it would be easy to enclose in one wall and it might make a good purchase"*. This reveals not only his wish to acquire a suitable outlying house for the family, but also concern about making a shrewd property investment.

"I have concluded purchase of the Lanfredini villa for 6880," we read in a later letter, *"another thousand will be needed for the garden annexes and farm buildings, and some major building work is needed and perhaps some enclosing walls are needed . . . the farm was once large but it has been broken up. Since G.D. sold some greenhouses to him we are negotiating with Giacomini for a nearby farm and house that could serve for the family. I have gone up to 2700 and they are standing firm at 3000; there is another on this road belonging to Conte del Maestro which could be had, with another two adjoining fields, if we want to occupy the whole site, which is bordered by the roads leading to Boldrone and Petraia which, being a fine place with two large farm . . .".*

These letters go on to describe the changes that were introduced to the area in terms of the formal layout we can still see today, despite the division of the property and the generally poor condition of the whole complex: *" . . . among other things, I thought of making an open space at the end of the avenue leading towards the Capuchin friars, where I thought of extending the grove of cypresses by building a small round court in front of the gate; but since the entrance or gates of the avenue are out of line, I thought of making a similar one on the road which, aligned with these cypresses, would meet the one coming from the Capuchins . . . "*

In the history of the villa's transformation we can clearly identify some important stages marking the process which, to greater or lesser degree, was common to all the conversions and rebuilding operations carried out on the properties of the wealthy classes.

The original core of the villa consisted of two houses, one for gentlefolk and one for workers, as we read in the contract of sale of 1460. We have no pictorial image of this original nucleus to add to the archival documents and we can only hypothesize on the shape of the 15th-century building on the basis of later remodellings.

The first recorded event occurred while it was owned by the Rinieri. The two buildings were joined with a central block with loggias on three sides, as is clearly shown plan of the parish of San Michele a Castello, and those of the Capitani di Parte (1580). The south face still has a 15th-century appearance with a rusticated entrance and two rows of windows with handsome surrounds supported on stone corbels. A still earlier feature is recognizable on the east elevation, probably the remains of the old dovecote tower once a structural part of the building. During this period the garden was ornamented by Tribolo and Pierino da Vinci, then engaged on Cosimo I's villa at Castello.

"Tribolo worked at the villa of Cristofano Rinieri at Castello while he was engaged on the duke's fountains, above a fish-pond which is at the top of a netting grove, a life-size grey stone river in a niche, which pours water into an enormous basin made of similar stone. This river, which is composed of several pieces, is made with such skill and care, that it seems to be one piece alone."

This is what Vasari writes in his *Life* of Tribolo. And moreover, as Vasari tells us, it was Cristofano Rinieri who introduced Tribolo to Cosimo I who was dissatisfied with the way Piero da San Casciano was carrying out the work at the Castello villa: *"One day, when*

His Excellency was talking to him at his place . . . with some gentlemen, Ottaviano de' Medici and Cristofano Rinieri, a friend of Tribolo and faithful servant of the lady Maria and of the Duke, they praised Tribolo as a man endowed with all the qualities required to lead work on such an operation, so that the Duke appealed to Cristofano, who sent for him from Bologna."

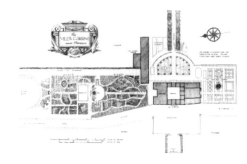

The statue personifying the river now stands in a niche, built in the 18th century and probably later altered, separated from its original basin and deprived of its symbolism. It once represented a source of water which, from the highest point in the garden, flowed from the pitcher between the figure's legs into the basin and the fish-pond, and right down to the fountains in the courtyard and the central basin. Cristofano Rinieri was also responsible for the what must once have been the appearance of the walled garden: a stone fountain in the centre surrounded by beds of orange and lemon trees bordered by box hedges. Another decisive moment for the villa's architectural style, and for the gardens, was the works conducted in the 17th and 18th centuries after the property had been bought by the Corsini family. The 17th-century intervention has been attributed to Antonio Ferri, who had worked for the Corsini in their city palazzo on the Lungarno, and this is supported by scholars who have studied the Villa Corsini. The discovery of the correspondence between Filippo Corsini, who lived chiefly in Rome, and the master of works, the priest Giuliano Leonardi, who acted as an emissary between the commissioner and the artists, craftsmen and gardeners working on the villa, has allowed the rebuilding operations to be restored to Giovan Battista Foggini.

The 18th-century conversion is an interesting example of the baroque style being superimposed on an originally 16th-century building. The villa's principal façade was given an elaborate new face, while preserving the earlier pattern of two rows of windows. These were now framed by slightly projecting pilaster strips and stucco ornamentations, while in the centre of the façade, above the ornamented doorway and overhead balcony, a coat of arms and festooned clock was added on a frontispiece starting from the two wings of the building and soaring upwards into a pedimented crown flanked by balustrades ornamented with urns. The façade on the garden side was ornamented in the same way, and a broad depressed arch inserted in the upper storey, above a loggia with stone columns on the ground floor. The 18th-century operations were extended to the villa's interior, with a handsome courtyard in 16th-century style, with arches on three sides, the fourth side being closed by a wall with pilaster strips and blind arches. The two-storey drawing-room has a barrel vault and large areas of wall are frescoed with landscapes and ornamented with elegant stucco decorations. And lastly, the small chapel added to the north side of the building (the Oratory of SS. Cosma e Damiano), whose furnishings have been lost. The copious and as yet only partly catalogued archives of the Corsini family have led to a close study of the works conducted at the villa from the time it was purchased by Filippo Corsini until his death in 1706 and, in particular, the role that Foggini played at the planning stage, and the contributions of the various craftsmen involved. The stucco ornamentation was produced by Carlo Maria and Passardo Passardi, the frescoes by Niccolò Lapi (replaced in 1905 by Niccolò Contestabile's bucolic scenes), decorations by Rinaldo Botti and Alessandro Gherardini (who painted the Corsini-Rinuccini arms in the main reception room), and building work was carried out by the stonemason Antonio Sandrini and a team led by Orazio Totti. The outside areas would also seem to be owed to Foggini even if the commissioner, in the exchange of letters, expresses his own opinions

firmly and includes ideas and sketches for the architect to consider. It was Corsini's idea to build a semi-ellipsoidal wall on the south side of the villa interspersed with pillars and stone benches, overlooking the vanishing perspective created by the avenue of evergreen oaks which connected the entrances to the villa and the stables.

" *when the grain has gone we shall have to begin enlarging the lawn in the rear, which I want to make oval in shape and furnish with benches to sit on and pot-stands for taller and shorter vases; tell Foggini of my ideas and send me a sketch.*" A month later, the correspondence continues: "*I have received the plants I was sent. I like the change… I like the idea of a lawn to draw water both from the 'wilderness', and of the semicircle, and can begin work, however I do not want any statues or urns but pots of flowering orange trees instead; and on the bases at the entrance to the path I want two stone basins to collect the water drawn from the courtyard, for sending it back to the garden; discuss it with Foggini.*"

In fact, this programme was later modified, perhaps at the architect's suggestion, because the water-basins were alternated with statues of the Four Seasons set on pillars, produced by Isodoro Franchi between 1702 and 1703. The same artist was commissioned for a putto and dolphin, now lost, for the water reservoir that was being built in the "wilderness". The proprietor also gives instructions on how these woods should be cut, giving a new shape to the 16th-century bird-netting area; a new position for the fountain from the courtyard; the placing of pillars at the entrance to Via di Castello, in line with the villa's principal entrance; the use of "*spugna di Valdimarina*" (a variety of tufa) to ornament the pillars "*in front as well as at the back*"; and the paving to surround the villa, which was to have "*some round holes for planting jasmine*" all along the south façade. In the "French- style" garden, a fountain was installed in the netting area flanked by a curving stairway, an interesting example of a scenic motif much used by Buontalenti. The marble basin was fed by water from a house's head framed in volutes and surmounted by a stone crowning. Above this was set a vast water basin fringed with maidenhair fern, beyond which a short path leads through the dense trees to Tribolo's statue. Today, the 18th-century garden ends here, though reduced to an untended dense thicket, but until the end of the 19th century it was continued by a riding ring, no longer in existence by the early 1900s. A grove of cypresses planted in rows separates the wood of ilex trees from the farm. Vines and olives once adjoined the formal garden, crossed by the majestic avenue that ran from the semicircular garden of the Four Seasons to the gate leading to the old Via di Mezzo. The garden of the Four Seasons is also in deplorable condition and the statues are badly damaged. The view from the walled garden is a sorry sight by comparison to its splendours a century ago.

Bibliography:
Tosi, *Rinieri Villa Corsini*, 1893.
Carocci, 1906, p. 280.
Elgood, 1907, pp. 96–98.
Eberlein, 1921, p. 76.
Wiles, 1933, pp. 35–36.
Lensi Orlandi, 1965, p. 19.
Dezzi Bardeschi, Zangheri, 1969.
Acton, 1973, pp. 57–58.
Fuscari, Prosperi Valenti Rondinò, 1982, pp. 81–118.
Castello campagna medicea periferia urbana, 1984, pp. 67–68.
I giardini della chimera, 1989, pp. 57–59.
Santangelo, 1996.

VILLA MAFFEI

This building is called "Villa Maffei" on the I.G.M. maps, but Carocci also refers to it as "Carelli or Quarto". It stands in a good position on the slopes of Rufignano and has a 19th-century appearance, with no notable features. There appears to have been no building here before the second half of the 16th century, when the Ruspoli family owned a farm on the site, later bought by Uguccione de' Ricci. The modest-sized villa was built by Lucrezia and Camilla di Vincenzo Ruspoli and later sold to Galeotti. In 1624 it was owned by Count Del Maestro, who also had other properties in the nearby parish of Castello. In 1653 it was bought by Francesco M. Vettori and until 1832 formed part of the Marchese Vettori's extensive estates at Quarto. On the right, slightly further along Via Dazzi, stands a somewhat reworked building which corresponds with the 19th-century Villa Alessandra (its name on the 1896 I.G.M. map). The villa belonged to the writer Pietro Dazzi, as both Carocci and Lensi Orlandi mention.

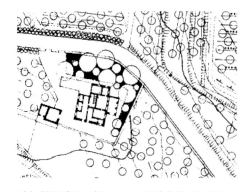

Bibliography:
Carocci, 1906, p. 272.
Lensi Orlandi, 1965, p. 16.

VILLA BELGIOIELLO

The building appears on the 1896 and 1923 I.G.M. maps as "Villa Belgioello", but the 1936 edition carries no reference to it. It has been subjected to numerous conversions and deprived of any particular architectural character. In the early Cinquecento it was the country house of the Buongirolami family from Perugia; in 1496 they sold it to Alessandro Pandolfini. A subsequent change of ownership in 1547 made it the property of Niccolò Stagnese who sold it to Giovanni di Niccolò Vettori, whose family continued to own it until the 19th century. During Vittorio Emmanuele II's reign, the "Lista Civile" bought it from the proprietor, Ottavio Gigli, who exchanged it for the Vivaio and Steccuto farms at Castello. On the 1896 I.G.M. map, the facing building on Via Dazzi, today with no architectural features of note, is referred to as "Il Pratello", and this would seem to correspond with the Baldesi villa on the Capitani di Parte map of the parish of Santa Maria a Quarto.

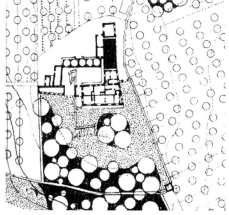

Bibliography:
Tosi, 1905, p. 9.
Carocci, 1906, pp. 271–272.
Lensi Orlandi, 1965, p. 17.
Mannini, 1984, pp. 152–153.

VILLA MALAFRASCA

The name on the three versions (1896, 1923, 1936) of the I.G.M. maps is "Villa Malafrasca".

This building, of little interest from an architectural point of view, was described by Lensi Orlandi as "*a dull looking rural house*". It faces the northern limits of the Petraia park, the trees of which cut off the view of the plain.

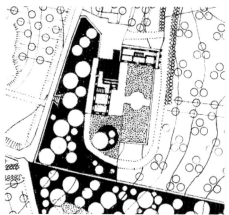

Bibliography:
Lensi Orlandi, 1965, p. 17.

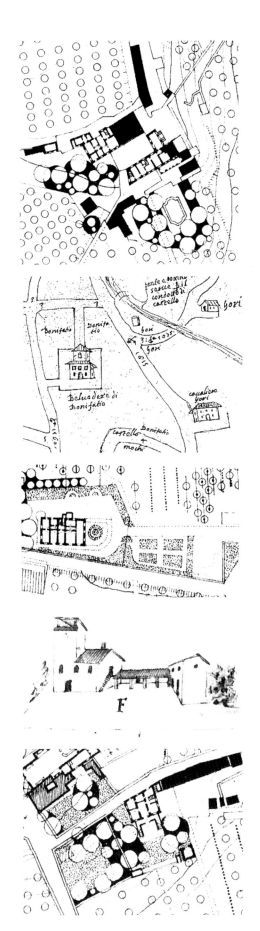

VILLA BELVEDERE

The 1896 and 1923 I.G.M. maps carry the names "Villa Luder" and "Villa Belvedere", the 1936 version only the latter. The complex has very early origins and is composed of a variety of rural buildings surrounded by olive trees in a wonderfully panoramic position. Remodellings of different periods have given it a unified appearance. In the early 15th century it belonged to Niccolò di Giovanni Gori di Careggi, and in 1470 it passed to Francesco d'Andrea Noferi who sold it in 1473 to Corrado Tedesco, known as Lupo. It was then owned by his wife Leonarda and went as a dowry to Alessandro Giannini who sold it in 1552 to Francesco di Giovan Battista Mochi. Subsequent owners included Ginevra di Andrea, sword-maker (1591), Jacopo di Bartolomeo, shoemaker, and Salvestro Magliani, who sold it to the Stiattesi in 1621. It was bought from the next owner, Andrea Baldanzi, in 1649 by Cosimo di Rodolfo Dei, whose family continue to own it for many years. During the 19th century it belonged to the Luder family. The map of the Capitani di Parte of the parish of San Silvestro at Ruffignano records the existence of a towered building, carefully illustrated with its surrounding land and called "Belvedere di Bonifatio", of which there is now no trace in the present building, after its repeated transformation.

Bibliography:
Carocci, 1906, p. 272.
Lensi Orlandi, 1965, p. 17.
Mannini, 1984, p. 155.

IL RIPOSO or BELRIPOSO

The 1896 I.G.M. map records the building as "Il Riposo Villa Naldini". The present entrance is on the road leading to Villa Petraia, opposite Villa Corsini.

The building's present 19th-century appearance, with a vaguely neo-gothic tower, conceals the traces of a much early construction, a house for a worker on the Arco farm, annexed to the Castello estate. The clear map of the Steccuto and Arco farms, included in the register of the Medici estate dated 1697, shows a plan and a small perspective view of the house prior to its 19th-century transformation, which altered the appearance of the dovecote tower without demolishing it. A farm track connected the house and the farmland behind it, running as far as the land belonging to the church of San Michele at Castello. These two farms, Steccuto and Arco, were turned into one farm, Steccuto, and the Arco house was used as an annex by the Castello estate. When the estate was broken up in 1869 the Steccuto farm was given to Ottavio Gigli in exchange for the land of Belgioiello and the buildings were turned into villas. The villa known as Steccuto, then Pallestrini and later Cini, was recently heavily converted and made indistinguishable from the new buildings that have sprung up on the old farm.

VILLA LAWLEY

This building on Via San Michele at Castello is called "Villa Lawley" on the 1896 and 1923 I.G.M. maps and "Villa Toja" on the 1936 version. This is probably a 19th-century conversion of a pre-existing building, once the property of the parish estate of San Michele at Castello. However, the maps carry no reference to it.

VILLA DI QUARTO

The Villa di Quarto, now divided into apartments, and its vast and magnificent park, provide a perfect example of a 19th-century transformation in the Florentine area. On the basis of existing documentation, the original nucleus of the villa goes back to the 15th century.

We have no visual record of the building at this time and can only presume that it was a *casa da signore* with a fairly simple layout, with neither interior courtyards nor loggias, since subsequent works of restructuring were usually conducted without totally altering the original planimetric design. Owned by the Pasquali family, doctors to the grand ducal court, the villa was remodelled in around 1713 on Alfonso Parigi's design. Its appearance after Parigi's intervention is displayed by an interesting anonymous 18th-century painting (formerly part of the Acton collection and later owned by Baron Ritter de Zahony) which presents a clear view of the villa and garden after the alterations. The façade on the garden side is regularly spanned by windows with handsome frames and stone corbels, thrown into relief by the white plaster. In the centre is a ground-floor loggia with three arches, immediately below the small dovecote tower high above. It has more in common with a late 16th-century villa than with the rocaille façades of Villa Corsini or Villa Corsi Salviati. The 18th-century intervention is most obvious in the landscaping of the garden and the grandiose lemon-house, which forms a screen on the garden's south side.

Subsequent change in proprietors (the sale early in the 19th century to Conte Caselli, then to Girolamo Bonaparte, ex-king of Westphalia who, after the fall of the Empire chose Florence as his place of exile, and later to the Russian Prince Anatolio Demidoff) mark the period during which the villa played a leading role in Florentine society gatherings, and together these owners were responsible for the villa's final appearance. Between 1840 and 1850 major changes were introduced to the complex and to the surrounding land. The estate was enlarged by the acquisition of the Gattaia farm (bought in 1851 from the Conservatorio degli Angiolini), a stretch of the San Silvestro road (between the cemetery and Via Nuova di Quarto, which was built at this time and to which the prince had contributed the sum of 10,000 lire), and finally, in 1852, by the annexation of a property called "La Gironda", from the administrators of the Reali Possessioni di Toscana.

The most remarkable operation on the land was to turn the farmland into a romantic park full of exotic rare plants, ornamented with statues, pavilions and a lake. The conversion into a park was speedily carried out, together with work on the adjacent Petraia park; its grandeur was praised in contemporary accounts.

The villa and its annexes were sold in 1865 to Grand Duchess Maria of Russia, the oldest daughter of Czar Nicholas; after her death in 1882 it was bought by the Marchese Capponi, passing in 1890 to Duke Massari and it continued to be a focal point of contemporary social life and a place for entertaining important visitors to Florence. In 1908 the villa was bought by Baron Ritter de Zahony who carried out substantial restoration work on the buildings.

The three-storey villa has a very simple planimetric layout with a two-storey main drawing-room in the centre with first-floor galleries on three sides, leading to the other rooms. The face on the garden side has an arched loggia on coupled columns, added during the course of the 19th-century conversion to replace the 18th-century loggia. However, the 19th-century work did not affect the nature of the earlier layout, or only as regards some details. The position of the windows remained unchanged, although

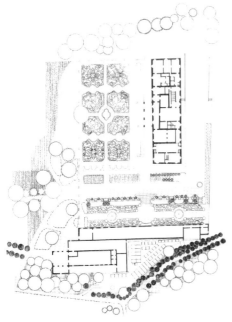

those on the ground floor illustrated by the 18th-century painting were turned into doorways, those on the first floor lengthened, and the small apertures on the mezzanine floor of the central block were closed.

The garden is an interesting contemporary interpretation of the traditional walled garden. It is surrounded by a stone balustrade bearing 18th-century statues, faithfully reproducing the image presented in the 18th-century painting. During the operations conducted by Demidoff this balustrade was replaced by a more up-to-date iron railing and short stone pedestals, still present on the north side of the building. The flower-beds, edged with box hedges in an elaborate "French" design, were introduced early in the 20th century by Baroness Ritter. In the 18th-century painting we see a simple lawned garden, with a central water-basin. The garden is landscaped to follow the natural lie of the land and has a raised level on the south side of the building, ornamented with patterned flower-beds and fountains. Stone steps, which become semicircular benches or surfaces for standing vases, link the two levels. On the south side the garden is closed off by the beautiful lemon-house with raised side-wings for housing the servants. This building is also connected to the enormous stables, approached though a large portico. Alterations to the lemon-house in the 19th century, which removed the crowing balustrade on the raised wings and the baroque framing of the windows, preserved the 18th-century clock in the centre.

The garden is surrounded by a thickly planted park with a broad view of the city to the east. In the opposite direction the high part includes a belvedere terrace which stands above the Quarto church.

Bibliography:
Da Prato, 1886.
Tosi, *Santa Maria a Quarto*, 1892.
Carocci, 1906, pp. 269–270.
Lensi Orlandi, 1965, p. 16.
Trionfi Honorati, 1966, p. 68ff.
Gobbi, 1974, pp. 19–21.
Castello campagna medicea periferia urbana, 1984, p. 90.

VILLA PETRAIA

Built like a small fortress, this was once the property of the Brunelleschi family, and it was here that Boccaccio Brunelleschi's sons reportedly fought off the Pisan troops led by Giovanni Acuto (the Englishman, Sir John Hawkwood) in 1364, as we are told in Chapter LXXXVIII of Matteo Villani's *Cronaca*. There is no record of the transfer of the property from the Brunelleschi, a family which lived in the parish of San Leo and owned property in the countryside near Sesto, to Palla Strozzi, the wealthiest citizen in Florence, whose declaration for the land register in 1427 included: *"A property called Petraia in the parish of San Michele at Castello, with a ruined gentleman's dwelling, worker's house and olive press with CXL staia of land, part vineyard, part arable and with olives and woods . . . worked by Bonuccio di Bruno who every year earns about twelve florins . . . .*

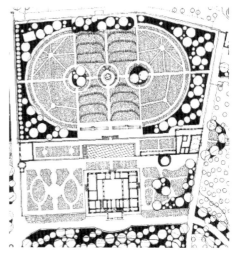

Annual production:
Grain: 74 bushels at 17 soldi a bushel, total L. 62 and 18 soldi
Wine: 31 barrels at 28 soldi a barrel, total L. 43 and 8 soldi
Oil: 14 jars at 100 the jar, total L. 70
Total revenue: L. 176 and 6 soldi."

We have no precise information on the transfer of the property from the Strozzi to the Medici but we know that in 1544 the villa belonged to Cosimo I and that in 1566 it first appeared in the Campione di Beni (register of goods and property).

On the south face of the tower appears Palla's coat of arms: a helm and the motto PAR.VOUS, left intact to display the noble origins of this Medici residence, though they were bitter enemies of the Strozzi. Despite the radical changes carried out from the late 16th century onwards, traces of the original building can still be seen in the lower part of the tower, the surrounding wall to the west which has blocked-in medieval-style windows, and the walls on the north side. In 1566 Cosimo I entrusted Davide Fortini with remodelling operations (he worked on some parts and on a loggia) for his son Ferdinando to whom he gave the villa and its possessions in 1568. From 1587 onwards more substantial alterations were entrusted by Ferdinando (now Grand Duke after the unexpected death of his brother Francesco I) to the architect Raffaello di Zanobi di Pagno, who had worked on the Medici villa in Rome. The intention was to make the whole building more rational and ordered. One major change was the addition of a new block in line with the tower, providing extra hallways and the space to install a new staircase. Another important event was the insertion of the new courtyard, on an out-dated plan that was probably influenced by the pre-existing one.

The tower was also raised. In the plans of the property on the Capitani di Parte for the parish of San Michele at Castello there is a view of the front of the villa topped with the familiar tower, but lower with only one row of windows. Moreover, the words "Cardinale Medici e S.A.S." evidently refer to the period prior to Cardinal Ferdinando's rise to the grand ducal throne, and therefore prior to the changes that he introduced. Further alterations were made to the farmland immediately adjoining the villa, now turned into a garden, as reported in Cosimo I's register of goods and properties. To the north of the palazzo a thick barrier of cypresses was planted to keep out the north wind. Two roads led to the property, one on the east and one on the west. The west road has been absorbed by the park while the east one is now partly public and partly in the park. On the death of Ferdinand I, use of the Petraia went to his younger son Don Lorenzo. At this time (1609) works were carried out on the garden – previously divided into beds outlined by box hedges – and in around 1622 operations began on the great underground passageway, leading from the villa to the road to the west and connecting the palazzo with the kitchens, positioned at the

end of this passageway. During this same period Giulio Parigi reinforced the tower and various artists were engaged to decorate rooms and loggias. Among these were Cosimo Daddi and, above all, Baldassarre Franceschini, better known as Volterrano, who painted the splendid cycle the *Glories of the House of Medici*, commissioned by Don Lorenzo who held court to learned men of letters and artists. On Don Lorenzo's death in 1649 the villa returned to the main branch of the Medici family. The inventories list many other paintings, including a Tintoretto. Great attention was also paid to the agricultural side of the property and to the various areas of the garden and the conduits which brought water from the Valcenni aqueduct to feed the fountains and the fish-pool. It would seem that the garden was given its final lay-out on three levels in the mid-17th century, despite the fact that, as we have said, work had begun a century earlier, as shown by the documents we have cited (1574). The upper garden, by the east side of the villa, was divided into four flower-beds for bulbs and a trellis of citrus trees was trained against the wall of the villa. On the level of the fish-pool were statues and box clipped into *opus topiarum*; in the lower part of the garden were eight large beds, two for growing flowers and the others vegetables; around this were four groves of ilex and paths covered by arching foliage. The agricultural part of the property consisted of three farms: Arco, Ragnaia and Topaia. When the property returned to the main branch of the family Petraia was no longer free be independently administered but remained tied to the Castello estate. Projects to adapt and change the villa are recorded in the Florentine State Archives. The most notable change to the villa's surroundings took place in 1836 when the land of the old Ragnaia farm and the land between the villa and the Quarto church were turned into a romantic park. By 1850 work on the garden was more or less complete. After this some changes were introduced, such as the greenhouse, built in 1833, and the "compartments" made on the "level with the *figurina*", the upper east garden adjoining the villa where Giambologna's *Venus* had been transferred from the Castello villa in 1788. When Florence was made the capital of the new Kingdom of Italy, the Petraia became the favourite outlying villa of Vittorio Emanuele II. Further changes and adjustments to suit the prevailing style were introduced to both the villa and the surroundings. The villa's courtyard was covered with a glass and iron roof to create a large ballroom; lakes were created in the higher area of the park, the formal garden was substantially altered to accord with the Victorian system of mass planting and the "level with the *figurina*" was set with large aviaries, designed by Ferdinando Lasinio in 1872. But all this was to be short-lived. In 1984 the villa was declared a national monument, restored, furnished and opened to the public.

Bibliography:
Acidini Luchinat, Galletti, 1995, and accompanying bibliography.

IL QUADRIVIO
The present building at the crossroads of Via di Castello and Via della Querciola looks just like any other 19th-century villa (the name which it bears on the 1896 and 1923 I.G.M. maps is "Quadrivio villa Rossi"). Formerly annexed to the Castello estate to be used by the laundry workers and later the wardrobe staff, the building was annexed to the Steccuto farm. Together with the land and the farmhouse it was ceded in perpetuity to Ottavio Gigli and converted into a villa.

Bibliography:
Carocci, 1906, p. 286.

VILLA RICCERI

The 1896 and 1923 I.G.M. maps record the name "villa Ricceri", while on the subsequent 1936 edition the name has disappeared. The connection between the villa and garden and the farm in the rear is clearly marked on the map, a path on an axis with Via di Mezzo.

This was a worker's house belonging to Aldobrando di Lorenzo of Steccuto, sold in 1482 to the Franceschi family who turned it into a villa with an elegant 16th-century architectural design. Carocci tells us that the villa was owned by Antonio di Benedetto Tarchiani, a secretary to Cosimo III, who bequeathed it to the Ricoveri. Margherita di Simone Ricoveri, wife of the courtly poet Bartolomeo Corsini, was separated from her husband and went to live on her property at Castello. Until the 18th century the Ricoveri family owned property at Arco, Querciola and along the Via Serezzano. The villa and attached farm passed in 1872 to Amerigo Ricceri, who bought it from the Pozzolini, who had received it as a dowry from the Magnelli. The name "Querciola", used by Carocci, comes from archival material that mentions the Querciola farm as being part of the Medici estate. In volume 37 of the maps of grand ducal properties (Piante delle Regie Possessioni) at c. 68 there is a map of the Villa Querciola farm "*bartered in exchange by S.A.S. to Diacinto Maria Marmi by in the year 1669, together with eight other pieces of land adjoining Via Maestra, as shown on the present map, etc.*". On this map we read the names of neighbouring proprietors and among them, adjacent to this farm, between Via Maestra, Via di Castello and the road leading to Petraia, lies the Tarchiani property. The farm and villa returned to the estate between 1747, the year of Bernardo Sgrilli's map recording it as Ricoveri's property, and 1810, the date of De Carcopino's map, which marks it as a grand ducal property.

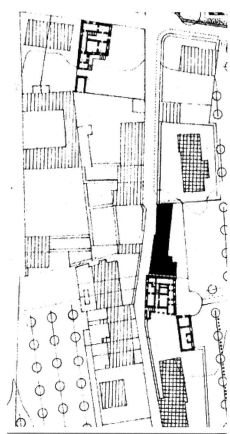

Bibliography:
Tosi, 1905, p. 3.
Carocci, 1906, p. 286.

VILLA DEL PANTA, BELVEDERE

The building is called "Villa Del Panta" on the 1896 and 1923 I.G.M. maps and "Villa Belvedere" on the 1936 edition. According to Tosi, Oduardo Del Panta bought the Gondo farm when part of the Castello estate was alienated (after 1868) and it seems likely that he built the villa. The better-preserved part has all the features of a later 19th-century building, and it fails to appear on earlier maps.

"*Notices bearing the coats of arms of the State and the Carabinieri have been installed simply to inform us that the old hillside villas, high on the narrow road, have been turned into a centre for breeding and training police dogs,*" states Lensi Orlandi. And indeed, the villa and the surrounding land which once formed part of the old farm are now used for this purpose.

Bibliography:
Tosi, 1905, p. 10.
Lensi Orlandi, 1965, p. 20.

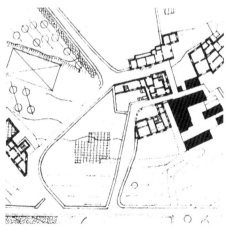

POGGIO SECCO

On the 1896 and 1923 I.G.M. maps this group of buildings is marked as "Poggio Secco" (the same name appears on the 1936 map, as well as "Villa Fava"). It also appears on the Capitani di Parte map of the parish of San Michele at Castello as a cluster of buildings with the words "Poggio" and "Arte dei Mercatanti".

The complex is included in the register of Medici properties at Castello for the year 1697, where it is called "Casa del Poggio", on the borders of the Steccuto and Arco farms. The map of the farms offers a plan of these houses for farm workers and a perspective view. According to Carocci, what the I.G.M. map defines as "Villa Fava" once belonged to the Giambullari family, of which the historian Pier Francesco Giambullari was a member. Part of it passed to the Arte del Cambio, after which for a lengthy period it became part of the Grand Duke's Castello estate.

On the map of the estate drawn up by Sgrilli in 1747 it is marked as "*Casa di Poggio with a piece of land now being worked by Pier Bellacci*". On a later map, drawn up by De Carcopino in 1810, the Poggio houses are not marked and on the land adjoining the property appears the name Chimidweller.

The building adjacent to Villa Fava, Villa Ribagli, belonged to the Sermanni family in the 15th and 16th centuries. Later it was the home of the Flemish painter Bilivert, who worked at the Medici court. In 1761 it was bought by the grand duchy and annexed to the estate, and later resold.

Bibliography:
Carocci, 1906, p. 284.
Lensi Orlandi, 1965, p. 21.
Gobbi, 1978, p. 10.

VILLA DI CASTELLO

In his *Life* of Tribolo, Vasari gives a vivid description of this villa (see notes 33, 36, 39, 44 in Chapter Four in this volume), one of the finest complexes in the Florentine area.

The name of the villa appears to come from the Latin *castellum*, meaning a water reservoir, indicating the collecting point for the water from the numerous sources in the area, feeding the Roman aqueduct of Florence, which passed close by. Its other name, "Vivaio" (fish-breeding pool), was used of the earlier residence on this spot, a further reference to the presence of water deposits. In Letter X of his *Notizie Istoriche dei Contorni di Firenze* Moreni states: "*It should be known that in our time there were still two large fish-breeding pools in the meadow in front of the villa.*" These two pools are clearly indicated on the Capitani di Parte's map of the *popolo* of San Michele at Castello, at the end of the avenue connecting the villa and Via Maestra (*viottolo di S.A.S.*, as it states on the map, while the two fish-pools are described as founts). The map of the adjacent parish of San Silvestro at Ruffignano shows a trench from the greenhouses marked "*bridge and cesspool of the Castello conduit*".

Castello became a Medici property in 1477 when Pier Francesco's sons, Lorenzo and Giovanni, bought the villa from Andrea di Lotteringo Della Stufa. Before this, in the early 15th century, the grand house had belonged to the Del Milanese before being sold to Dionigi da Mangona in 1440 who resold it to the Della Stufa family fourteen years later. During this time the property also included, as well as a forge and several houses, three farms near the owner's house. This was the original nucleus of what a century later was to become one of the Grand Duke's most splendid extra-urban residences. The property passed to Giovanni's son, the future Giovanni delle Bande Nere who lived there with his mother as a boy when the family was banished from Florence. After being enlarged by new acquisitions it became the property of his son Cosimo (see the declaration in the 1534 Land Register where the grand house is described as, "*A palazzo with its appurtenances called Vivaio*"). The villa had been much enlarged before being purchased by the Medici but it had not yet achieved sufficient grandeur to satisfy Cosimo. However, it was already used for State occasions since Varchi reports, "*Monsignor Silvio Passerini, Cardinal of Cortona, who governed Florence at this time in the name of Pope Clement VII for the magnificent Ippolito with the 'Magnifico', left Florence on 26 April 1527, with two cardinals, the Magnificent, Count Pietro Noferi and the whole court and went to Signor Cosimo's villa at Castello to meet and pay their respects to the Duke of Urbino and other leading figures of the League*". Having recovered the villa, looted and sacked when the Medici were driven from the city, Cosimo paid great attention to its restoration. Buontalenti was engaged for rebuilding operations and Vasari decorated the villa with new paintings and works of art, including Botticelli's *Venus* and *Primavera* and the *Chimera da' Arezzo*. The original building and interior courtyard were doubled in size by Buontalenti's extension which encapsulated the existing building in a plan that stressed its linear development. The central courtyard was no longer in line with the main entrance or with the garden path, something that Utens "corrected" in his painting. The main façade is very simple, two storeys, a mezzanine, attic and basement, revealed by the small openings in line with the windows above. The ground-floor windows are barred and the stone doorway is built of square ashlars and topped by a balcony. Zocchi's view reveals a change in the part of the building to the left of the entrance, with three windows on the ground floor and four on the upper storey (now five). The elevation on the garden side has similar architectural elements to those of the main façade. But the most remarkable feature here is the magnificent garden, only partly realized by Tribolo, which aimed to celebrated the glories of the House of Medici. According to Benedetto Varchi's plan the statuary, grottoes, water and vegetation formed an elaborate pattern covering the slope behind the villa and this was to lead, in Varchi's plan, to an avenue connecting Castello and the river Arno.

After various events, in 1974 the Villa became the seat of the Accademia della Crusca, and the interior still has 17th-century decorations including Volterrano's fresco the *Allegory of Sleep and Vigilance*, commissioned in 1636 by Grand Duke Ferdinando II.

Bibliography:
Acidini Luchinat, Galletti, 1992, and accompanying bibliography.

IL GONDO

We have no precise records of the origins of this building which still preserves, despite various uses and repeated alterations, the stately features of a gentleman's 15th-century country house. In the plan of the Capitani di Parte of the parish of San Michele at Castello, the building is marked with the name "Gondi". On the general map of all the palazzi, gardens, vineyards and farms of the Castello, Petraia and Topaia villas in the year 1697, on the border of the Castello garden is written: "property of Signor Ferdinando Gondi"; and the map of farms, vineyards and buildings of the S.M.I.'s Castello estate, drawn up by Bernardo Sgrilli in 1747 when the House of Lorraine was in power, shows Gondi as the proprietor of the property adjoining the Castello garden. Tosi tells us that it was occupied for

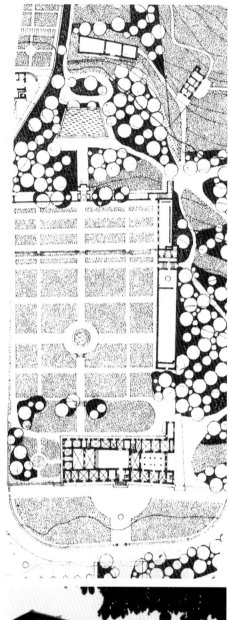

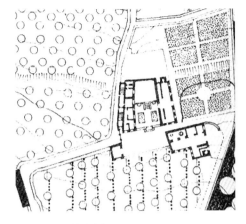

a time by Francesco Redi, a man of letters and doctor to the penultimate Medici court, but we do not know if he owned the villa or simply enjoyed its use. According to the maps we have mentioned, the villa remained in the Gondi family until the mid-18th century. The villa later formed part of the grand ducal estate, although not earlier than 1747, the date of Bernardo Sgrilli's map. In the *Pianta dei terreni che formano l'Imperiale Fattoria di Castello*, drawn up in 1810 by Jérôme De Carcopino, the Gondo villa is shown as part of the property. This is probably the time of operations to convert the villa into a service annex for the Castello estate. In the first decades of the 19th century Grand Duke Leopoldo II of Lorraine, who had a keen interest in agriculture, erected a building immediately in front of the villa *"fitted with a hydraulic press, designed to serve as a model to landowners for improving oil production"*.

Gondo, having become annexed to the grand ducal estate, followed the same fate and, after the First World War, with Vittorio Emanuele III's donation of the crown's possessions, it became the property of the Opera dei Combattenti. In 1928 the villa and the farm were bought by the Baldi, a farming family who used it for purposes that were inappropriate to the elegance of the building, besides making apartments for labourers.

The building is of great architectural interest, with all the typical features of a 15th-16th century villa in the outlying areas of Florence, with a loggia, courtyard and dovecote tower. The layout is an irregular U-shape: the central courtyard, surrounded on three sides by the building, is closed on the fourth side by a wall with the entrance. This wall is higher at the ends where it joins the side-wings of the building, a design we find elsewhere (see Villa La Corte). At the end is a beautiful ground-floor loggia with arches on stone columns and Tuscan-style capitals ornamented with a rosette motif, repeated on the corbels of the vaults. The pattern of these capitals was widespread in Florence in the 16th century, and can be found, albeit with variations, in some of Baccio d'Agnolo's work (courtyards of the Bartolini Salimbeni, Gerini and Taddei palazzi). Similar capitals also appear on the portico of the nearby church of the ex-monastery of Boldrone. The windows and doors are handsomely framed in stone, while other more recent openings mar the harmony of the façade. On the upper floor a spacious covered loggia is continued in a side-wing of the building which, at the opposite end, is crowned by a handsome dovecote tower. In the interior, in order to make more letting space, the old vaulted rooms were much altered and divided by partition walls. But the many changes introduced during the 1930s do not prevent a reading of the original layout. On the façade overlooking the garden a vast lemon-house, incorporated into the building at ground level on this side, has been turned into stables. The garden, once divided into a regular pattern of beds with a fountain in the centre, is today neglected and overgrown, the old beds bordered with pergolas of vines. Restoration work in 1968 only concerned the exterior plastering.

The intrinsic quality of this building and its proximity to the vast Castello complex make it worthy of more suitable use, and of restoration work which would reveal its original features, now damaged by the unsuitable way that the complex has been used for decades.

Bibliography:
Tosi, 1905, p. 10.
Lensi Orlandi, 1965, p. 23.
Gobbi, 1978, p. 13.
Castello campagna medicea periferia urbana, 1984, pp. 73–74.

VILLA IL POZZINO

It seems probable that the Pozzino villa, with its imposing tower, is the result of a series of additions around a central nucleus, a frequent practice when remodelling buildings into grander residences. According to Carocci, in the 15th century it became the country house of the noble Carnesecchi family, and in 1576 was bought by Carlo di Galgano Campana, a physician from Montepulciano. The Capitani di Parte map of the parish of San Michele at Castello shows a house rising behind a wall on the banks of the Termine stream, with a meadow in the rear and the name of the proprietor, Campana. The Pozzino took on its present form when it was bought by Zanobi Grazzini's children, a family of which the comic poet Anton Francesco, better known as Lasca, was a member. They converted the villa and had it decorated with paintings by Giovanni da San Giovanni and Piero Salvestrini. The main façade on the road leading from Quarto to Quinto is 15th-century in style and has traces of decorative graffito work and handsome barred windows with acanthus leaf corbels in *pietra serena*. An imposing tower faces the side overlooking the garden and is capped by a covered roof-terrace and columns with Tuscan capitals embellished with Ionic side volutes; on this face the tower has three 13th-century windows. The main body of the adjoining structure also has a covered roof-terrace, columns with Tuscan capitals, similar to those in the tower, and ceilings with grotesque decorations. The walls in the interior courtyard have frescoes by Giovanni da San Giovanni, already engaged nearby on the Quiete and Casale villas. The frescoes were commissioned by Giovan Francesco Grazzini and completed by 1630. The subjects depicted in the fresco cycle (satyrs and nymphs) were in keeping with plans for the villa, as Baldinucci records: "*since they were to ornament a palazzo in the country, all surrounded by agreeable pleasures, Giovanni wanted them to be pleasing and amusing*". The fresco cycle, unfortunately in very poor condition, reflects the iconographic programme adopted by genre painters, mythological and pastoral scenes and views of country and town, in which local themes are combined with classical ones: Apollo and Marsyas, the Triumph of Galatea, the story of Cupid and Psyche and the Golden Ass alternate with rural scenes, allegorical figures and grotesque decorations. The city street with the figure of a peasant being arrested by the guards is Via Calzaioli; in the background stands Giotto's tower and the dome of the cathedral, stressing the link between life in the country and life in the city. (Again, according to Baldinucci, Giovanni da San Giovanni produced an oil painting entitled *La beffa del pievano Arlotto*, now in Viscount Scarsdale's collection at Kedlestone Hall in Derbyshire.)

The grotesque decorations in the covered roof-terrace were done by Piero Salvestrini, pupil and collaborator of Poccetti, a specialist in the grotesque, who had already worked at Torre (Villa Franceschi), Casale and at the Strozzino villa. "*The presence of similar series of grotesques confirms the hypothesis that Salvestrini was the first choice for this form of decoration, further favoured by the close contact that existed between the wealthier and more important clients and families in this area and the Medici court*" (M. P. Mannini). The villa, surrounded by agricultural land adjoining the Medici estate, has interesting open-air features including an Italian garden, a lemon-house with the remains of a late mannerist nymphaeum with rustic decorations ornamented with sculpture, now lost, and a small oriental garden with a fountain with polychrome decorations and anthropomorphic figures. A surviving inscription bears the date 1588 and the arms of the commissioners. After the Grazzini family the villa was inherited by Bartolini Baldelli and later by Mori Ubaldini Alberti, from whom it was bought by a lawyer, Alessandro Lucii. After

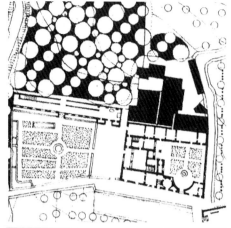

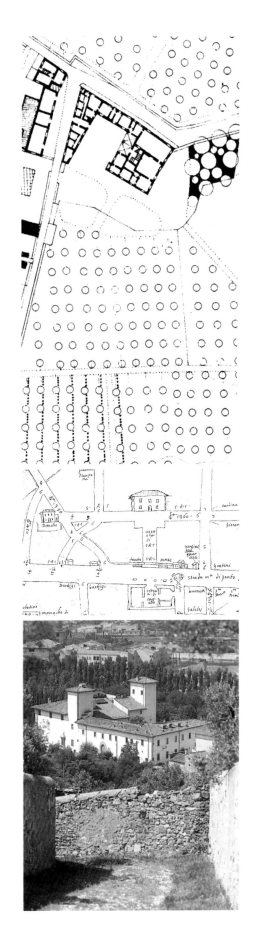

passing from Gilli to Naldini Bordoni it was sold in 1946 to the Sisters of Divine Zeal, becoming the seat of the women's Istituto Antoniano of the Canonico Annibale Maria of France. Repeated changes in ownership and in use, led to radical alterations and particularly serious damage to the decorations which still, nevertheless, make this villa one of the most interesting in the area, deserving a full work of restoration.

Bibliography:
Castello campagna medicea periferia urbana, 1984, pp. 75–76 and accompanying bibliography.
Vezzosi, 1989, pp. 66–74.

BELLAGIO, VILLA LE BRACHE
Down a lane bordered with unkempt vegetation, once the road connecting the convent of Castellina and Via Giovanni da San Giovanni, the majestic towered and fortified structure of Le Brache springs into view. The origin of the name is uncertain and was later changed to "Bellagio" (but the Capitani di Parte's map of the *popolo* of San Michele at Castello bears the name "Brache" to indicate an imposing building with a small projection on the old Via Quintigiana, a diagonal connection between Via Maestra and Via di Castello). This is one of the most remarkably interesting examples of a 15th-century residence in the outskirts of Florence. Carocci says: "*this would seem to preserve traces of an ancient fortified building, capable of repulsing the threat of attack*", and its appearance with two towers and heavy exterior walls might indeed suggest an early origin, common enough to many establishments in the area. The severity of the façade on Via di Castello is counterbalanced by the insertion of a broad loggia in the upper floor on the side overlooking the garden, with a view of the surrounding countryside. The complex is built round an interior courtyard, a typical plan of extra-urban Florentine constructions, and surrounded on three sides by the building, the fourth side being originally closed by a wall. We see this in Vasari the Younger's drawing, which presents a planimetric map, a great deal more regular in layout than the real one. The now missing wall was still there during the 19th century, as we see from the plan drawn by Martelli. The large stairway that once projected from the body of the building, giving the courtyard an irregular shape, has also disappeared. Three buildings of different dates can be identified in the complex: the central block of the building, with a façade on Via di Castello is Renaissance in design and has a large arched doorway framed with sandstone blocks; the main entrance and three small windows on the first floor, framed in sandstone with frescoed sills. On the ground floor to the right of the façade are two ashlar doorposts, the remains of a 14th-century doorway. In general this part can be dated to the early Cinquecento, as we see from the plaster, smoothed with a trowel in preparation for graffiti and monochrome decorations. The present entrance is on Via di Bellagio through an 18th-century doorway leading into the area once used for stabling and services. This is the earliest, 14th-century part, of which there remains a portico with two arches on octagonal pillars and half-pillars with "shield" capitals. This leads to the residential part of the villa. In the centre of the paved courtyard stood the familiar stone well, removed early in the 20th century. The Renaissance part of the complex is to the right of the loggia: on the ground floor an arched doorway is surrounded by sandstone ashlars with four barred windows and supporting corbels; on the upper floor the large roofed loggia has four spans on one side and six on the other, and columns with composite capitals. The roof-loggia has been rebuilt on the original pattern. Beside

this, on the short side, are two simple 16th-century windows framed in sandstone; on the long side, under the roof, two 14th-century round-arched windows framed with stone blocks. The Martelli collection, in the Department of Drawings and Prints of the Uffizi Galleries has a series of drawings by Giuseppe Martelli (1791–1876) which concern a project to transform the villa. Apart from alterations to the interior this included plans to regularize the façades; open a loggia along the length of the central part of the façade and add a crowning pediment; open new symmetrically placed windows and a main rusticated entrance. This interpretation of the classical style would have had an adverse effect on the complex's original character. Martelli also prepared a design for the gates and railings. This project may have been entrusted to Martelli by Count Dainelli Da Bagnano's family, which owned the property during the 19th-century. Numerous changes in ownership are recorded in the land register from 1427 onwards, when the proprietor was Jacopo di Giovanni Aldobrandini; it then passed to Francesco di Simone Tornabuoni who sold it in 1482 to the Monte officers, on behalf of Michele Attendolo, Count of Cotignola, *condottiero* of the Commune. After returning to the Aldobrandini in 1488, the villa passed again to the Tornabuoni family who sold it in 1546 to Maria, widow of Jacopo Gualterotti. Her heirs resold it in 1571 to Camilla Martelli, second wife of Cosimo I, and it was then inherited by her daughter Virginia who married Grand Duke Cesare d'Este in 1586. In 1614 the Duke's procurator sold it to Del Tovaglia from whom it was bought by Jacopo Ricciardi in 1629. From Del Tovaglia it passed to Dainelli Da Bagnano, to the Masetti family and then to Francalanci Buscioni, after being used as a military hospital during the First World War.

The garden has an irregular shape and the traditional planting beds have disappeared, the result of 19th-century changes. The villa is surrounded by an agricultural property of about ten hectares, made up of fields and olive trees stretching down to Via Reginaldo Giuliani, where a pathway leads to the majestic entrance gates. The building has lost its original context having been recently transformed into the main centre of the Buddhist community in Italy.

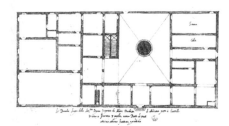

Bibliography:

Stegmann, Geymüller, 1885–1908, p. 14.
Tosi, Le Brache, Villa Masetti, 1893.
Carocci, 1906, p. 288.
Patzak,1912, p. 104.
Thiem, 1964, pp. 82–83.
Lensi Orlandi, 1965, p. 25.
Castello campagna medicea periferia urbana, 1984, pp. 88–89.

TERRIO, VILLA GIRALDI

Carocci describes this villa as a "*charming and well-situated holiday-house*". Now of little interest in architectural terms, it was one of the many properties that the Carnesecchi family owned in the district of Castello until the early 17th century. It then became the property of Bandieri and in 1762 passed as a dowry to the Giraldi family, who remained the proprietors until the early 1900s. In the "*Geographic description of all goods and property that are enjoyed and owned by the S.mo Grand Duke, etc.*" dated 1697, the farm called Terrio has a clear drawing of a gentleman's residence, both a ground-plan and a perspective view, comprising a tower, an adjoining lower building and a walled garden extending on two sides. This was the core of

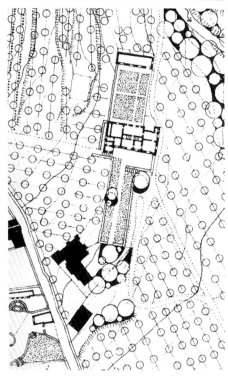

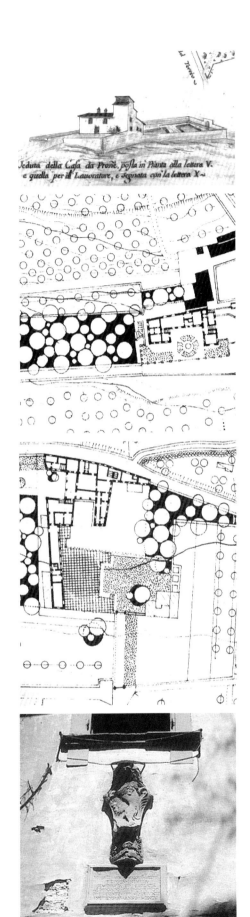

Seduta della Casa da Prone, posta in Pianta alla lettera V. e quella per il Lauoratore, e segnata con la lettera X

the present villa, which underwent a large-scale conversion during the 19th century which almost totally destroyed the building's early origins.

Bibliography:
Carocci, 1906, p. 291.
Lensi Orlandi, 1965, p. 23.
Gobbi, 1978, pp. 10–11.

POGGIO ALLEGRO, POGGIOCHIARO

The path connecting the Castellina convent and Via del Lasca, the lower part of which is now impassable and overrun with brambles, separates the agricultural land surrounding the villa and Poggiochiaro's annexed farmhouses from the nearby Terrio villa.

The name "Poggio Allegro" appears on the 1896 and 1923 I.G.M. maps, while the 1936 edition refers to it as "Poggiochiaro". It stands on a knoll below the Castellina convent and although greatly transformed in the 19th century it still has the elegant loggias of the original building, the property of the Sali, a family of wealthy grain-merchants; it went to the Belli, and in 1769 to the Picchianti. It was next occupied by the tenor Niccolò Tacchinardi and then the Ricceri. According to Carocci's account, from 1860 until 1876 it was the home of the lawyer Vincenzo Ginanneschi, a keen agronomist, who changed the original name Poggio Secco to Poggio Allegro, probably to accord with the improved condition of the land after his skilful ministrations. It later belonged to a Capitano Pessuti, who made further changes to the building. Subsequent owners were the Sforni, the Leggets and the Migliorini. Today, the farming land around the house has an abandoned look and the old gateway giving onto the lane leading down from the Castellina appears to have fallen into disuse.

Bibliography:
Carocci, 1906, p. 291.
Lensi Orlandi, 1965, p. 23.

VILLA FONTENUOVA

The building stands halfway up a slope on the road between Castello and Quinto and is today in a deplorable condition. Among the ruins of the 17th-century complex some traces of fine architecture still remain under the alterations the villa was subjected to when it was last occupied, as a nursing home. The farming property, which until the 1950s extended from Via di Castello to Viale Gramsci, began to be turned into building lots in 1958, greatly affecting the existing balance between the elegant houses and the agrarian and productive structure of the area.

In the early 15th century the villa was the property of the Da Fortuna family, from Mugello, passing in around the middle of the century to the Boni of the *popolo* of Santa Maria Maggiore, who embarked on a complete restoration in 1595, as recorded by the still existing plaque set below the arms above the entrance. In 1648, the Boni family died out and the property passed to the Michelozzi, who continued to own it for a long period. During the 19th century it was the property of the Bartolini and, in 1876, the Ragionieri family.

Bibliography:
Carocci, 1906, p. 289.
Il parco territoriale di Monte Morello, 1979, p. 94.
Villoresi, 1988, pp. 128–129.

VILLA COVACCHIA

This name, which in early times was "Canovaja", is recorded in the 14th century. The first document, dated 8 August 1394, is a contract of sale with which Cristofano of the late Lippo Doni of the parish of San Frediano sold the farm and worker's house, called Canovaja, to Cante of the late Giovanni Compagni. At the end of the 15th century the villa was the property of Rosso Cerretani from whom it passed early in the following century to Cristofano di Bartolomeo Rinieri. On the Capitani di Parte map of the parish of San Michele at Castello, alongside the building recorded as "Covachia" appears the name Guidi, a family which also owned land abutting on Topaia. In the 17th century, the Castello and Petraia villas were the favourite residences of the court, Covacchia was bought by Ippolito Bassetti, the Grand Duke's secretary. It then became a grand ducal property, as is recorded in the property inventories and related papers drawn up on the passing of the House of Medici. We can set the alienation of this property to the period between 1747, when the *Map of farms vineyards and buildings of the Castello Estate* was produced by Bernardo Sgrilli, where the Covacchia farm and villa are included as part of the estate, and 1810, when the *Plan of the Imperial Estate*, prepared by Jérôme De Carcopino, no longer records this property, later bought by the Uzielli, the Giannini and, in 1961, the Morino family.

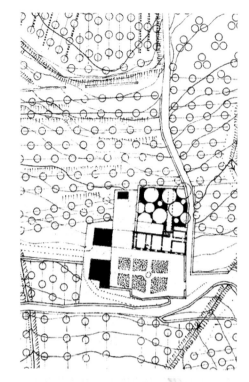

Numerous changes have altered the 15th-century character of this country villa. It stands on the northern slopes of Poggio Secco, to the north of Castello; we are afforded an early view of it by the drawing in Volume II of the Properties (A.S.F.). The sheet describing the Covacchia farm includes a ground-plan and a perspective view of the master's house, consisting of a tower, a loggia on two sides and a colonnaded portico on the ground-floor façade. Today, the complex is very different in appearance to this 17th-century view. The ground-floor portico has gone, the loggia on the upper floor is closed and only the castellated tower remains to record some slight echo of the original building, the layout of which has been destroyed by both old and recent rebuilding operations. The garden has the same perimeter and "walled" character of the 17th-century sketch. Even the straight road leading from the house to a thickly planted area on the edge of the wood marking the property's boundary has survived. Today it leads to a ruined belvedere tower among the olives, a 19th-century conversion in Gothic style of an earlier chapel. Two rooms in the villa still have their fine coffered wooden ceilings. On the 17th-century map a fountain (now gone) is clearly marked in front of the entrance to the villa, which gave its name to the old road, now almost impassable. The Covacchia farm was broken up and the farmer's house, once the country house of the monks of Santa Maria Novella, no longer belongs to the villa.

Bibliography:
Carocci, 1906, pp. 284–285.
Lensi Orlandi, 1965, p. 22.
Gobbi, 1978, pp. 10–11.

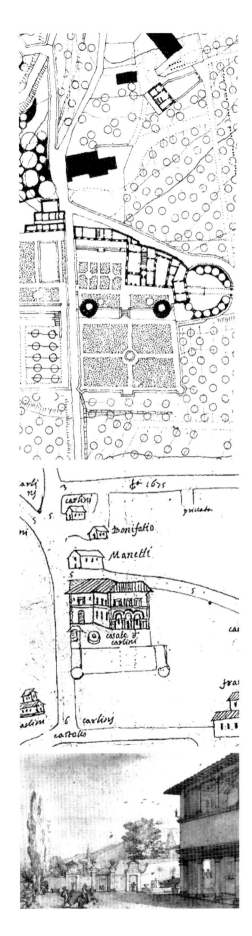

VILLA IL CASALE

The complex is one of the most interesting examples of the villa-farm in this area from the point of view of its architecture, the diverse typological pattern of its farm buildings, the important position it occupies and the overall layout of its surrounding land. The villa's present typology is the result of successive building operations.

In reality, the greatest mark was made by the particular kind of family it belonged to, members of the grand duchy's bureaucracy who moved to this area because the Medici were there. Carocci tells us that the first mention of the villa is recorded in the 14th century and some windows and the doorway of the earliest building still reveal traces of this period. The first alterations were carried out in the following century when the property was bought by the family of the Grand Duke's secretary, Lorenzo Pagni. In the latter half of the century the villa was purchased by the Carlini family, also in the employ of the ruling family, restructured and made the centre of production for an agricultural estate which included surrounding farms, farm buildings around the villa and the gentlemanly residence La Torre. When the Carlini family died out during the 19th century the villa and the farm holdings passed through the female line to the De Saint Seigne and subsequently to the Tosini, until 1952. After some upheavals and changes in ownership of a speculative character, it was bought by the Principe family whose heirs still own it today, caring for it attentively in terms of both its architecture and its surroundings.

The layout has a linear development on the road leading up the hill, and this façade has a rural white-plastered face broken by small simple stone-framed windows. The south façade is more elaborate with a horizontal movement emphasized by broad loggias that span the façade overlooking the garden and the plain. The central L-shaped body is developed around the first level of the formal garden and is opened on the south side by loggias on two storeys of the projecting section, and a one-storey loggia in the recessed block. A second lower body, separated from the first by a small "secret garden" of herbs, seems to be a later addition. This would be confirmed by the villa's late 16th-century iconography. On the Capitani di Parte map of the parish of San Silvestro at Ruffignano, the illustration of the "Casale dei Carlini" (with an arched elevation rather than a loggia with an architrave) stops short at the central part. The later addition of the east block was connected with the circular pattern of the forecourt and the ramp leading to the impressive avenue of cypresses. This is an interesting instance of a late 16th-century work of complete reorganization, besides being one of the few surviving examples in the Florentine area of a layout based on a perspective axis, after Tribolo's design for the avenue at Villa di Castello. These operations, carried out during the very last years of the 16th century, also extended to the area west of the villa. An annex was built, on the other side of the road which skirted the garden, and this became an integral part of the structural organization of the villa. The building, modest in scale, was provided with all the accoutrements for the pastimes and pleasures of a grand 17th-century country house, including an underground nymphaeum, or grotto, a large covered fish-pool connected to a main outside pool which was surrounded by another garden with a theatre above. The layout of the park adjoining the garden on the west side was truly remarkable. Crossed by avenues of tall walls of ilex, the park was ornamented with statues and marble artefacts, some arising from archaeological finds in the area. Today, most of the statuary has been removed and all that remains is the *Tempietto*, crowned with a single large stone which is traditionally held to come from an Etruscan tumulus, while the 17th-century garden looks like a natural wood, in the romantic style. In the villa there are scenes painted by an unknown water-colourist which record, albeit in an idealized manner, the former appearance of the park. The garden on the south side of the villa is of the traditional kind and, though laid out relatively recently, its design is modelled on the traditional Tuscan garden: geometric beds surrounded by box hedges, tubs of citrus trees and water basins, all enhanced by the changing levels of three terraces which extend to the boundary wall.

The second edition of the Capitani di Parte map for the parish of San Silvestro at Ruffignano depicts "Casale dei Carlini" as a building with a three-arched loggia on the ground floor and a garden with a round fountain and a boundary wall and embankment ending in two small towers. The Carlini property is shown as extending to the surrounding terrain, with a bird-snaring area stretching as far as the Torre dei Franceschi.

A drawing of the villa attributed to Baccio del Bianco allows us to compare the present situation with the garden's 17th-century appearance. The drawing shows a simple lawned area, without partitions, while the arrangement of the boundary wall on the road side, appears almost unchanged. One view, among those mentioned earlier, reveals the changes made to the façade overlooking the garden, with the closing of the first-floor loggias. The loggias were re-opened in the 20th-century, restoring the building's true character, but the opening of large ground-floor windows towards the lemon-house, has marred the original façade's harmonious pattern of volumes and spaces. The finely proportioned rooms in the interior are well known for the fresco decorations by Piero Salvestrini and Giovanni da San Giovanni, painted in about 1616 and therefore among the artist's early work. Below the loggia and above the principal entrance a grandiose Medici coat of arms appears alongside the Austrian arms, decorated with two small cherubs seated on volutes supporting the grand ducal crown, and a scroll with the words *Magnus Etruriae quartus* with two pendent festoons of flowers and fruits. In the hall are two frescoes, an oval on the ceiling framing a male figure with a club in the right hand and a shield in the left, and a young man bearing a garland which is doubtless a portrait of Grand Duke Cosimo II.

The entire ceiling of the small chapel is decorated with graceful ornamental motifs and in the centre a garland encircles the Carlini arms. On the intrados of the window are head-and-shoulders portraits in ovals of the two commissioners and the date 1616. On the upper part of the intrados two cherubs support a tondo with a view of the villa and landscapes in ovals. On the outer faces are paintings symbolizing the theological virtues: Meekness, the lamb; Purity, the dove; Chastity, the unicorn, accompanied by festoons and scrolls with Biblical scenes supported by cherubs.

Bibliography:
Carocci, 1906, pp. 273–274.
Giglioli, 1949, pp. 19–20.
Lensi Orlandi, 1965, pp. 18–19.
Mannini, *Valori storici, artistici e archeologici di Sesto Fiorentino*, 1965.
Gobbi, 1975.
Gobbi, Gobbò, Capaccioli, Lazzareschi, 1977.
Mannini, 1979.
Cenci, Peroni, 1990, pp. 15–26.
Mannini, 1991.

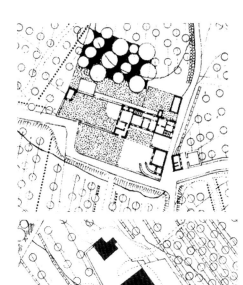

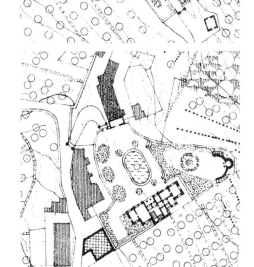

VILLA LA TORRE

This dates back to the 14th century and traces of the original structure are recognizable despite the late 16th-century conversion. The property belonged to the Franceschi family, and is clearly depicted on the map of the Capitani di Parte of the parish of San Silvestro at Ruffignano. The image shows a tower, the original nucleus of the building, and a clear boundary marked by rows of trees in front of the building.

The ceiling of the great entrance hall in the interior is particularly interesting, entirely frescoed with motifs typical of late-mannerist decoration. The wooden coffered ceiling has square lacunae with pale blue and gold ornamentations in relief and beams painted with trailing vines, birds and snakes, similar to the plant motifs frescoed in 1580 in the Uffizi corridor. The decoration's unusual typology is divided into three sections: the Four Continents at the sides and Heaven and Earth in the main panels in the centre. The decoration's subject matter focuses particularly on the various features and figures in "*la vita in villa*", huntsmen, shepherds, peasants and musicians, rural landscapes which serve as backgrounds to hunting and fishing scenes, differentiating them from the decorative cycles in the city palazzo. In the allegory of the Four Continents there are some interesting scenes of festivities in 16th-century Florence and eight scenes of pursuits and pastimes at the villa. The commissioner's inscription *Franciscus di Franciscis faciendum curavit AD MDLXXXXVII* appears below a depiction of the flight of Phaethon, the epitome of audacity, and this and the whole decorative cycle reflect the intellectual taste and boldness of a wealthy merchant of the time.

Bibliography:
Carocci, 1906, p. 274.
Lensi Orlandi, 1965, p. 18.
Mannini, 1979, p. 25.

VILLA DELLA CASTELLINA

The name marked on both the 1896 and 1923 editions of the I.G.M. maps is "Villa Servadio", while on the 1936 map it is called "Villa della Castellina". This late 19th-century complex is only remarkable for its spectacularly panoramic position, surrounded by peaceful olive groves, on the slopes of the hilltop north of the convent of Castellina.

Bibliography:
Lensi Orlandi, 1965, p. 23.

VILLA PALASTRETO

This is an amusing example of a melange of architectural styles, a late 19th-century holiday house which combines neo-Gothic and Moorish features, including castellations around the top of the building, combined with some innovations, such as the cast iron columns of the entrance portico. The villa stands high on the hilly slopes and has a superb panoramic view of woods alternating with cultivated terraces.

Bibliography:
Lensi Orlandi, 1965, p. 24.

VILLA TOPAIA

The building became part of the Medici property of Castello between about 1500 and 1534. The declaration to the Land Register for that year includes among the properties of Cosimo, "di signor Giovanni de' Medici", "*a farm with house for farmer and worker at a place called La Topaia with several pieces of land, some level, and in many ways similar to another two small farms at the place called Casale*" (A.S.F. Campione dei Secolari Q.S.M. Novella 1534). In Cosimo I's register of properties for 1566, the words have been changed to "*A farm with a house for signori and workers at a place called La Topaia, with about one hundred and twenty staiora of arable with olive groves and vineyards*". The change in the description would suggest that the building had been converted into the "manor house". According to Moreni, the "*small villa called the Topaia*" was built by Cosimo I "*as is shown by the arms in the left-hand corner and the handsome motto:* Exaltabo te Domine et exultabo", and in fact the villa was used as a guest house by the Grand Duke to accommodate illustrious people, before use was ceded to Benedetto Varchi in 1558 so that he could concentrate on his work in the peace and quiet of the villa. That Varchi wrote his *Istoria* in this retreat would seem to be confirmed by Francesco Vinta's lines, when he says in his poem:

"*Varchi cui favet, otiumque Cosmus*
Thuscorum Dominus facit, perenne,
Ut res tradere bellicas, suosque
Annales calamo elegantior
Posteris queat, interim, ac beate
Rus colat procul Urbe."

Varchi describes this villa in his *Ercolano* or *Dialogo delle Lingue*, where he makes it the setting for the action: "*Count Cesare Ercolano . . . went to the villa above Castello, where he lived, and where I was, arriving at lunchtime and after the usual greetings . . . strolling on the lawn in front of the house for a while and taking a turn around the garden, which he liked very much, he wished he could spend more days with his brother Count Ercole, and highly complimented and praised the great liberality and courtesy of his Excellency our Illustrious Duke, his commodious rooms and pleasingly arranged garden beds; we went to dine on a small terrace set above a loggia from which there is a wonderful and most entertaining view, as well as many other beautiful things including Florence and Fiesole . . .*"

The humorous poet Anton Francesco Grazzini, known as Lasca, wrote a sonnet praising the villa:

"*Varchi, la vostra Villa è posto in loco*
Che ella volge le spalle al tramontano,
Sicché soffi a usa posta o forte, or piano,
Che nuocer non vi può molto né poco
Penso doman venire (e non è baia)
Con esso voi a starmi alla Topaia."

After Varchi's death in 1566, use of the villa was conceded to Scipione Ammirato who, in the *incipit* to his *Storia Fiorentina*, states: "*Above this [Villa Petraia] is the Topaia villa, where much of our work will be written, conceded to us by Grand Duke Cosimo for this purpose.*" On the Capitani di Parte maps a small building called Topaia appears in two places: the first in the parish of San Michele at Castello, where a now impassable track leads from Poggio Secco to the "Topaia houses"; the second in the parish of San Silvestro at Ruffignano on the road now called Via di Malafrasca. The building was converted into a grand country house by Cosimo III, becoming his favourite holiday retreat, and given his predi-

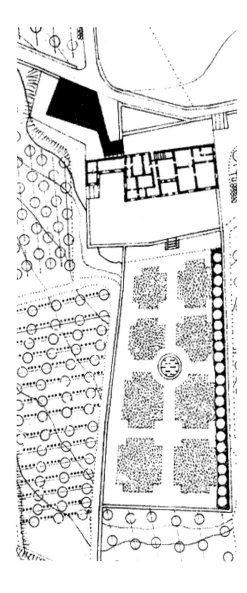

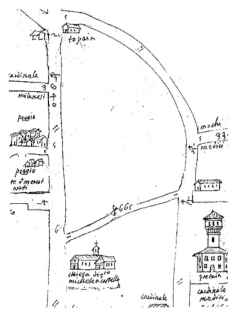

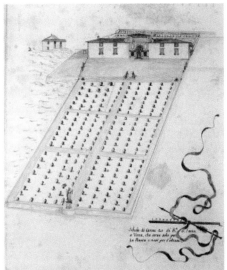

lection for rare plants he had an orchard made in the French style with dwarf pear and apple trees. The garden itself he dedicated St. Fiacre, traditionally believed to have devoted himself to the cultivation and study of medicinal herbs. The Grand Duke commissioned a marble statue of this saint, carved by the Florentine artist Giovan Battista Piamontini, bearing a commemorative inscription to record his reverence, and the date 1696. The villa was further embellished with a series of paintings by Bartolomeo Bimbi of life-size images of rare varieties of fruit. This series of paintings was later removed from Topaia and installed in the Castello villa. The group of paintings was part of an overall scenic design, as emerges from the Life of Bartolomeo Bimbi as recounted by Baldinucci: "*His Royal Highness Cosimo III, having built a fine country house at the place called Topaia, at the top of the slope of the famous vineyards of the Royal Villa of Castello, to give himself a resting-place when he wished to make outings in the area, since this place was and is full of all kinds of fruit, oranges and lemons, grapes and flowers which until then had been left in a wild state, bizarre and freakish abortions of nature, so he wanted the place adorned with pictures illustrating things as they should be, not only so that if the original plants were lost there would still be a living record of the shapes and colours of all varieties of their fruits, but also primarily that note be taken of their correct names, formerly often confused, and copies and engravings made of these. Thus, as soon as a foreign and bizarre fruit appears H.R.H. sends it to be painted by Bimbi, to be then placed in the country house in its proper order and position.*"

In the description of the Grand Duke's goods and property in the list drawn up for the property register in the year 1697 there are clear drawings of both the villa's plan and elevation, its orchard and adjoining agricultural land, and these give a good idea of the house's appearance. A low building with a façade overlooking the garden, broken in the centre by a ground-floor portico with a central arch in *pietra serena* (a local grey stone) and side-columns supporting the architraved apertures, while above is a covered roof-terrace. The masonry separating the two storeys of apertures has a pattern of geometric shapes in *pietra serena* against a white plaster background. Each side-wing has two curving barred windows with simple stone frames. The upper floor has two small rectangular windows with stone frames, set in line with the lower ones. A low wall separates the garden beyond the villa from the old orchard, turned into a formal garden and divided into simple compartments with trimmed box hedges and a central fountain. A bank of cypresses separates the garden from the surrounding land and shelters it from the wind.

Bibliography:
Moreni, 1791 and 1795, pp. 94–101.
Carocci, 1906, p. 283.
Lensi Orlandi, 1965, pp. 17–18.
Godoli, Natali, 1980, p. 44.
Castello campagna medicea periferia urbana, 1984, p. 72.

IL CANTONE, VILLA BILLI

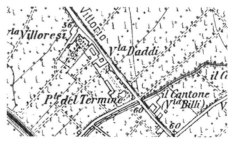

The name recorded on the three I.G.M. maps is "Il Cantone Villa Billi". "Cantone" refers to its position, bounded by the Termine stream that marks the border of Florentine territory. The façade on the road has been completely remodelled several times. The complex once belonged to the Aldobrandini del Lion d'Oro family, known as Aldobrandini di Madonna, a gift from Grand Duke Ferdinando I on 20 March 1587 to Cardinal Ippolito Aldobrandini (later Pope Clement VIII), to his nephew Pietro, and to his legitimate and illegitimate offspring. This gift, according to what Tosi tells us, concerned "*two-sevenths of a property in the parish of San Michele at Castello, in the region of Sesto, a place called Il Cantone, with gentleman's residence and farmhouse, with fields, vineyards and other appurtenances formed of two parcels of land, one close to the house, about twenty-nine* stiora, *and the second on the other side of the Termine stream, towards Sesto, of about sixteen* stiora" (A.S.F. Privilegi Granducali, Vol. IV, c. 59). The property then passed to the Torrigiani, the Rapi and, in 1878, to the Billi family. The land across the stream was annexed to the Villa Fontenuova farm and in the 1950s it was sold for building lots. The land immediately above the villa has also been built on.

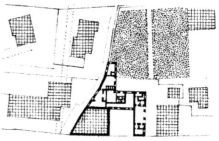

Bibliography:
Tosi, 1905, pp. 46–48.
Carocci, 1906, p. 279.

VILLA VILLORESI

The 1896 and 1923 I.G.M. maps carry the name "Villa Villoresi" and the 1936 version "Podere S. Alberto". The existence of a property called "La Strada" is recorded in 1427, when it belonged to the Ambrogi who continued to own it into the 19th century. The façade on the road has 16th-century windows and a small 17th-century doorway. Adjoining the villa is the chapel of San Reginaldo, which received an endowment for its officiation and the obligation to maintain a free school. Because of the recent encroachment of new buildings there remains no trace of the spatial layout that once linked the villa to the garden in the rear and the farm.

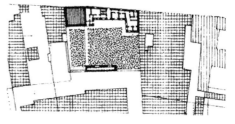

Bibliography:
Carocci, 1906, p. 297.
I dintorni di Firenze. Arte, storia, paesaggio, 1983, p. 209.
Villoresi, 1988, p. 129.

LA FONTE

On the 1896 and 1923 I.G.M. maps this is called "Villa Daddi", "Villa Fonte" in the 1936 edition. It stands next to the "La Strada" villa and, according to Carocci, was once owned by the Guidacci family. During the 17th century it was rebuilt by the Frilli.

Bibliography:
Carocci, 1906, p. 297.
Villoresi, 1988, p. 129.

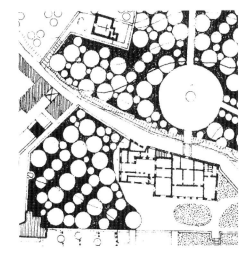

VILLA BALDINI-BORGHESE

This building, whose early name was "Poggio or San Poteto" (the I.G.M. maps record it as "Villa Baldini" or "Villa Bellavista"), is a remarkable and rare example of a conversion in neo-classical style in the Florentine area. First references to it are from the 15th century (the date of the original structure), when it was the property of the heirs of Doctor Ugolino di Montecatini. Towards the end of the century the property was transferred to Lorenzo Petrucci, a member of an old Florentine family with a town house in Via della Scala. In 1553 it passed from Petrucci to Antonio di Raffaele Torrigiani, the owner of other properties in the area. As the Capitani di Parte map for the district of Santa Maria at Quinto records, the building at the end of the road running between Via Maestra and a shrine marked "Vergine di Torrigiani" (now the course of Via Taddeo Gaddi) marks the villa's 16th century nucleus, below which appears the name Torrigiani. In June 1659 Senator Carlo di Raffaello Torrigiani sold the property to Cavaliere Benedetto Dragomanni and, according to Moreni, this family is to be ascribed with the alterations and embellishments. Moreni tells us that in the 1700s the villa was already furnished with *"an extremely handsome gallery with admirable ornamentations skilfully carried out, and the well-studied architectural arrangements and perspective views, and the elegant manner that the famous Jacopo Chiavistelli, a pupil of Fabrizio Boschi and of Baccio del Bianco, has of highlighting in oils. . . . . The aforementioned gallery having suffered greatly, it was restored in 1738 and returned to its original splendour by the skill of Niccolò Pintucci."*

In 1820 the villa was sold to Prince Camillo Borghese. Governor of the transalpine departments under the Empire, he lived in Paris. After the fall of Napoleon, whose brother-in-law he was, having married his sister Paolina, he settled in Florence where he inherited property from his mother's family, the Dukes Salviati. The land register of the 1830s enables us to uncover the extent of this property which included, beyond the garden and to the north of the park, other scattered pieces of land on the plain south of Via Pratese. However, despite the size of its agricultural property, about twenty hectares, the importance of the complex certainly rests on its stately character, the extra-urban residence of the nobility, a *pendant* to their urban palazzo in Via Ghibellina, sumptuously converted by Baccani. We do not know who was responsible for the architectural remodelling of the Dragomanni's old villa, or for the outdoor layout which included the creation of a romantic park full of rare plants, pools and fountains, a main avenue lined with statues, now lost, and an amphitheatre, boldly connected to the house by means of an iron suspension bridge spanning Via di Castello. This was in keeping with the prevailing interest in technical innovations, and probably inspired by a similar iron bridge already installed in the Poggio a Caiano park, one of the few exemplars in the Florentine area. The north face of the building follows the course of Via di Castello while the south façade overlooks the garden. The house is symmetrically laid out with rooms leading off the ground and first-floor halls which fill most of the space on the side overlooking the garden and the plain. In restructuring the building the unknown architect sought to adjust the block pattern of the traditional Tuscan villa to accord with the new aesthetic canons. This shows particularly clearly in the new design for the main façade, on the garden side, where the rhythm of volumes and apertures of the lower floor is counterbalanced by a first-floor storey, more chiaroscuro in tone and spanned with simple windows whose vertical movement is emphasized by the decorative stucco panels beneath, while the end windows are flanked by figures in niches. The idea of adding the band of simulated, painted rustications along the lower part of the main façade was an undemanding device introduced to keep abreast of the general fashion for modernizing the design of earlier buildings. A similar, if simpler, form of modernization appears on the Via di Castello façade, where the regular spacing of the windows, emphasized by a double cornice marking the dividing line between the storeys, is only broken by the central window, where the iron bridge leads across to the park. On the ground floor of this façade, works of conversion seem to have been kept to a minimum and among the irregularly spaced openings, for the service rooms, is the doorway to the chapel, crowned with an 18th-century style broken pediment, the remains of the earlier façade. The desire to remodel the structure on neo-classical lines is particularly clear from the roof, where the tiles and overhanging eaves were replaced by a pediment on each side. A simplified version of these pediments also appears on the farmhouses belonging to the estate. If, as information concerning the Borghese property in the 1834 inventory for the land register would suggest, two of these houses were not part of the property, it seem probable that they were rebuilt at a later date for the subsequent proprietor, Count Baldini, a visible sign that these rural houses were part of the estate.

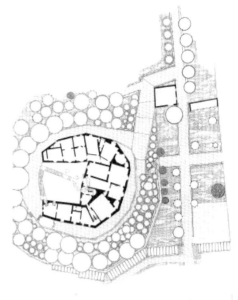

The decorative details, particularly in the interior, are extremely elegant. On the gallery walls are a series of bas-reliefs by Costoli, who also produced the statues on the façade. The gallery is also the position of the very fine frescoes depicting an allegory of Triumph, the work of Bezzuoli, who was also engaged on the decoration of the palazzo in Via Ghibellina. The rooms are all furnished in perfect neo-classical style, preserved in every detail.

Bibliography:
Moreni, 1795, pp. 126–127.
Carocci, 1906, p. 294.
Lensi Orlandi, 1965, p. 23.
Gobbi, 1974, pp. 17–18.
I dintorni di Firenze. Arte, storia, paesaggio, 1983, p. 96.
Villoresi, 1988, p. 123.
Cresti, 1992, pp. 406–409.

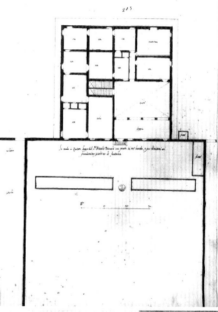

VILLA LA MULA

This building has the air of a castle and there is a good view of its towered and fortified appearance from Via Gramsci. The irregular plan is dictated by the shape of the burial mound on which it stands, very different from the regular, almost square, layout which forms an L-shape round the courtyard and loggia, as we see from Giorgio Vasari the Younger's plan. The name of this unusually shaped complex is etymologically uncertain and it cannot be given a precise date since it would seem to be the outcome of a series of conversions of a 13th-century fortified structure spanning a long period. It apparently belonged to the powerful Guelph family Della Tosa who owned several properties in this area and in Sesto, and who, having moved to this parish in the mid-14th century changed the name to Della Mula da Quinto. The uniqueness of this early structure rests on the fact that it stands on a 7th-century BC. Etruscan tomb, marking the site's unbroken occupation. The tomb still preserves the great *tholus*, 8.95 metres in diameter, with a mock cupola and no central pillar. The present height of about 5 metres is due to the floor being repaved in terracotta when the space was used as a wine-cellar. The tower stands only slightly higher than the rest of the building which is crowned with crenellations on one side, continuing those on the tower. There is an intriguing 17th-century

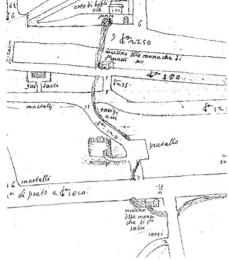

view of the old loggia (now closed) in a painting by Giovanni da San Giovanni which uses the villa as a background. The rooms still preserve their elegant 17th-century additions, with murals of pastoral scenes and landscapes. One of the rooms looking towards Florence has a wooden ceiling, the corbels supporting the beams carved with water leaves and the joists and dust-excluders painted with geometric patterns, still intact after five centuries. The name is difficult to explain. Moreni cites a Florentine saying: "*Tra Quinto Sesto e Colonnata / Una Mula d'oro è sotterrata*", referring to the unearthing of ancient treasure, and probably related to the name of the original proprietors. The two maps of the Capitani di Parte illustrate this building differently. One carries the word "Mula" on a wall encircling a tower and a lower block, the other shows a more compact view of the surrounding wall. On both maps there is a gateway in the outer wall and a short path leads to the field below and opens onto the adjoining road. The name Martelli is repeated along the borders with Via Maestra and Via di Castello. One map carries the words "Caccalese Martelli" on Via Maestra. The agricultural land that once surrounded the complex, made up of three separate share-cropping farms until 1974, has shrunk and the use and character of the farmhouses has changed.

Bibliography:
Moreni, 1795.
Carocci, 1906, pp. 298–299.
Lensi Orlandi, 1965, pp. 25–26.
Mannini, *Gli Etruschi a Nord dell'Arno*, Florence, 1965.
Gobbi, Gobbò, Capaccioli, Lazzareschi, 1977.
Stefanelli, 1978.

VILLA EUGENIA-NENCETTI

The 19th-century name on the 1896 and 1923 I.G.M. maps is "Villa Eugenia"; on the 1936 map the house is called "Villa Nencetti", from the name of the family who owned it for many years. Although the present appearance of the villa resembles a 19th-century conversion, according to information supplied by Carocci, the site was previously occupied by a 15th-century building, the property of the Pescioni family. In the 17th century it belonged to the Sisters of Faenza, and the Strozzi who declared its ruined condition to the Decima officials. The property was subsequently rebuilt. The land of the "Ai Muli" farm which surrounded the villa and extended to Villa Gramsci has been recently encroached on by the building of a church.

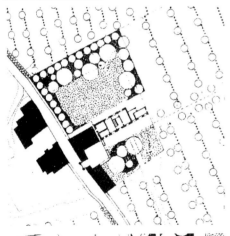

Bibliography:
Carocci, 1906, p. 295.
Villoresi, 1988, p. 124.

VILLA LAPI-WINTELER

This modest-sized building stands on the Via degli Strozzi, overlooking the Villa Torrigiani park, surrounded by a small amount of land which appears to have been "cut out" of the Villa Manfredi farm. The absence of any reference to this building on the Capitani di Parte map of the parish of Santa Maria a Quinto would suggest it is of later date, based on a farm building and turned into a holiday house towards the end of the 19th century. On the 1896 and 1923 I.G.M. maps it is called "Villa Lapi", on the 1936 edition "Villa Winteler". This type of conversion is one of the last instances of the occupation of this area, but although constructed on harmonizing traditional lines, it displays some very different features from the early examples.

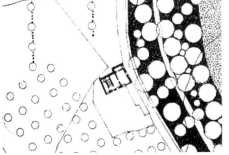

BOGLIOLO, VILLA MORENI

The villa stands in the centre of Quinto. What we see today is the result of the alterations, carried out in various periods, on a very early central nucleus. The restoration conducted some decades ago revealed 14th-century masonry. The building stands on the site of Roman baths, as was shown by finds such as paving, remains of buildings, fragments of statuary and columns and marble steps discovered during archaeological digs in the 19th century. "Le Pergole" was originally called "a Bogliole", as is recorded on the Capitani di Parte map of the parish of Santa Maria at Quinto, where a fountain is marked in an area surrounded by the road which circles the property, below the building marked "Palazo". The two editions of the map differ slightly, with one bearing the words "*orto di Bogliole*" (garden of Bogliole) and the other simply "Bogliole". On the latter, a spring of water is shown inside the surrounding wall, and in the other against the wall. On both maps the spring flows into a stream – the Gora di Quinto – which fed the mill of the Sisters of San Martino and, further south, the mill of the Sisters of San Salvi. The building belonged to the Bartolini Salimbeni family which, apart from this and other buildings, also owned a great quantity of land in the area of Quinto. The map carries the name Bartolini on the land in front of the building, which ends at the border with the church. In about the middle of the 15th century Leonardo di Bartolomeo Bartolini bought it from Antonio and Domenico di Piero of the "Gonfalone delle Chiavi". The villa remained the property of this aristocratic family for a long period and they embellished it with handsome ornamentions, perhaps carried out by the architect Baccio d'Agnolo, who also worked on their city palazzo. The family coat of arms, three poppies and the motto "*Per non dormire*", still appears on the architraves of the doorways to some rooms, which have beautiful 16th-century ceilings. In front of the villa is a giant fish-breeding pool, continually replenished with fresh water flowing, as in Roman times, from the Seppi spring. As Abbot Moreni records, this water, which served the Roman baths, was also used for working porphyry. It would seem that this was the site of "the ingenious construction for marble at Quinto and plentiful water to drive it". According to this account: "*At the time of Grand Duke Cosimo I, overcoming the hardness of porphyry was a closely guarded secret, and its working is almost attributed to him. Today it is widespread in Rome and in other Italian towns, including Florence, where the distinguished foundry-man Signor Alessandro Moreni makes beautiful objects using jets of water. Many years have passed since he invented and built an ingenious machine, the mechanism of which could carry out several operations at the same time, such as pulling metal wire, drilling tubes, turning mortars etc., at his villa at Quinto, a place with an abundant supply of water.*"

The surrounding agricultural property, which included a farm of five hectares, is now as neglected as the beautiful house which it surrounds.

Bibliography:
Moreni, 1795.
Carocci, 1906, p. 295.
Lensi Orlandi, 1965, p. 24.
Il parco territoriale di Monte Morello, 1979, pp. 82–83.

VILLA TORRIGIANI

Before this building was turned into a clinic, which notably affected its appearance, it had all the features of a grand 19th-century house in the traditional style of Florentine villas, but its origins are 15th century. The

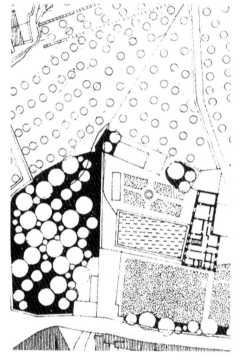

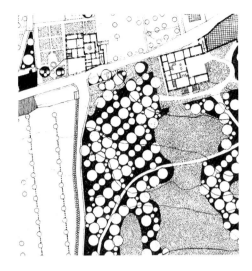

land register for 1427 records it as the property of the Guidacci family. As Carocci tells us: "*In 1474 Vieri Guidacci sold this ancient property to Francesco Boninsegni, but in 1485 Guidacci's sons bought it back and it remained the property of the family without interruption until the line died out. On the 28th of April 1650 the Quinto villa passed to Luca Torrigiani, archbishop of Ravenna, and to the brothers, Raffaello's children, who inherited it from their mother Camilla, daughter of Senator Carlo Guidacci.*" On the map of the parish of Santa Maria at Quinto, datable to around 1580, in the area on the boundary of the Zambra stream, the name Simone Guidacci appears beside a building, the nucleus of what was to become Villa Torrigani. The Torrigiani family already owned other properties in the Quinto area, as we see from this same map which shows their name across a vast stretch of land, running from Via di Castello to Via Maestra, opposite Villa La Mula. The shrine at the corner of Via Maestra and Via Taddeo Gaddi is known as the "Virgin of Torrigiani". The Torrigiani properties in this area are further recorded by the licence granted in 1556 to Antonio Torrigiani, by the Sisters of San Martino al Prato of Florence, to pipe water from a spring on their Tassinaia farm, and by a grand ducal rescript of 1587 allowing the lady Lucrezia Capponi nei Torrigiani to close a road which crossed one of her properties in the parish of Santa Maria at Quinto, on payment of fifteen *scudi*. During the 19th century the old villa-farm was transformed into a grandiose summer residence for one of Florence's leading titled families. The remodelling operations, which involved not only the building but also the surrounding land, took place a few years after the transformation of their city residence. The Torrigiani house in Via del Campuccio was built by Marchese Pietro, an aristocratic cosmopolitan figure who had links with Napoleonic circles, who "*in 1817, with the aim of giving work and bread to the poor afflicted by famine and typhoid, opened the enormous garden on the left bank of the Arno and engaged them to build a small villa with a tower*".

The villa has a U-shaped plan and the façades have two rows of windows, with corbels on the ground floor, and a double-ramped stone stairway on the face overlooking the garden; possibly an attempt to interpret the kind of villa derived from Buontalenti's style which had become part of local tradition. Another large staircase was installed in the interior. A local 19th-century scholar describes the building as follows: "*The principal entrance to the Quinto villa is on the north side; on entering we soon reach a spacious courtyard which gives access to a magnificent entrance-hall. Here is a handsome stone staircase which despite its great scale has something light and ethereal about it which catches the eye. The architect was the aforementioned Marchese Pietro and he was so pleased with his work – quite rightly – that he had his portrait painted showing him sitting in an armchair studying the plans and instructing the master builder – a certain Bacherini of Quinto – whom he had engaged to build the staircase . . . . Considering the period, this staircase was an extremely bold venture and it roused much discussion, wherefore it seemed not unfitting to record the fact with the following inscription:*"

NELL'IMMAGINARE E DIRIGERE
LA COSTRUZIONE DI QUESTA SCALA
E GLI ABBELLIMENTI DELLA VILLA DI QUINTO
IL MARCHESE PIETRO TORRIGIANI
GUIDATO DA SOLO AMORE
DELL'ARTE ARCHITETTONICA
SI STUDIÒ DI EMULARE CHI LA PROFESSA
L'ANNO 1843

On the south side are 6 large rooms which lead to the wonderful park which the Marchese Pietro made to embellish the villa, taking over two adjoining farms for the purpose."

Creation of this romantic park was the operation that made most impact on the surrounding terrain. It followed a gentle slope, thick vegetation alternating with clearings, lemon-houses, greenhouses and a small lake, dug out, unfortunately, from the ruins of an Etruscan tumulus. The park, which covers six hectares to the south of the villa, is now neglected and overgrown. The only larger park was that of the Villa Petraia, which it must once have rivalled in splendour. The main body of the villa, which became the property of an estate agent in the 1970s, is currently undergoing radical restoration.

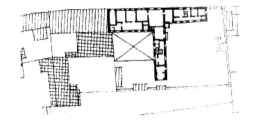

Bibliography:
Tosi, 1885.
Torrigiani, 1889.
Tosi, *La villa Torrigiani a Quinto*, 1892.
Tosi, Santa Maria a Qiunto, 1893, pp. 8–9.
Carocci, 1906, p. 296.
Lensi Orlandi, 1965, pp. 18–19.
Gobbi, 1974, pp. 18–19.

LA ZAMBRA

This building on Via Gramsci, with its elegant ornamented 18th-century façade, is one of a series of grand villas standing along the old Via Maestra, centres of agricultural estates stretching down to the plain, which, owing to their position, have suffered severe transformations or even disappeared. This villa is marked as "La Zambra" on the 1896 and 1923 I.G.M. maps while on the 1936 version it is called "Villa Bianchini". Its earlier name was derived from the Zambra stream which flows from the peaks above Quinto Alto, on the border of the property's land. Recorded in the 1427 land register as belonging to the Tempi family (as Carocci reports), over the course of the centuries it changed hands several times. In the 17th century it was the property of the Aldobrandini, Del Mazza and the Ginori family whose arms, combined with those of the Ricasoli, appear on the ceiling of one of the rooms.

Bibliography:
Carocci, 1906, p. 299.
Villoresi, 1988, p. 128.

IL POZZACCIO, VILLA PARENTINI

The building stands on the border of the Strozzino property, with access on Via Fontemezzina, and appears to be a late 19th-century conversion of a pre-existing structure which is shown on the Capitani di Parte map of the parish of Santa Maria at Quinto as a house with a dovecote tower to the north of the Strozzino property, and the name "Simone Guidacci".

Bibliography:
Il parco territoriale di Monte Morello, 1979, p. 88.

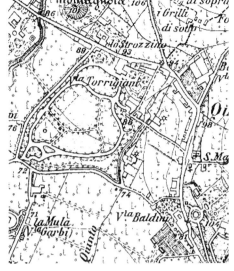

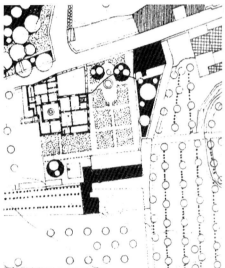

LO STROZZINO, VILLA MANFREDI

This imposing 17th-century style building stands on Via F.lli Rosselli. It was earlier called "Via Erbosa" and "La Petrosa", before becoming "Lo Strozzino". Like almost all the buildings in this area it is the result of a series of additions and alterations to a much earlier central core. According to Carocci, the first records that we have go back to 1340 with the bill of sale for: "*a piece of land and two houses in Via Erbosa, drawn up by the sons of the former Barone di Cappello to Niccolò of the late Andrea of the parish of San Michele at Bertelde.*" In the following century the property belonged to the Galli, a family from the south side of the Arno, in the gonfalon of Fersa, and they continued to own it until the 16th century. The Capitani di Parte map of the parish of Santa Maria at Quinto marks two buildings called "la Botte" and "Pedoni". The manuscript accompanying the map describes the road corresponding to the present Via degli Strozzi as follows: "*The said road begins from the main road to Prato between the Ambrogi and Martelli properties, is b.a 6 wide [3.50 metres], b.a 1150 [671 m.] long and finishes at the* botte *and near the* Vergine del Pedone, *width b.a. 7° [4.38 m.]*". The chapel in the villa has a fresco of the Virgin and this may be the roadside shrine, now incorporated in the family chapel built some decades later when the villa was realized. Indeed, in 1652 Luigi di Alessandro Strozzi's sons, who had purchased the property, declared a ruined landlord's house, the *botte* referred to on the 16th-century map. It was at this time, when the proprietors were called Strozzino, a branch of the Strozzi family, that the villa was rebuilt and given its present appearance. When the family died out the villa was inherited by the Samminiatelli who sold it to the Corsi family. Early in the 20th century it was bought by Senator Manfredi, before passing to the Cantagalli. In the garden of the villa is the "Montagnola", an Etruscan domed tomb or tholus, of great importance in recording the presence of Etruscan settlements in the Quinto area, like the other nearby tombs at the Mula, Palastreto and Torrigiani villas. A *studiolo* in the villa has a particularly interesting grotesque decoration, frescoed according to a pattern which recurs in other villas in the area and attributable, according to A. M. Mannini, to the Salvestrini workshop of Castello, which was engaged in other villas, Pozzino, Casale, Torre, Corsi Salviati at Sesto, and Chiavacci at Colonnata. "*In the friezes we find again the charming figures painted on the ceiling of the Torre: sturdy serving-maids bearing lamps and peasant girls with straw hats and spinning distaffs. The rectangular panels show pastoral scenes and the delights of a visit to a country villa: walks, concerts and falcon hunting. The images in the corners of the frieze are interesting, showing skilfully painted young peasants out hunting. The grotesque decoration here is more crowded with figures, coloured streamers and canopies, than the earlier examples in the other villas and is datable to the third decade of the 17th century.*"

The property's agricultural land, consisting of two farms in the 1940s, remains unchanged in size if not in administration and management.

Bibliography:
Tosi, 1902.
Carocci, 1906, p. 295.
Mannini, *Gli etruschi a Nord dell'Arno*, 1965.
Stefanelli, 1978.
Mannini, 1979.
Il parco territoriale di Monte Morello, 1979.
Villoresi, 1988, pp. 124–125.
Mannini, 1991, p. 62.

John Singer Sargent, *Scene in a garden at Villa Torre Galli,* 1910, Royal Academy of Art, London.

APPENDIX

Six villas to visit
with original perspective views by
Giovanna Balzanetti Steiner

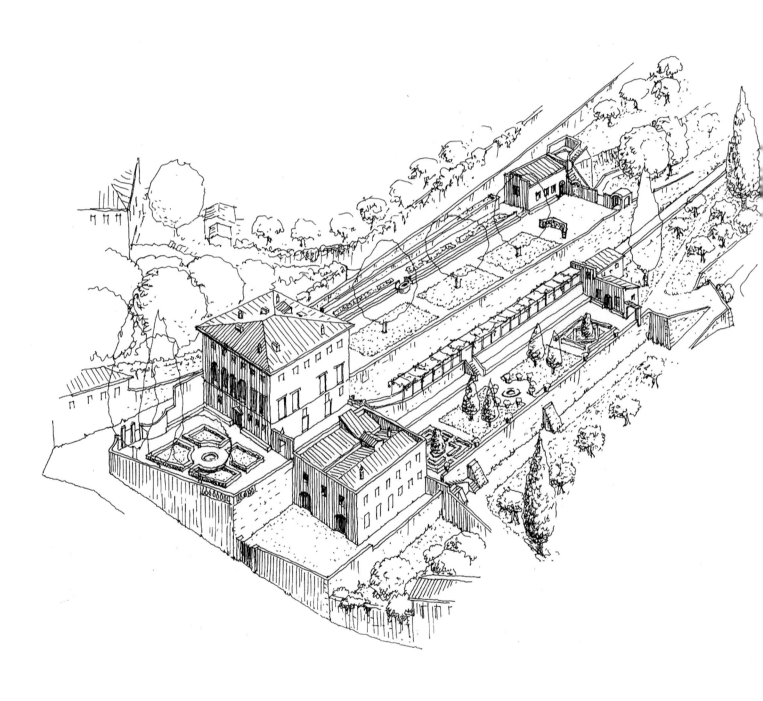

According to Giorgio Vasari, Cosimo the Elder built the Medici villa at Fiesole for his son Giovanni, giving the commission to Michelozzo in about 1450 although building work was delayed until between 1458 and 1461. For the first time in the history of the Medici villas this was not an adaptation of a pre-existing structure, but an entirely new building. Moreover, the villa was not connected with any farming activity, the site being chosen for its panoramic view on a steeply sloping hillside. This position made it necessary to build a massive substructure to support the building and garden and Vasari tells us that tremendous expense was involved in building the foundations on the steep hill. In fact, the location of the villa, about 250 metres above the valley of the Arno, is most dramatic with steeply sloping ground in front and in the rear the even more precipitous south-facing hillside. From a distance the façade stands out sharply against the background. The garden area was designed according to a new idea: the creation of a terraced garden which followed the contours of the steeply sloping land. The villa is a cubic block. The absence of an interior court was the first radically new element in the spatial conception of the villa plan. Interest is focused on what is outside the house, towards views near and far, and not inwards, as is implied by an interior courtyard. This absence is also an indication of an entirely new design, unrelated to either pre-existing models or completed buildings. A central reception room gives onto the two loggias on the east and west faces, with no direct contact with the outside; inside, the surrounding landscape is reproduced in the painted murals. The layout is basically resolved on three levels: a central one, the level of the garden on the west side and the two loggias; an upper floor with private apartments and bedchambers; a lower level, on the same plain as the lower garden and the "secret garden" on the east side of the villa. It was not possible to move from one level to another without passing through the villa. A recent study by D. Mazzini and S. Martini suggests the attribution of the project to L. B. Alberti.

Historical events and subsequent changes in ownership were responsible for some alterations. In 1469 the villa became the property of Lorenzo the Magnificent who visited it in the company of poets and men of letters. There are numerous reports of the villa and of the important people who were guests during this period. We can see the original appearance of the building in a fresco by Domenico Ghirlandaio, *The Assumption of the Virgin*, in the choir of Santa Maria Novella, and in an *Annunciation* attributed to Lorenzo di Credi, now ascribed to Biagio d'Antonio Tucci in the Accademia di San Luca in Rome. On the basis of these, it seems likely that there was once a loggia with four arches on the west face of the building. The Medici sold the villa in 1671, when its modest proportions were deemed inadequate for the pomp and splendour of court

life. After further changes in ownership it was bought in the 1770s by an unconventional Englishwoman, Lady Margaret Orford, Horace Walpole's sister-in-law, who made some changes including a driveway for carriages (the original entrance gave onto Via Vecchia Fiesolana) and additions to the garden on that side, with a belvedere decorated with rustic mosaics, a shrine and a lemon-house designed by Gaspero Paoletti. The building was extended on the north side, towards the hill, to create service quarters and a loggia was opened in the building's new façade, altered by the closing of the arcade to the south, to give symmetry to the ends of the façade; above the doorway we can see the change in masonry which marks the closing of this opening. In the mid-1800s the villa was bought by William Blundell Spence, a collector and art lover, and it became a centre for society gatherings. When work was being done to widen the access road some Etruscan masonry was unearthed, as is recorded on a plaque at the entrance. In 1911 the villa was bought by Lady Sybil Cutting, wife of Geoffrey Scott and Percy Lubbock and the mother of the writer Iris Origo. This new owner commissioned the architect Cecil Pinsent to restore the garden. Pinsent recreated a lower 15th-century garden, divided into four simple beds with two magnolia trees and clipped box hedges, with a central stone fountain; he made a path linking the two terraces and a pergola of Banksia roses along the wall supporting the upper terrace and altered the secret garden to the west by installing a central fountain, eliminating the flowering plants and introducing classic lawns and box hedges. According to inventories of the time, the characteristic espaliers of orange trees date to the Medici period, when bitter orange trees were imported from the Kingdom of Naples.

In 1959 the villa was bought by the Mazzini family.

Bibliography:
B. Patzak, *Die Renaissance und Barockvilla in Italien*, Leipzig 1913.
G. Masson, *Italian Gardens*, London 1961, pp. 73–76.
C. Bargellini and P. De La Ruffinière du Prey, "Sources for a reconstruction of the Villa Medici, Fiesole", in "The Burlington Magazine", CXI, 799, October 1969.
P. Van de Ree, G. Smienk, C. Steenbergen, *Italian Villas and their Gardens*, Amsterdam 1992.
D. Mazzini, S. Martini, *Villa Medici, Fiesole, Leon Battista Alberti and the Prototype of the Renaissance villa*, Città di Castello 2004.
A. Lillie, "Giovanni di Cosimo and the villa Medici at Fiesole" in *Piero de' Medici il Gottoso (1416–1469)*, Berlin 1993, pp. 190–205.

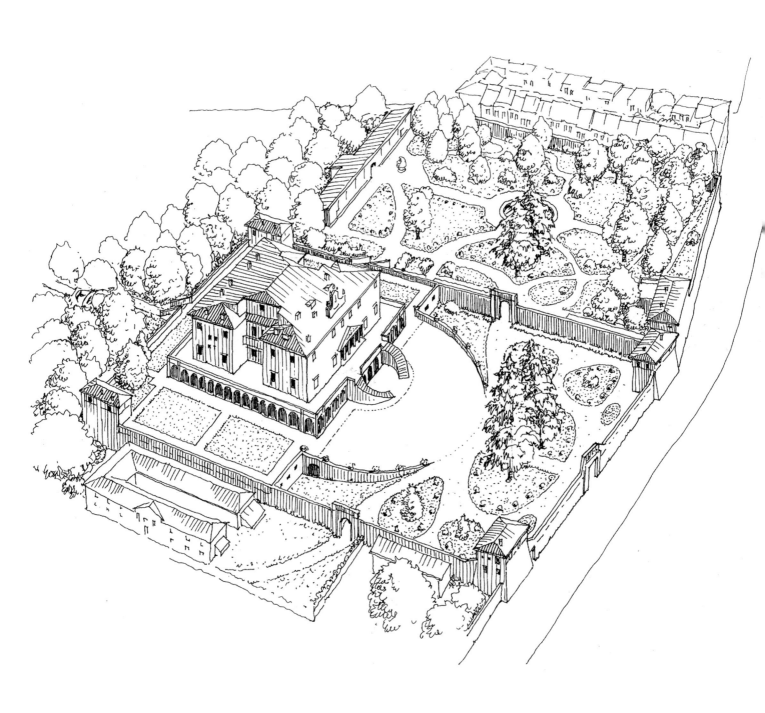

The Medici villa of Poggio a Caiano is the most remarkable example of a new type of villa, one not realized from a pre-existing building or a model. Although the typological innovations introduced at the Fiesole villa, with no central courtyard and thus oriented to face a view of the surrounding landscape, introduced a new goal for the ideology of the villa and its relationship to the landscape, these aspects were most coherently developed in the architecture of the Poggio a Caiano villa. It was designed by Giuliano da Sangallo for Lorenzo the Magnificent and became a prototype that was to be later developed by Palladio and become a universal model.

The architect, Giuliano da Sangallo, came from a family of architects and artists, later famous for their classical erudition, which bequeathed to posterity one of the largest known collections of architectural designs and sketches.

The Poggio estate was acquired by Lorenzo the Magnificent towards the end of the 1470s and the commission to built the villa was given to Giuliano da Sangallo in the early 1480s. Building work began in around 1485 but we have few contemporary accounts. Two poems by Poliziano and one letter of Michele Verino include references to the villa and these would suggest that in 1485 the new villa occupied much of Lorenzo's attention and that it gave rise to great expectations. In 1492, the year of Lorenzo's death, the new villa was still unfinished. It seems likely that building work was continued under the direction of Piero de' Medici, until his exile in 1495. By 1495 one part of the main building had been completed and of the two remaining parts, only the foundations and some sections of wall had been produced. Loggias, surrounding porticoes, the balustraded platform and exterior staircase had also been built. Work came to a halt between 1495 and 1513 when the Medici family was in exile, resuming in 1515 and continuing until about 1520. During this final phase of activity, the two unfinished sections of the building were finally completed. Other parts were not finished until the time of Pope Leo X, Lorenzo's son.

The villa's hillside position protected the foundations from the Ombrone's floods and exposed it to cool and refreshing summer breezes, while the high hills to the south shielded it from the cold winter blasts. This raised, flood-protected, healthy site with a splendid view had all the prerequisites recommended by early writers, later reiterated by de' Crescenzi and Alberti.

On its low isolated hill, the building appears to stand on a terrace supported by arches, forming an ambulatory, or walkway, round all four sides. In fact, this "terrace" is part of the basement storey immediately below, and the *piano nobile* has several doors and windows communicating with this terrace. The openings give the impression of leading directly outwards to the distant countryside, with no contact with the ground beneath. The state rooms and their surrounding terrace thus seem to float like a ship over the beautiful landscape with views of the distant valley and the surrounding hills.

The ground plan is strictly symmetrical with a main axis that runs through the large front staircase, the centre of the terrace, the loggia, the central hallway, the great hall and, finally, a room in the rear giving onto the terrace on the opposite side. The main axis thus runs through a series of spatial forms, all of different proportions, but with a single unifying principle. Against the main axis we can trace a second system of symmetry, two secondary transeptal axes, which, unlike the main axis, repeat the same unity on both sides. All smaller rooms are placed at the four corners while the larger ones, intended for collective use or state occasions, are positioned along the main axis. The centrepiece of the whole structure is the great hall which, like a covered courtyard, fills the full height of the building with its stupendous barrel vault, mentioned by Vasari as being an unusually daring construction. The corner rooms are grouped together to form separate apartments,

each suitable for some distinguished guest and his personal servants. Sangallo's combination of private chambers and state rooms created an entirely new pattern, where symmetry and harmony were put before the demands of pure practical convenience.

The centre of the Poggio a Caiano façade is ornamented by a loggia in the form of a hexastyle temple front with a triangular pediment. In classical architecture this motif was almost exclusively used for sacred buildings. It was later adopted, precisely for its sacred character, for the ceremonial architecture of the late Roman emperors when they wanted to stress the divine nature of their power. It is not easy to say what this feature implied in early Italian Renaissance architecture, although it would seem to have retained its religious significance. This originally sacred motif thus acquired a new symbolic value, a vestibulum leading to a grand secular residence. The fact that the temple façade later became one of the most popular themes in secular architecture does not weaken the supposition that Sangallo's use of it at Poggio a Caiano must have made a tremendous impact on his contemporaries, a remarkable fresh idea. For late 15th-century Florentine architects this was a way of giving a domestic building a higher level of aesthetic dignity, and a symbolic value. The Medici villa at Poggio is the first example of a compact and almost symmetrical Florentine villa based on a centralized plan. Vasari tells us that Lorenzo asked Sangallo to "*make a model of what was in his mind*". In the sketches this centralized plan is carried much further than in the actual building. In fact, the sketches hold an intermediate position between Lorenzo's villa and a fully-fledged Palladian design such as the Villa Rotonda near Vicenza, Andrea Palladio's masterpiece, a villa formed of a square with classical porticoes on all four sides, while the interior is developed around a circular two-storey *salone*.

The loggia has a lofty appearance with widely spaced columns. A majolica frieze with figures on a blue ground enlivens the regularity of the columns. This is crowned by a simple, slightly heavy, pediment bearing the Medici coat of arms, in both conception and form the majolica frieze is strictly classical in character. In the middle of the two central columns is the temple of Janus. The figures have been interpreted as a sophisticated allegory of the seasons in the countryside but the scene must allude, in some fashion, to the political achievements of the Medici family, in the service of peace and prosperity.

Windows are set on either side of the loggia, not regularly spaced, but the same on both sides. This corresponds with Alberti's dictum: "*let such ornaments as are proper to the middle be placed in the middle, and let those which are at equal distances on each side, be proportioned exactly alike*." Giuliano da Sangallo did not create a new architecture from nothing. We can see that this Medici villa closely follows the general ideas concerning villas expressed by Leon Battista Alberti in his work on architecture. This was the first in a long line of outlying villas which together form one of the most glorious chapters in European architecture.

Bibliography:
P. G. Hamberg, "The Villa of Lorenzo il Magnifico at Poggio a Caiano and the Origin of Palladianism" in "Idea and Form. Studies in the History of Art", Stockholm 1959, pp. 76–87.
Ph. E. Foster, *A Study of Lorenzo de' Medici's Villa at Poggio a Caiano*, Yale University Ph.D. 1976.
S. Bardazzi, E. Castellani, *La villa Medicea di Poggio a Caiano*, Florence 1981.
J. S. Ackerman, *The Villa*, London, New York 1990, pp. 78–82.

VILLA GUICCIARDINI CORSI SALVIATI AT SESTO FIORENTINO

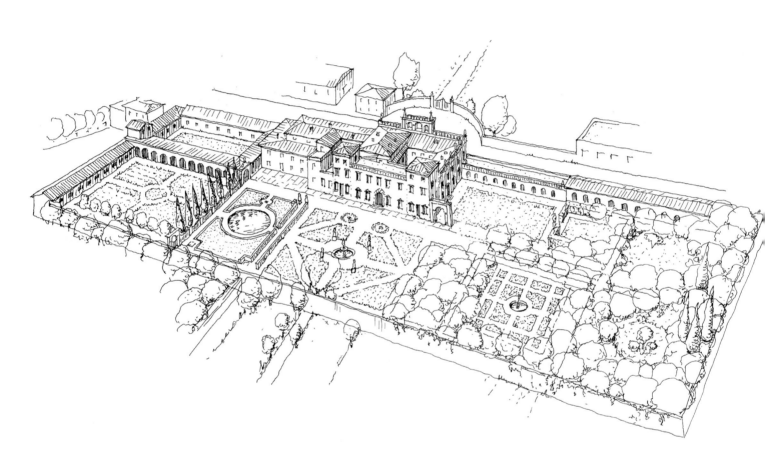

The roadside position on the plain and the baroque style make this an unusual villa. Villas were normally built on a slope, in accordance with the precepts of the writers of architectural treatises. This villa belongs to a group of numerous villas and farmhouses that once stood along the road linking Florence to Sesto Fiorentino, on the plain. Indeed, the old road marks the boundary between the hills to the north-west of Florence and the large plain that runs from the road to the Arno river. Many villas were built off the right-hand side of this road, the old Via Maestra, including the Villa Medici at Castello, Villa Petraia and Villa Corsini, while still others sprang up on the left, towards Sesto. These villas had a common purpose since they were designed to form the centres of management of the large agricultural estates which stretched across the plain as far as the river. Like Villa Guicciardini, many had long façades on the road side and, at the rear, were gardens, orchards and the farms making up the estate. Maps of the 19th-century show many interesting villas along this road but a number were destroyed, many more were remodelled and changed, and almost all lost their relationship with the countryside and with their land in the mid-19th century when the railway was built connecting Florence, Pisa and Livorno. This was a determining factor for the changes in the landscape and the rash of new buildings along the plain. This was the chief direction of Florence's expansion and the city advanced inexorably towards the villas, still in the open countryside. As its name implies, Sesto Fiorentino marked the sixth milestone on the old Roman road to Prato, beyond today's industrialized Rifredi and the Medici villas above, now a crowded thoroughfare lined with modern constructions encroaching on the former vineyards and olive groves.

Villa Guicciardini's position on a plain certainly offers no memorable views of countryside or city but the house is nonetheless splendid for the balanced linking of its spaces and its carefully planned detail.

" *You might pass to and fro a thousand times through the dusty little street of Sesto without ever dreaming of what certain walls along the south side of that busy thoroughfare conceal unless, by a fortunate chance, several doors at one particular spot happened to be open simultaneously, revealing the barest glimpse of the loveliness within*", these are the words used by Harold Donaldson Eberlein to express his admiration for this villa in his book on Tuscan villas published in 1922, and he continues: " *Seen from the street, the villa Corsi Salviati presents a bleak, uninteresting grey stucco wall, pierced at intervals by windows that utterly fail to intrigue the imagination. For ought of promise conveyed by its northern or road aspect, it might

as well be a tenement or a factory. But enter a door, pass through a court and out through another doorway, and the sudden change is astounding. It is like being transported in the twinkling of an eye from purgatory into paradise. You find yourself unexpectedly in the midst of a garden which, as Guido Carocci rightly says 'is amongst the most beautiful and delightful of those created in that seventeenth century, in which everything had to be in keeping with the pomp of life, and with the magnificence of costumes and customs'. This garden*", he continues, "*lies to the south of the buildings, occupying a long tract of level ground, embellished with ponds and pools, with fountains and ingeniously contrived jets of water, with shady groves enriched with statues, vases, grottoes and rustic adornments, with thickets and with borders wherein grow luxuriantly the most beautiful flowers and where the rarest plants are cultivated.*" This reads almost like one of the fanciful descriptions of the fabled garden of classical antiquity, penned by the Italian writers of romances during the Renaissance, but it is simply an incomplete and entirely veracious account to which more might have been added without any risk of exaggeration.

From the earliest times, "*to which the memory of man runneth not back*", the Carnesecchi family owned a house and land on this spot. In January 1502 Luca di Andrea Carnesecchi sold the house, with walled garden, dovecotes and other appurtenances to Simone di Jacopo Corsi. The villa was remodelled and embellished by the Corsi family during the following century "*with all that pomp and magnificence which the taste and the elegance of the period demanded and which the wealth of that illustrious family made possible*". We are told by Carocci that the most celebrated artists "*were engaged on the new buildings and on the stucco decorations and frescoes*". Among these "*should be recorded the names of two pleasing and brilliant painters: Federigo Zuccari and Baccio del Bianco*".

The fresco decorations have disappeared, except for those on the ceiling of a 16th-century study and library painted with mythological scenes and grotesque motifs, in the style of Pierin del Vaga, in which appear two scenes of the villa before the 17th-century alterations. In the painting, the face on the garden side has a loggia on the upper floor where pieces of silk are hanging up to dry in the sun, an allusion to the proprietor's manufacturing activity. The loggia was flanked by a taller block with an unequal saddle roof and a dovecote in the rear, in keeping with the 15th-century typology of many houses in the countryside around Florence. In the fresco the villa has a doorway of ashlars and, on either side,

two stone dogs in niches. The garden in front has a simple lawn divided into beds and a central fountain ornamented with tritons. The other painting is a view of the courtyard and loggia, with an elegant stone fountain in the middle, the bowl crowned with a figure of "*the spirit of fame*". The fresco decoration is of great historical interest and was formerly attributed to Bernardino Poccetti, but more recently it has been ascribed to Alessandro Fei Barbieri, who had worked for the Corsi family in 1575 in the Chapel of the Flagellation in the church of Santa Croce, and is therefore fully 16th-century in period.

In 1632 Giovanni and Lorenzo di Jacopo Corsi embarked on a second series of operations which may have involved Gherardo Silvani, for the architectural work, although we do not have the names of the architects and sculptors concerned. Between 1640 and 1641 Baccio del Bianco decorated some rooms with paintings, but alas these have disappeared. At this time the garden was laid out with simple rectangular sections bordered with box hedges, a central fountain and a shady grove on one side and, on the other, a fish-pond, a small orchard and a grassy expanse with bases for pots of lemon trees and a rabbit house.

One of the major innovations in the garden was a system of irrigation, with underground pipes carrying water from the Gora, making it possible to create a large round pool. At the same time, Antonio Corsi enlarged the villa and built the rectangular pool and the channel with thirteen little waterfalls. A 1644 map records the work in the garden, which appears divided into sections separated by walls into a flower garden, wilderness, orchard, a fish-pond with an exedra and a rabbit-warren.

The result was a handsome villa, with subsidiary buildings and gardens, all in perfect 17th-century baroque style. The interior still has many traces of its original design but the exterior has been repeatedly altered to accord with prevailing architectural styles. The villa was designed to fit its situation. "*There was nothing to be gained by considering the road front on the north*", states Eberlein, "*so the architecture on the side was left ungraced by any amenity and all the buildings were placed squarely on the line of the street so that the ground might be saved for the south side, where it would count most. All the architectural graces were lavished on the garden side of both the dwelling and the various dependencies. Directly adjoining the south front of the dwelling is the parterre, geometrically laid out with gravelled walks and box-edged beds, such adjuncts as fountains, statuary, and the usual lemon trees in great earthen pots, which always serve to give accent and definition, being freely employed but disposed with excellent judgement. To the west of the parterre is the long pool or vasca, one end coming near to the loggia at the west end of the house. West of the pool are flower gardens and other delights, the architectural setting of every item being duly considered. To the south of the parterre is the park. The joy of an extensive outlook being denied by the flatness of the ground, a compensation for this lack is provided by the belevedere on top of the house.*"

During the first decades of the 18th century major works were carried out on the building and in the garden. All the façades were embellished with statues and balustrades and on the façade on the road a great coat of arms of the Corsi family was added. One dovecote was turned into a loggia and a great arch was

built flanked by statues of mythological deities. A long fish-pond was built and a labyrinth, on the east side, and in the middle of the century a bird-netting area was set out. The new owner, Antonio Corsi, swept away the boundaries separating the three main "rooms" in the garden and enlarged the semicircular pool of the rabbit island to form a large round pond. To provide space for these innovations, the fish-pond was converted into a rectangular pool, flanked by urns on pedestals and with statues of the Four Seasons at the corners. The old aviary was converted into a loggia and its walls decorated with classical ruins. This is probably when the old square parterres behind the house were replaced by the present diamond-shaped pattern, while smaller beds were added around the fountain near the house. The whole kitchen garden was planted with trees and somewhere in this same area a maze was created, now lost.

Giuseppe Zocchi's engraving supplies the most authoritative records of the appearance of the house and garden in the 18th century. The perspective is exaggerated, the space dilated in a way that was common in 18th-century scenes. The villa is given its particular character by the terraces, to create which building material was taken from the two pre-existing towers overlooking the garden. The villa had a semicircular forecourt, lost in the mid-19th century when the road was straightened.

Later, both house and garden fell victim to 19th-century fashion: in 1865 the great hall on the ground floor was frescoed with the Four Elements, while statues, box hedges and topiary work were removed, being considered insufficiently romantic, and replaced with palm trees and other exotic plants. These included double jasmine from Goa, the Arabian jasmine, camellias, gardenias and the "rosellino di Firenze", the ranunclus, and these became the specialities of this new type of landscaped garden. The wood was extended and converted into a small park with a lake, grassy mount and mock castle in the romantic style.

Marchese Giulio began restoring the garden in 1907. He attempted to recreate the original traditional layout without obliterating all traces of the successive interventions. In 1922 he restored the layout of the parterre on the south side of the villa.

In her book on Italian gardens Georgina Masson states: "*He with great pains and admirable taste set about the restoration of as much as possible of its eighteenth-century character. Though, as he points out in his beautifully documented monograph of the villa, he 'took warning from the mania that possesses some people for re-doing their villas and gardens too much and, in their desire to bring them back to one period, depriving them of the traces left by the passage of time that give them a human and living character'.*"

Today this villa, like several others in the outskirts of Florence, is occupied by an American institution, Michigan University, and the garden, which is in need of attention and upkeep, can be visited by appointment.

Bibliography:
H. Donaldson Eberlein, *Villas of Florence and Tuscany*, Philadelphia, London, New York 1922.
G. Guicciardini Corsi Salviati, *La Villa Corsi a Sesto*, Florence 1937.
G. Masson, *Italian Gardens*, London 1961.
H. Acton, *Tuscan Villas*, London 1973.

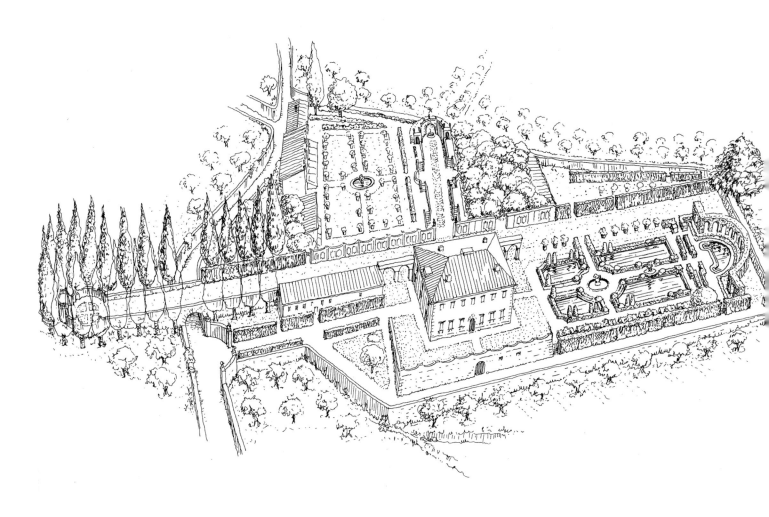

In his book *Tuscan Villas* Harold Acton tells us that Villa Gamberaia has *"the most poetical garden near Florence. In its homely simplicity Villa Gamberaia is a perfect foil, as it were, to the elaborate embroidery of its garden. From a distance, as in Zocchi's engraving, the latter is invisible, approached by a narrow lane from Settignano. With its projecting eaves, and coigned angles in pietra serena [limestone], the two-storey structure differs from others of the species by the addition of flying arcades to north and south. Though it has the characteristics of a sixteenth-century building, it dates from the beginning of the seventeenth. One would never guess that it has arisen like the phoenix from its ashes [since it was wholly gutted during the last world war] because its present owner has restored it with such scrupulous integrity that it is, if anything, finer than it was before – a miracle of aesthetic reconstruction."*

Recorded in the 14th century as a country house for the Benedictine Sisters of San Martino a Mensola, in the next century we discover, from the land register declarations, that it was the property of the Gambarelli family, two of whose members were the sculptors Antonio and Bernardo Gambarelli, better known as Rossellino. In the following century the property was alienated from their heirs and passed to Andrea di Zanobi Lapi who enlarged it with further acquisitions and turned it into a fine residence, as we see from the inscriptions on the building's architraves: *Zenobius Lapius erexit ac fundavit AD MDCX.* In 1630 there were further works to enhance the complex, still further enlarged by the purchase of adjacent buildings. The property passed to the Capponi family in 1718 when the Lapi were faced with financial difficulties. This is the year of the following declaration to the land registry: *"A gentleman's villa in the borough of Santa Maria at Settignano, called Gamberaia, with all the rooms and cellars, a fountain, garden, groves of trees, avenues, chapel, ball-court, bowling green, gardener's house, vases and pots and storage rooms, citrus trees and flowering plants and another small house called Lottino, including also all forms of shelter and appurtenances, usages and services."*

The new owners conducted further operations on the villa, giving it the appearance it has in Giuseppe Zocchi's 1744 engraving. It stands on a broad terrace, finishing in a massive wall to support the steeply sloping terrain. The villa has a restrained design, a compact two-storey block with handsome windows framed in stone, broken by central rusticated doorways. The corners are reinforced with ashlars. The south façade opens onto a loggia, set at a slight angle to the formal garden. The planimetric layout revolves round a central courtyard giving access to the interior, set at the crossing of two axes which connect the avenue with the formal garden and, at right angles with this with the front terrace and the rocaille *studiolo* in the rear. At either side of the façade are two arcaded extensions, one with a terrace connecting the main building with the chapel and outside buildings, the other leading towards the parterre of the formal garden.

The villa has a similar position to the Medici villa in Fiesole, both as regards distance from the centre of Florence and because it is invisible from the approach road. Again, both buildings are modest in scale and both command a spectacular view of the city, from terraces which in both cases serve as foundations for the buildings, built on steep slopes. The design of the villa and garden is based on different uses of spatial features, linked and unified by a sweep of greenery. One end of this finishes in a grotto dug out of the hill, an arched fountain of rusticated stonework encrusted with stalactites. The other end looks out into space: a balustrade supports a statue of Diana between two stone obelisks and commands a vast panoramic view of the Arno valley and the distant hills.

The site's abundant supplies of water, due to the proprietor's acquisition of nearby sources, made it possible to maintain the villa's wealth of greenery, including the groves and the bowling green. Quoting Harold Acton: *"Rococo statues, obelisks and balustraded steps lead up to a lemon orchard and a sheltering stanzone. This grotto garden is one of the prettiest open-air boudoirs imaginable. But the main salon of the garden is spectacular: an oblong parterre of geometrical pools framed in box of varied design round a circular central fountain, divided by paths with terracotta jars of lemons and stone vases of geraniums. The pools reflect such a feast of shimmering colour that the eye is dazzled before it can absorb so many precious details: the star in mosaic on the pavement, the carved stone and the immaculate topiary work. It is a hall of horizontal mirrors terminating in a theatrical arcade of clipped cypresses, with stone benches for contemplation above a semi-circular pool of water-lilies."*

When the famous American writer Edith Wharton saw the garden in the early 1900s the most remarkable transformation, introduced by the pools of water, had not yet taken place but she was so struck by place that she described it as *"probably the most perfect example even in Italy of great effect on a small scale"*.

A few years later the villa was bought by Princess Catherine Ghyka, the sister of Natalia of Serbia, who restored the villa and garden with the help of the garden experts Luigi Messeri and Martino Porcinai, father of the well-known landscape gardener Pietro Porcinai. Although the villa subsequently changed hands several times the garden maintained the layout which had been introduced at the beginning of the century.

As G. Masson states: *"From the grassy terrace in front of the house the domes and spires of Florence are seen in the distance across the olive groves and vineyards that, as in Pliny's Tuscan villa, come close up to the house. But the crowning glory of the whole place is the water parterre which lies spread out like some shimmering flower-strewn Persian carpet representing a 'paradise' garden, covering the floor of the beautiful garden room that extends from the house to the end of the terrace upon which it stands, terminating in one of the most breath-taking views in Tuscany. The layout is still the traditional Renaissance one of four parterres, divided by paths, with a circular open space containing a fountain at the crossing. Here and there terracotta urns filled with flowers and orange trees laden with golden fruit, provide vertical accents that are reflected in the pools. At all seasons of the year this garden is a place of surpassing loveliness, but perhaps it is at its most beautiful either when seen on a misty April day, when the fresh spring green provides a perfect foil for the brilliance of the tulips, or in the height of summer with the pink of the oleander blossom silhouetted against the brilliant blue sky, and the same colour scheme repeated in the great lotus blossoms mirrored in the waters of the semicircular pool."*

Bibliography:
E. Wharton, *Italian Villas*, London 1903.
J. C. Sheperd, G. A. Jellicoe, *Italian Gardens of the Renaissance*, London 1925 (1993).
G. Masson, *Italian Gardens*, Thames and Hudson, London 1961.
H. Acton, *Gamberaia*, Florence 1971; *Tuscan Villas*, London 1974.
P. van der Ree, G. Smienk and C. Steenbergen, *Italian Villas and Gardens*, Amsterdam 1992.
M. Pozzana, *A Guide to Villa Gamberaia*, Florence 1999.
Revisiting the Gamberaia. An Anthology of Essays, ed. by P. J. Osmond, Florence 2004.

VILLA LA PIETRA

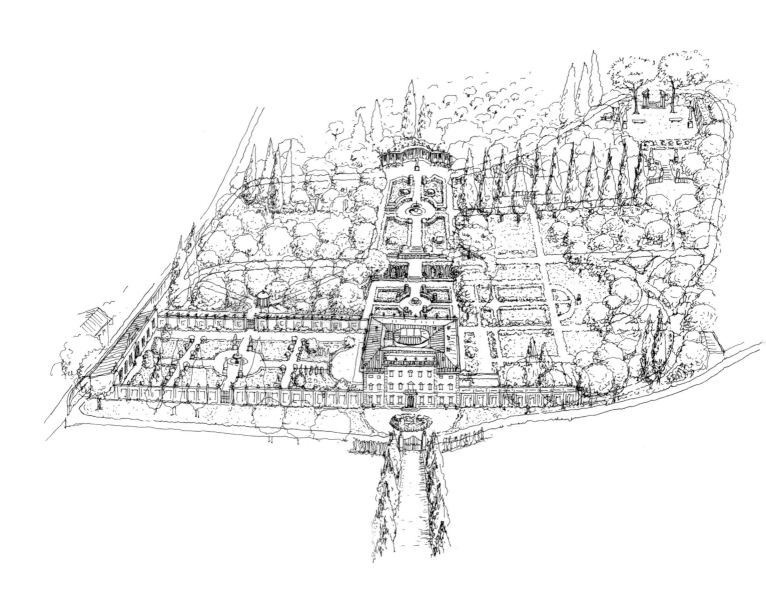

On Via Bolognese, at the level of the junction with Via di Montughi, is a gateway flanked by two buildings, formerly a farmhouse and a gatehouse, and here begins a magnificent avenue of cypresses on a slope dotted with olive trees. At the end of this rises the ochre façade of Villa la Pietra, crowned with a balustrade ornamented with vases. The villa takes its name from the place and from the milestone (*pietra* = stone) marking the distance from the San Gallo gate in the walls surrounding the city of Florence. This ancient house, formerly the property of the Macinghi, a powerful family which had provided the Republic with no fewer than eight *priori*, became the property of the Sassetti in the mid-15th century. The most influential member of this family, Francesco Sassetti, was extremely able in financial matters, a banker and a patron, a friend of literary men and philosophers including Marsilio Ficino, and a business associate of Cosimo the Elder and later Lorenzo the Magnificent. Returning from his bank in Lyon in France in 1468, he married Nera de' Corsi and they both appear in Domenico Ghirlandaio's fresco in the Sassetti chapel in Santa Trinita, which houses their tombs. Francesco Sassetti, a man of substantial means, must have invested a sizeable sum of money in remodelling the old house into a grand residence if, as Harold Acton reports in his memoirs, in his *De illustratione Urbis Florentiae* Ugolino Verino writes: "*Montuguas Saxetti si videris aedes / Regis opus credes . . .*" (If you saw the Montughi villa of Sassetti / You would think it the work of a king . . .). Francesco died in 1491 and in 1546 his heirs sold the property to Giuliano di Gino di Piero Capponi and the villa remained in this family's possession for the following three hundred years. The villa was Luigi Capponi's favourite residence and he was responsible for the baroque "up-dating" of the exterior as well as for the interior decorations. Becoming a cardinal in 1608, he gave up his position as papal legate in Romagna and at the Vatican Library in Rome and retired to La Pietra, where he continued to live until his death in 1659.

Further alterations were carried out during the early 18th century, probably by the architects Carlo Fontana and Giuseppe Ruggeri, who were also engaged for work on the city palazzo, in Via Capponi. The façade on the garden side bears the family coat of arms crowned with the cardinal's hat, while lower down are the Sassetti arms, retained to record the building's ancient noble past. The baroque ornamentations, the moulded curvilinear framing of the windows, the crowning balustrade and the stucco decorations in the interior, are only superficial and the building's 15th-century structure is plain to see. The building could thus be described as an "architectural palimpsest", clearly revealing the distribution of rooms, the vaulted ceilings on 15th-century corbels and the tall narrow windows of some ground-floor rooms. The only substantial alterations to the building were the transformation of the quadrangular courtyard, turned into an oval atrium and later covered, and the subsequent addition of a curving staircase to replace the early straight one. One further major change involved the closing of the loggia and its conversion into a drawing-room, opening onto the garden in the rear and ornamented with a wealth of stucco decorations.

The late 16th-century layout of the villa is illustrated in the collection of plans of "Chiese, palazzi e ville di Toscana e d'Italia disegnate dal cav. Giorgio Vasari in 1598" in the Gabinetto Disegni e Stampe in the Uffizi. Drawing n. 200 is described as "Palazzo of s.re Franc.o Capponi at Montuvi, a place called 'a' sassetti' with a meadow in front, and one behind". The description of the extra-urban residence as a "palazzo" emphasizes the stately character of this building with a planimetric layout closely resembling that of a city palazzo, closed off and inward-looking, with a central quadrangular courtyard with an open loggia. The 17th and 18th-century alterations highlight the axial layout of the building which connects, on a single perspective axis, the tree-lined avenue, entrance corridor, atrium, former loggia, converted into a drawing-room and the garden in the rear, coming to an end in a semicircular exedra with a panoramic view of the hills. We have an image of the villa after its 18th-century alterations in a monochrome fresco which, together with other illustrations of the Capponi's outlying properties, including Villa Gamberaia, are painted in one of the villa's ground-floor rooms. An enormous space lies in front of the main façade, once connected with the original approach. The gardens at the sides of the villa were surrounded by walls ornamented with geometric motifs and topped with statues.

The interior alterations may only have had a superficial effect on the pre-existing structure but changing fashions brought greater changes to the outside spaces, adapted to suit the tastes of various periods. Giorgio Vasari's plan reveals a "secret garden" on the right of the building, divided into quadrangular flower-beds, and a large garden on the left, while the rear is referred to as meadow. A stall and a hen-house appear beyond the pathway. The large garden, an "orchard-garden", was closed with an encircling wall and completed with a lemon-house, the visual termination of the second axis shown in the layout. This walled garden largely retained its former pattern, albeit now embellished

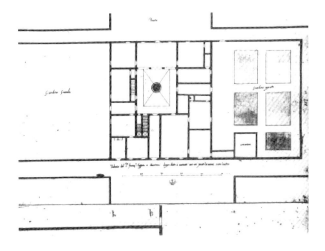

with sculptural works on the surrounding walls, with statues and *mascaron*, alternated with geometric patterns in full baroque style. On the opposite side a drawing-room leads to a man-made grotto decorated in late-Renaissance style with porous rock and shells. Every door and window frames a particular view of the spectacular garden surrounding the villa. In the mid-18th century further changes were made to the annexes, the buildings on Via Bolognese and the great gateway to the villa were put in order, some mural painting in the interior also belongs to this period. In the mid-19th century the villa was inherited by the Incontri and in 1860 the prevailing taste for the romantic garden brought radical changes to La Pietra too, the baroque garden being transformed into an English-style park. Early in the 20th century the villa was first rented, in 1904, and then bought, in 1908, by a young Anglo-American couple, Hortense Mitchell and Arthur Acton, who made it their permanent home. He was a collector, art lover and dealer of Anglo-Neapolitan descent, she the daughter of a Chicago banker and heiress to a considerable fortune. La Pietra was used to house the works of art they collected and became the centre of the busy social life of the international set of expatriates who had chosen Florence as the place to pass their lives of leisure. The most unusual work to be carried out during this period was the transformation of the garden to accord with the canons of the Tuscan Renaissance garden, freshly interpreted with Anglo-Saxon sensibility. An inscription on a wall of La Pietra reads: "*Arthur Acton agli inizi del secolo transformando il parco inglese di Villa La Pietra in giardino all'italiana ne ristabilì l'armonia col poetico paesaggio toscano*". In an isolated corner of the garden another inscriptions records the names of those

who took part in the more than twenty-year long operation: gardeners and architects and the landscape architects Mariano Ambroziewicz, Pasquale Bonaiuti, Giuseppe Castellucci, Edwin Dodge and H. O. Watson.

From the approach road, originally lined with false-acacias and replanted with cypresses as being more in keeping with the predominantly Tuscan character of the villa, the garden is arranged on a series of terraces which take advantage of the natural slope at the rear of the building. We shall leave the task of describing the garden to the pen of Sir Harold Acton, the last proprietor, a cultured aesthete, historian and writer and "*one of the consummate conversationalists of his time*". "*The main plan consists of a series of broad terraces, each like a separate garden, levelled from a slope descending behind the hill. The first is a long platform with a grey stone balustrade for statues at regular intervals, flanked by stairs on either side, which run down the central terrace, enclosed by low walls and clipped hedges with niches for other statues. In the centre of this and the lowest terrace are ancient fountains with circular basins, surrounded by stone benches and geometrical plots of grass hemmed in by clipped hedges of box. A mossy staircase paved with coloured pebbles descends to the long valley below, with a colonnade roofed in by creepers on the right. Both terraces are planted mainly with evergreens. A peristyle of Corinthian columns screens the lowest terrace from the adjacent vineyard and a statue of Hercules stands vigorously in the centre with a pair of venerable cypresses behind him. Many paths running parallel with the hill-side lead to stone arches and circular plots enclosed by hedges and statues. The whole garden is essentially green; other colours are episodic and incidental. Sunlight and shade are as carefully distributed as the fountains, terraces and statues, and in no other private Florentine garden have I seen statues of such individual grace, from the lone colossus by Orazio Marinali, to the Venetian figures by Francesco Bonazza which have stepped on to the open-air theatre as for one of Goldoni's comedies. The wings of this little theatre are evergreen, also the globed footlights. The statues collected by my father for many years deserve a separate monologue; there are over a hundred of them, exclusive of what Nollekens called 'bustos'. It is a garden for all times and seasons, independent of flowers. The central axis faces Vallombrosa; Fiesole and San Domenico loom on the extreme left."*

The particular features of this garden are those typical of a late Renaissance Florentine garden: greenery, with the art of topiary used as an architectural material to form walls, recesses or volumes; water in its different forms, and stone in a variety of ways. The geometric axial plan is expanded outwards along secondary ones. The first, on a level with the first water basin, has a green bower on one side containing the gigantic statue of Hercules by Marinali, and on the other a *tempietto*; on the lower level a green path connects a clearing on the right, ending with the vista of a rotunda, with the opposite side where there is a small theatre of greenery adorned with states depicting *commedia dell'arte* characters, once the setting for theatrical and musical performances, staged to entertain the proprietors and their numerous guests. On the level between these two is a covered pathway with columns on one side and, on the other, bordering the green theatre beneath, a winding path that leads to the back of the lemon-house.

When describing this garden, created by his father, Sir Harold Acton writes: "*The decision to Tuscanize the so-called English garden was taken in 1904 . . . . The garden looking to the south was demolished in the last century and restored by my father as he imagined it must have been."* The uniqueness of this garden lies less in the scale of the undertaking than in its particular approach. This is a 20th-century interpretation, or re-creation, of a Renaissance garden, according to the taste and sensibility of an Anglo-Saxon art lover, where nature and artifice are used and combined in a completely original manner, yet one which observes the canons of the traditional Tuscan garden.

Sir Harold Acton, the last Anglo-Florentine, died in 1994, leaving La Pietra to a leading American academic institution, New York University. The university has made it a centre for their Studies Abroad programme and for conferences, while the faithful work that has been carried out on restoring the villa and garden, and the numerous works of art they contain, to their original splendour, offers the public a major example of the "museum-house", a record of the elegant and eclectic taste of an early 20th-century collector.

Bibliography:
Harold Acton, *More Memoirs of an Aesthete*, London 1970.
Harold Acton, *Tuscan Villas*, London 1974.
J. C. Sheperd, G. A. Jellicoe, *Italian Gardens of the Renaissance*, London 1925 (1993).
M. Pozzana, *Gardens of Florence and Tuscany*, Florence 2001.
A. Richard Turner, *La Pietra, Florence, a Family and a Villa*, Milan 2002.
A. Lillie, *Florentine Villas in the Fifteenth Century: An Architectural and Social History*, New York 2005.

VILLA LE BALZE

Villa Le Balze is undoubtedly one of the most interesting examples of the early 20th-century movement to revive the formal garden. The achievement owes much to the character and training of the designer and his close rapport with the commissioner and with the cosmopolitan and cultured circles to which they both belonged. The English landscape architect, Cecil Pinsent, was commissioned for the villa in 1911 by the American philosopher Charles Augustus Strong. The site chosen by Strong on a steep slope on the Fiesole hillside, not far from the Villa Medici, was a long narrow strip of land with a breathtaking view over the plain and the city below, obliging the young architect to evolve a very specific planimetric design for both the villa and the garden.

The close attention to the rules of geometry which characterizes Pinsent's work is clearly displayed in the plan of the villa and garden of Le Balze and both are developed on a line running lengthwise along the plot of land. The building is long and narrow, opening in the centre with a 15th-century style loggia giving access to the library and leading onto an open terrace with a broad view of the city. Inside the villa is a long corridor, running parallel with the terrace and connecting all the ground-floor rooms, which open onto a loggia on the garden side, opposite the entrance. A first-floor loggia opens at the opposite end of the building, facing the garden.

The building's particular architectural features are related to a revival of a 15th-century style which adopted the vocabulary of the early Renaissance: plastered walls, enhancing the *pietra serena* frames of the doors and windows and the columns and capitals. On the architect's propensity to draw inspiration from local Tuscan architecture see the essay by Yoi Maraini, for whom Pinsent worked, who states: "*On the hills of Florence there are a few modern houses that fit perfectly with the olives and cypresses of the landscape. These houses are designed by Cecil Pinsent, a young English architect, and though they are in no way imitations either of older farmhouses . . . or of the dignified villas near them, yet they are so much part of the Tuscan scene that Italian architects often stop to admire the manner in which an Englishman has understood their architecture, but how to use its characteristic lines for entirely modern needs.*"

Both the interior and exterior spaces are developed in a careful balance of masses and openings, a subtle play of parts, based on an informed understanding of the relationship between architecture and landscape. The parallel axes along which the spatial sequence of both the interior and the exterior are organized on different levels are the keystone of the design, and they carry through the succession of developments. The garden is conceived as a succession of outdoor rooms, enclosed by walls of greenery holding well-positioned openings for viewing the panorama of the plain below. Moving from one leafy chamber to another is achieved in such a way that a space's characteristics are only fully revealed on entering. The spatial continuity of the whole complex is entrusted to the pattern of parallel axes, real view-finders, which end in eye-catching features, sculptural works used as vanishing points, such as statues, niches and exedrae, etc. The 15th-century style which the architect is re-evoking here is joined by mannerist and baroque touches in the stairway at the rear of the building which seem to echo the secret garden at Villa Gamberaia, and the aedicules which form the background to the first green chamber. The layout ends with what is known as the "philosopher's walk", a pathway lined with ilex, iris and lavender. The present entrance on the old Via Fiesolana replaces the original one on Viuzzo degli Angeli which was set above the level of the villa to allow easy access to the proprietor, who suffered from trouble with his legs. Thus, the smaller villa which was annexed to the property is now linked at the entrance and the level of the walkway beneath the pergola that joins the loggia on the upper floor and extends over the whole garden.

In line with the principal axes which follow the natural lie of the land, on a level with the loggia overlooking the terrace is the central feature in this sequence of open spaces: the grotto. Ornamented with statues of philosophers, it opens from the centre of the pergola on the upper level and is carved out of the rock at the height of the original entrance. This feature, reminiscent of the baroque, forms a perfect fulcrum in the sequence of outdoor rooms and it alludes, along with the busts of philosophers, to the villa's significance as the residence of a modern philosopher like the commissioner. Features of a traditional Tuscan garden are interpreted in a new spirit which in some way enhances their character. Geometrically divided flower-beds, walls of greenery which have real windows opening onto the outside world, glades, statues, grotto and niches faced with porous rock and mosaic, some produced by Pinsent himself, and tubs of lemon trees, all form one amazingly varied whole, the beauty of which is enhanced by the careful attention with which the complex, now the seat of Georgetown University, is maintained.

Bibliography:
Y. Maraini, *The English Architect Abroad*, in "The Architectural Review", LXXI, January–June 1932, pp. 6–7.
Cecil Pinsent and his Gardens in Tuscany, edited by M. Fantoni, H. Flores, J. P. Pfordresher, Florence 1996.
G. Galletti, "Cecil Pinsent architetto dell'Umanesimo" in *Il giardino europeo del Novecento 1900–1940*, edited by A. Tagliolini, Florence 1993, pp. 183–198.
I. Romitti, M. Zoppi, *Gardens of Fiesole*, Florence 2000, pp. 52–58.
M. Pozzana, *Gardens of Florence and Tuscany. A Complete Guide*, Florence 2001, pp. 72–73.

BIBLIOGRAPHY

This bibliography does not include the books quoted in the notes of the first part and in the appendix.

1791 and 1795
D. MORENI, *Notizie Istoriche dei contorni di Firenze*, Florence.

1885
C. O. TOSI, *Sesto Fiorentino. Note e documenti*, Florence.
C. VON STEGMANN, H. VON GEYMÜLLER, Die Architektur der Renaissance in Toscana, Munich.

1886
C. DA PRATO, *Firenze ai Demidoff. Pratolino e San Donato*, Florence.

1889
L. TORRIGIANI, *Descrizione delle ville di Quinto, Panna e Camigliano*, Florence.

1892
C. O. TOSI, *Santa Maria a Quarto*, Sesto Fiorentino.
C. O. TOSI, *La villa Torrigiani a Quinto*, Sesto Fiorentino.

1893
C. O. TOSI, *Santa Maria a Quinto*, Sesto Fiorentino.
C. O. TOSI, *Le Brache, Villa Masetti*, Sesto Fiorentino.
C. O. TOSI, *Rinieri, Villa Corsini*, Sesto Fiorentino.

1902
C. O. TOSI, *Villa Corsi a Quinto "Lo Strozzino"* "Corriere Italiano" 139, 142.

1905
C. O. TOSI, *Castello nel comune di Sesto Fiorentino*, Florence.

1906
G. CAROCCI, *I dintorni di Firenze* vol. 2, Florence.

1907
G. S. ELGOOD, *Italian Gardens after drawings by C.G. with notes by the artist*, London.

1933
B. H. WILES, *The Fountains of Florentine Sculptors and their Followers from Donatello to Bernini*, Cambridge.

1949
O. H. GIGLIOLI, *Giovanni da San Giovanni*, Florence.

1964
C. UND C. THIEM, *Toskanische Fassaden-Dekoration in Sgraffito und Fresco*, Munich.

1965
M. MANNINI, *Valori storici, artistici e archeologici di Sesto Fiorentino*, Sesto Fiorentino.
M. MANNINI, *Gli Etruschi a Nord dell'Arno*, Florence.
G. C. LENSI ORLANDI, *Le Ville di Firenze*, 2 vols., Florence.

1966
M. TRIONFI HONORATI, *Le case dei Bonaparte a Firenze negli anni dell'esilio* in "Antichità Viva" 2, pp. 64–80.

1969
M. DEZZI BARDESCHI, L. ZANGHERI, *La villa Corsini a Castello*, in "Bollettino degli Ingegneri" 11, Florence.

1973
H. ACTON, *Ville Toscane*, Florence.

1974
T. CARUNCHIO, *Origini della villa rinascimentale: la ricerca di una tipologia. Studi di storia dell'arte*, Rome, vol. 4.
K. W. FORSTER, *Back to the farm. Vernacular Architecture and the Development of the Renaissance Villa*, "Architectura", pp. 1–12.
G. GOBBI, *Alcuni interventi ottocenteschi sul territorio fiorentio* in "Bollettino degli Ingegneri" 10, pp. 15–21.

1975
G. GOBBI, *Strutture storiche nel territorio fiorentino: la villa del Casale*, in "Bollettino degli Ingegneri", 6, Florence, pp. 10–13.

1976
D. R. WRIGHT, *The Medici Villa at Olmo a Castello: Its History and Iconography*, 2 vols, Ann Harbor.

1977
R. STOPANI, *Medievali "case da signore" nella campagna fiorentina*, Florence.
A. BANTI, *Giovanni da San Giovanni, pittore della contraddizione*, Florence.
G. GOBBI, T. GOBBÒ, L. CAPACCIOLI, L. LAZZARESCHI, *Interpretazioni grafiche del sistema collinare fiorentino*, "Controspazio" 2, pp. 25–36.

1978
G. GOBBI, *Documenti per una storia del terriorio: interventi granducali nell'area fioentino* in "Bollettino degli Ingegneri" 7, pp. 6–13.
Città, ville e fortezze nella Toscana del XVIII secolo, Florence.
G. LENSI ORLANDI CARDINI, *Le ville di Firenze, di qua d'Arno, di là d'Arno*, 2 vols, Florence 3rd ed.
R. STOPANI, *Medievali "case da lavoratore" nella campagna fiorentina*, Florence.
V. STEFANELLI, *Territorio e architettura etrusca a Sesto Fiorentino*, Florence.

1979
D. COFFIN, *The Villa in the Life of Renaissance Rome*, Princeton University Press.
Il parco territoriale di Monte Morello, Florence.
M. P. MANNINI, *Le decorazioni in villa fra Sesto e Castello nei secoli XVI e XVII*, Sesto Fiorentino.
L. ZANGHERI, *Pratolino il giardino delle meraviglie*, Florence.

1980
A. GODOLI, A. NATALI, *Luoghi della Toscana medicea*, Florence.

R. A. GOLDTHWAITE, *The Building of Renaissance Florence*, Baltimore and London.

F. GURRIERI, D. LAMBERINI, *Le scuderie della villa medicea di Poggio a Caiano*, Prato.

P. J. JONES, *Economia e società nell'Italia Medievale*, Turin.

Il potere e lo spazio. La città del Principe, Exhibition Catalogue, Florence.

La città effimera e l'universo artificiale del giardino, 2 vol. edn, M. Fagiolo, Rome.

D. MIGNANI, *Le Ville Medicee di Giusto Utens*, Florence.

A. PAOLUCCI, *L'aurora dell'anima.*, in *Il primato del disegno, Catalogue of the Exhibition*, Florence.

Palazzo Vecchio: committenza e collezionismo medicei, Florence.

1981

S. BARDAZZI, E. CASTELLANI, *La villa medicea di Poggio a Caiano*, Prato, 2 vols.

Giardini italiani. Note di storia e di conservazione, Ministero per i beni culturali e ambientali, Rome.

Il giardino storico italiano. Problemi di indagine, fonti letterarie e storiche, Atti del Convegno di Studi Regione Toscana, Siena - S. Quirico d'Orcia 6–8 October 1978, ed. G. Ragionieri, Florence.

C. KLAPISCH-ZUBER, *Mezzadria e insediamenti rurali alla fine del medioevo*, in *Civiltà ed economia agricola in Toscana nei secoli XIII–XIV: Problemi della vita delle campagne nel tardo medioevo*, Pistoia.

R. M. MASON, *Vedute di Firenze e della Toscana di Giuseppe Zocchi*, Florence.

M. MASTROROCCO, *Le mutazioni di Proteo. I giardini medicei del Cinquecento*, Florence.

1982

P. F. BAGATTI VALSECCHI, S. LANGE', *La Villa*, in *Storia dell'arte Italiana, Forme e modelli*, vol. XI, Turin.

C. CANEVA, *Il giardino di Boboli*, Florence.

F. CHIOSTRI, *Parchi della Toscana*, Genoa.

G. FUSCARI, S. PROSPERI VALENTI RONDINÒ, *Note in margine ad una schedatura: i disegni del fondo Corsini nel Gabinetto nazionale delle stampe*, in "Bollettino d'Arte" 16.

I valori geografico-storici del paesaggio fiorentino, Atti dell'Istituto di Geografia dell'Università di Firenze, Florence.

La città degli Uffizi, I musei del futuro, Catalogue of the Exhibition, Florence.

N. MILLER, *Heavenly Caves. Reflections on the Garden Grotto*, London.

G. C. SCIOLLA, *Ville medicee*, Novara.

1983

L. BEVERLY BROWN, *Leonardo and the Tale of Three Villas: Poggio a Caiano, the Villa Tovaglia in Florence and Poggio Reale in Mantova*, in *Atti del Convegno Firenze e la Toscana dei Medici nell'Europa del Cinquecento*, Florence, vol. III.

A. CONTI, *I dintorni di Firenze*, Florence.

I dintorni di Firenze. Arte, storia, paesaggio, Florence.

1984

H. ACTON, *Ville toscane*, Milan (London 1973).

E. BORSI, C. PAMPALONI, *Monumenti d'Italia Ville e Giardini*, Novara.

Castello campagna medicea periferia urbana, Florence.

M. FERRARA, F. QUINTERIO, *Michelozzo di Bartolomeo*, Florence.

Il giardino come labirinto della storia, Atti del convegno, Palermo.

A. LILLIE, *Francesco Sassetti and his Villa at La Pietra*, in *Oxford, China and Italy. Writings in Honour of Sir Harold Acton on his Eightieth Birthday*, ed. E. Chaney and N. Ritchie, London.

M. MANNINI, *Le strade e i popoli della podesteria di Sesto nel XVI secolo*, Florence.

P. MINUCCI DEL ROSSO, *La Loggia de' Bianchi*, Florence.

C. VASIC VATOVEC, *L'Ambrogiana. Una villa dai Medici ai Lorena*, Florence.

L. ZANGHERI, *Joseph Frietsch un "giardiniere" boemo*, in "Antichità Viva", n. 3.

1985

J. S. ACKERMAN, *Il paradigma della villa*, in "Casabella", n. 509/510.

M. CATALANO, E. PANZINI, *Giardini storici. Teorie e tecniche di conservazione e restauro*, Rome.

Il ritorno di Pan. Ricerche e progetti per il futuro di Pratolino, ed. A. Vezzosi, Florence.

La fonte delle fonti. Iconologia degli artifizi d'acqua, Atti del Convegno, Pratolino, Florence.

1986

Capolavori e restauri, Catalogo della mostra, Florence.

J. DIXON HUNT, *Garden and Grove, The Italian Renaissance Garden in the English Imagination: 1600–1750*, London.

Il giardino romantico, ed. A. Vezzosi, Florence.

Il giardino d'Europa. Pratolino come modello nella cultura europea, Milan.

L. MEDRI, P. MAZZONI, M. DE VICO FALLANI, *La villa di Poggio a Caiano*, Florence.

M. MURARO, *Civiltà delle ville venete*, Udine.

1987

C. CRESTI, *La Toscana dei Lorena. Politica del territorio e architettura*, Milan.

Fiorenza in villa, ed. C. Acidini Luchinat, Florence.

Il giardino: idea, natura, realtà. Colloquio internazionale, Pietrasanta 22–23 July 1987, ed. A. Tagliolini, M. Venturi Ferriolo, Rome.

D. LAMBERINI, *Calenzano e la Val di Marina. Storia di un territorio fiorentino*, Prato.

Natura e architettura. La conservazione del patrimonio paesistico, ed. M. Boriani, L. Scazzosi, Milan.

L. ZANGHERI, *Pratolino, il giardino delle meraviglie*, Florence.

1988

R. ASSUNTO, *Ontologia e teleologia del giardino*, Milan.

M. BAXANDALL, *Painting and Experience in Fifteenth Century Italy: A Primer in the Social History of Pictorial Style*, Oxford (1972).

J. CHATFIELD, *A Tour of Italian Gardens*, New York.

A. FARA *Bernardo Buontalenti. L'architettura, la guerra e l'elemento geometrico*, Genoa.

M. MOSCO, *Flora medicea in Florentia*, in *Floralia, florilegio delle collezioni fiorentine del Sei-Settecento*. Catalogue of the Exhibition, Florence.

A. TAGLIOLINI, *Storia del giardino italiano. Gli artisti, l'invenzione, le forme dall'antichità al XIX secolo*, Florence.

A. VILLORESI, *Sesto Fiorentino. Notizie di storia geografia arte*, Sesto Fiorentino.

1989

Antico e futuro nel territorio mediceo di Castello. I giardini della Chimera, ed. A. Vezzosi, Florence.

A. CARNEMOLLA, *Il giardino analogo. Considerazioni sull'Architettura dei giardini*, Florence.

M. C. POZZANA, *Materia e cultura dei giardini storici*, Florence.

L. ZANGHERI, *Ville della Povincia di Firenze. La città*, Milan.

1990

J. S. ACKERMAN, *The Villa. Form and Ideology of Country Houses*, London.

E. CASSARINO, *La villa medicea di Artinino*, Florence.

E. CENCI, C. PERONI, *Il palazzo di città e il "Casale" dei Carlini. Ragguagli archivistici*, in "QUA.SA.R" 3.

Il giardino come labirinto della storia, 2° Convegno Internazionale 1985, Palermo.

C. LAZZARO, *The Italian Renaissance Garden: From the Conventions of Planning, Design and Ornament to the Grand Gardens of Sixteenth-Century Central Italy*, New Haven, London.

M. MOSSER, G. TEYSSOT, *L'architettura dei giardini d'Occidente, dal Rinascimento al Novecento*, Milan.

M.C. POZZANA, *Il giardino dei frutti*, Florence.

Pratolino Villa Demidoff. Storia, arte, natura, ed. Z. Ciuffoletti, Florence.

P. ROCCASECCA, *Ricerca sul lessico di parchi e giardini*, Istituto Centrale per il Catalogo e la Documentazione, Rome.

G. P. TROTTA, *Villa Strozzi "al Boschetto"*, Florence.

V. VERCELLONI, *Atlante storico dell'idea del giardino europeo*, Milan.

M. VISONÀ, *Giovanni Battista Foggini egli altri artisti nella villa Corsini a Castello*, in "Rivista d'Arte", XLII, IV, vol. VI.

1991

Boboli '90, ed. C. Acidini Luchinat, E. Garbero Zorzi, Florence.

D. COFFIN, *Gardens and Gardening in Papal Rome*, Princeton University Press.

La Villa Médicis ed A. Chastel, P. Morel, Rome.

A. LILLIE, *Vita di palazzo, vita in villa: l'attività edilizia di Filippo il Vecchio*, in *Palazzo Strozzi. Metà Millennio 1489–1989*, Atti del Convegno di studi, Florence 3–6 July 1989.

Parchi e giardini storici. Conoscenza tutela e valorizzazione, Ministero per i beni culturali e ambientali, Comitato Nazionale per lo studio e la conservazione dei giardini storici, Catalogue of the Exhibition Certosa di Padule 8 June–29 September l991, Rome.

M. MANNINI, *Lestrade e i popoli della podesteria di sestio nel XV1 secolo*, Florence.

E. TESTA, *Spazio e allegoria nel giardino manierista*, Florence.

1992

C. ACIDINI LUCHINAT, *I complessi delle ville di Castello e Petraia. Spunti di problematica*, in "Storia Urbana", 60.

C. ACIDINI LUCHINAT, G. GALLETTI, *Le ville e i giardini di Castello e Petraia a Firenze*, Pisa.

R. BENTMANN, M. MÜLLER, *The Villa as Hegemonic Architecture*, New Jersey and London.

C. CONTORNI, *La villa medicea di Careggi*, Florence.

C. CRESTI, *Civiltà delle ville toscane*, Udine.

P. E. FOSTER, *La villa di Lorenzo de' Medici a Poggio a Caiano*, Poggio a Caiano.

Il giardino storico all'italiana, Atti dei Convegno, St. Vincent 22–26 April 1991, ed. E. Nuvolari, Milan.

Il giardino e il tempo. Conservazione e manutenzione delle architetture vegetali, Atti del Convegno, Milan 29–30 November 1990, ed. M. Boriani, L. Scazzosi, Milan.

Parchi e giardini storici, parchi letterari, conoscenza, tutela e valorizzazione, Atti del Il Convegno Nazionale, Monza Villa Reale 24–26 June 1992, Monza.

M. J. POOL, *The Gardens of Florence*, photos by A. Albrizzi, New York.

Ville, parchi e giardini per un atlante del patrimonio vincolato, ed. V. Cazzato, Rome.

1993

S. BAJARD, R. BENCINI, *Villas and Gardens of Tuscany*, Paris.

A. CAPECCHI, *Il giardino di Boboli. Un anfiteatro per la gioia dei granduchi*, Florence.

V. CAZZATO, M. FAGIOLO, A.M. GIUSTI, *Teatri di verzura. La scena del giardino dal Barocco al Novecento*, Florence.

R. WILLIAMS, *The Country and the City*, London.

1994

A.G. CAUCCI, *Il paesaggio dei giardini storici, Firenze e il suo territorio*, Florence.

M.C. POZZANA, *Firenze, giardini di città*, Florence.

1995

C. ACIDINI LUCHINAT, G. GAULETTI, *La villa e il giardino della Petraid*, Florence

M. AZZI VISENTINI, *La villa in Italia, Quattrocento e Cinquecento*, Milan.

G. CAPECCHI, *Un anfiteatro di verzura*, in "Antichità Viva", n. 516.

O. GUAITA, *Ville e giardini storici in Italia*, Milan.

Il giardino delle Muse. Arti e artifici nel barocco europeo, Atti dei IV Colloquio internazionale di Pietrasanta, ed. A. M. Giusti, A. Tagliolini, Florence.

A. LILLIE, *The Humanist Villa Revisited*, in *Language and Images of Renaissance Italy*, ed. A. Brown, Oxford.

M. ZOPPI, *Storia del giardino europeo*, Bari.

1996

J. DIXON HUNT, *The Italian Gardens. Art, Design and Culture*, Cambridge University Press.

M. FAGIOLO, A.M. GIUSTI, *Lo specchio del paradiso. L'innmagine del giardino dall'antico al Novecento*, Cinisello Balsamo.

A. FARA, *Bernardo Buontalenti*, Milan.

Giardini Medicei. Giardini di palazzo e di villa nella Firenze del Quattrocento, ed. C. Acidini Luchinat, Milan.

O. GUAITA, *Le ville di Firenze*, Rome.

Il Giardino Botanico di Boboli, Florence.

Il giardino delle Esperidi, ed. A. Tagliolini, Florence.

Vegetazione e giardino storico. Atti della giornata di studio, Genova 22 April 1996, ed. C. Rezza, M. Devecchi, Molteno.

P. SANTANGELO, *Il giardino di villa Corsini a Castello, indagine conoscitiva e ipotesi per unrecupero,* doctoral thesis, Department of Architecture of Florence University, academic year 1995–1996.

M. ZOPPI, *Guida ai giardini di Firenze,* Florence.

1997

Villa La Quiete. Il patrimonio artistico del conservatorio delle Montalve, ed. C. De Benedictis, Florence.

1998

Bernardo Buontalenti e Firenze. Architettura e Disegno dal 1576 al 1607, Catalogue of the Exhibition, ed. A. Fara, Florence.

Giardini, parchi, paesaggi. L'avventura delle idee in Toscana dall'Ottocento a oggi, ed. G. Pettena, P. Pietrogrande, M. C. Pozzana, Florence.

Giardini regali. Fascino e immagini del verde nelle grandi dinastie: dai Medici agli Asburgo, Milan.

A. SEGRE, *Untangling the knot: garden design in Francesco Colonna's Hypnerotomachia Poliphili,* in "Word & Image", XIV, 1–2.

1999

Artifici d'acque e giardini. La cultura delle grotte e dei ninfei in Italia e in Europa, ed. I. Lapi Ballerini, L.M. Medri, Florence.

2000

Art, Memory and Family in Renaissance Florence, ed. G. Ciappelli, P. L. Rubin, Cambridge.

2001

I giardini di Toscana, Florence.

M. C. POZZANA, *Gardens of Florence and Tuscany, a complete guide,* Florence.

2003

G. CLARKE, *Roman House – Renaissance Palaces: Inventing Antiquity in Fifteenth Century Italy,* Cambridge.

I. LAPI BALLERINI, *Medicean Villas,* Florence.

2005

A. LILLIE, *Florentine Villas in the Fifteenth Century. An Architectural and Social History,* Cambridge.

The Classical Tradition in Architecture
Series Editor: Caroline van Eck, *Leiden University, Netherlands*

Classical architecture not only provided a repertoire of forms and building types capable of endless transformation; it was also a cultural actor and provided cultural capital, and was used to create political and religious identities. This series provides a forum for its interdisciplinary study, from antiquity to the present day. It aims to publish first-class and groundbreaking scholarship that re-examines, reinterprets or revalues the classical tradition in the widest sense. The series will deal with classicism as a cultural phenomenon, a formal language of design, but also with its role in establishing the agenda, method and grammar of inquiry in Western history of art and architecture and recent reconsiderations of these roles.